Entities

Entities

ANGELS, SPIRITS,
DEMONS, AND OTHER
ALIEN BEINGS

Joe Nickell

PB Prometheus Books
59 John Glenn Drive
Amherst, New York 14228-2197

Published 1995 by Prometheus Books

99 98 97 96 95   5 4 3 2 1

Library of Congress Cataloging-in-Publication Data

Nickell, Joe
     Entities : angels, spirits, demons, and other alien beings /
by Joe Nickell.
         p.   cm.
     Includes bibliographical references and index.
     ISBN 0-87975-961-5
     1. Parapsychology—Case studies. 2. Supernatural—Case studies.
3. Spirits—Case studies. 4. Angels—Case studies. 5. Ghosts—Case
studies. 6. Life on other planets. I. Title.
BF1040.N47   1995
133.1—dc20   94-44761
                                                              CIP

Printed in the United States of America on acid-free paper.

Contents

Acknowledgments

I am grateful to the many people who assisted me in researching and writing this book. I am especially grateful to Robert A. Baker (Lexington, Kentucky), Herbert G. Schapiro (Warren, New Jersey), and John F. Fischer (Orlando, Florida).

I also wish to thank the staff members of the Margaret I. King Library, University of Kentucky, for their assistance, particularly Rob Aken; the staff of the John F. Kennedy Memorial Library, West Liberty, Kentucky; the staff and members of the Executive Council of the Committee for the Scientific Investigation of Claims of the Paranormal; and, as always, my mother, Ella T. Nickell, for typing the manuscript.

To the many others who assisted in some way I also want to express my appreciation.

Introduction

I have settled on the word *entity*, a term meaning "being," to describe the assorted creatures, spirits, and other supposedly real existents that inhabit this book. I say supposedly real, because in every instance skeptics question whether they do in fact exist, and debunkers assert flatly that they do not.

Yet believers cite a large body of evidence, much of it based on personal experience, in favor of the reality of one or more entities. To be sure, belief need not be all-inclusive: one may be firmly convinced of the existence of ghosts while dismissing angels out of hand. Then again, one may discount all such otherworldly beings yet see persuasive evidence for the reality of Bigfoot, a manlike creature many believe roams the northwestern coastal areas of North America.

It is necessary, then, to take up the matter of belief. History shows that one man's deity is often another's devil, and clearly people are influenced by their upbringing. Catholics, for instance, are demonstrably more prone to experiencing apparitions of the Virgin Mary than are Protestants—let alone non-Christians. And a predisposition to believe in ghosts may be largely cultural. States one authority, for example:

> Eighteenth-century ghosts carried on many of the menial, workaday tasks that their seventeenth-century predecessors had performed, apparently unaware that great changes were going on down among the living, particularly in the realm of ideas.

Percipients, consequently, went on reporting the same old motifs, depending on their Protestant or Catholic inclinations.[1]

Belief can also stem from one's own specific needs—whether they be for certainty and security, control, novelty, attention, companionship, or any of a number of other human motives and desires (as we shall see on occasion throughout this book).[2]

The problem with belief, then, is that it may have no basis in fact. Only conclusions based on solid evidence can be treated and defended. It is sound argument, not emotional outpourings, that should be used to convey truths to others.

Therefore, in the chapters that follow, let us approach the subjects with an open mind, believing that claims should be neither hyped nor suppressed, rather that they should be thoroughly examined with an aim toward solving them. That is, let us be neither mindless "believers" nor close-minded "debunkers" but instead be *investigators* who follow the evidence wherever it may lead.

In that respect, let us avoid the pitfalls of those who start with the desired answer and then work backward to the facts, selecting only those which fit their preconceived notion and dismissing or rationalizing away the others. (Such an approach was taken by many of those who insisted the Shroud of Turin—the alleged burial cloth of Jesus—was authentic. They dismissed its lack of historical record, a medieval bishop's report that the forger had confessed, the presence of paint instead of blood, and much additional evidence, including radiocarbon testing by three laboratories that dated the cloth to the fourteenth century.[3])

And let us not mistake for objectivity the chronic timidity of some researchers who are unable (or unwilling) to reach a conclusion even when the evidence clearly warrants it. (In some instances it appears they are not investigators at all but merely mystery-mongering writers, even sometimes crypto-researchers who are actually in collusion with advocates and claimants.) Such fence-sitters, it may be hoped, will get much-deserved splinters in an uncomfortable place.

In investigating, let us follow some accepted ground rules:

1. Extraordinary claims require extraordinary proof. That is, evidence must be commensurate with a given claim. For example, while personal testimony might be sufficient to credit a person with travel to Honolulu, it would be inadequate to establish that he or she had taken a flying-saucer trip to Mars.

2. The burden of proof is on the advocate of a claim, not on anyone who would question it. In other words, a skeptic does not have to prove a claimant did *not* engage in extraterrestrial travel, it being difficult or even impossible to prove a negative; rather, the claimant has the burden of proving his or her assertion. This is the established principle in United States legal proceedings, just as it is the acknowledged rule in scholarship and science.

3. The simplest tenable explanation—that is, the one with the fewest assumptions—is most likely to be correct. This is a principle that philosophers of science term "Occam's razor" (named for fourteenth-century philosopher William of Ockham), which is expressed as *non sunt multiplicanda entia praeter necessitatem*: "things must not be multiplied beyond necessity." It is not, of course, a guarantee of absolute truth, but is a prescription for determining the preferred hypothesis among competing hypotheses.

My emphasis on investigation and the rules of evidence stems from my background as an investigator. Formerly an operative for a world-famous detective agency, I have for many years since been an investigative writer. Having earlier been a professional stage magician (including three years as resident magician at the Houdini Magical Hall of Fame in Niagara Falls, Ontario), I have naturally devoted much of my time to investigating magical or "paranormal" phenomena—those supposedly beyond the range of nature and normal human experience. My books include *Secrets of the Supernatural: Investigating the World's Occult Mysteries* (1988), *Looking for a Miracle: Weeping Icons, Relics, Stigmata, Visions and Healing Cures* (1993), and *Psychic Sleuths: ESP and Sensational Cases* (1994), as well as other books on the paranormal, including two for children, *The Magic Detectives* (1989) and *Wonder-workers!* (1991), all published by Prometheus Books.

I have also been associated for many years with the Committee for the Scientific Investigation of Claims of the Paranormal (CSICOP), founded by philosopher Paul Kurtz, astronomer Carl Sagan, writer Isaac Asimov, and other luminaries. CSICOP "attempts to encourage the critical investigation of paranormal and fringe-science claims from a responsible, scientific point of view and to disseminate factual information about the results of such inquiries to the scientific community and the public. It also encourages critical thinking, an appreciation of science, and the use of reason in examining important issues."[4]

Although I am a Fellow of the Committee and serve on its Executive Council, I consider my most important role to be that of a field investigator. As such, I have visited countless "haunted" places; investigated reputed psychics and other paranormal claimants, including UFO "abductees"; and carefully researched a wide variety of other allegedly mystical or magical phenomena.

In the course of such work I have—perhaps not surprisingly— exposed numerous hoaxes and explained various deceptive illusions. I have also encountered many seemingly credible people telling incredible tales—tales that could not readily be explained. The chapters that follow treat all such instances and represent a fair sampling of the cases that my colleagues and I have investigated over the years.

I have grouped the chapters into three parts as follows:

Part One, "Spirits," treats aspects of such phenomena: "Spirit Manifestations" (or the phenomena allegedly produced during spiritualistic séances); "Ghostly Habitations" (i.e., hauntings of houses, cemeteries, and other places); and "Poltergeist Disturbances" (the disruptive antics of so-called "noisy spirits").

Part Two, "Theological Beings," discusses in turn "Demonic Attacks" (such as allegedly occurred at a funeral-parlor-turned-residence in Connecticut) and "Divine Visitations" (including guardian-angel reports, the effects of near-death experiences, and apparitions of the Virgin Mary).

Part Three, "Alien Creatures," examines claims of "Extraterrestrial Invasions" (as supposedly represented by crashed saucers and alien abductions); "Monster Sightings" (including stories of werewolves, Bigfoot, and other creatures); and "Fairyland Encounters" (featuring the strange story of the Cottingley fairies and other wee creatures).

Are such beings real? How many of the claims are fact and how many fiction? How definitive is the evidence? For answers to these and other questions, turn to the pages that follow, enter the other-worldly realm of *Entities*, and be prepared for strange encounters.

Recommended Works

Baker, Robert A., and Joe Nickell. *Missing Pieces: How to Investigate Ghosts, UFOs, Psychics, and Other Mysteries.* Amherst, N.Y.: Prometheus Books, 1992. An investigative manual containing rules of evidence, investigative tactics, case synopses, and other fundamentals.

Binder, David A., and Paul Bergman. *Fact Investigation: From Hypothesis to Proof.* St. Paul, Minn.: West, 1984. Legally oriented text treating the gathering and evaluation of evidence, the formulation of hypotheses, etc.

Frazier, Kendrick, ed. *Science Confronts the Paranormal.* Amherst, N.Y.: Prometheus Books, 1986. Investigative articles and skeptical essays reprinted from the *Skeptical Inquirer* (the official journal of the Committee for the Scientific Investigation of Claims of the Paranormal).

Schultz, Ted, ed. *The Fringes of Reason: A Whole Earth Catalog.* New York: Harmony Books, 1989. An attempt at a balanced treatment of various fringe subjects described as "A Field Guide to New Age Frontiers, Unusual Beliefs & Eccentric Sciences."

Notes

1. R. C. Finucane, *Appearances of the Dead: A Cultural History of Ghosts* (Amherst, N.Y.: Prometheus Books, 1984), p. 153.

2. Robert A. Baker and Joe Nickell, *Missing Pieces: How to Investigate Ghosts, UFOs, Psychics, and Other Mysteries* (Amherst, N.Y.: Prometheus Books, 1992), pp. 25–26.

3. Joe Nickell, *Inquest on the Shroud of Turin*, 2d updated ed. (Amherst, N.Y.: Prometheus Books, 1988).

4. Official statement of CSICOP, which accompanies each issue of its journal, *Skeptical Inquirer*.

Part One

Spirits

1

Spirit Manifestations

Spiritualism

Belief in spirits of the dead is as old as the biblical story of the "witch of Endor" (1 Sam. 28: 7-20). She had a "familiar spirit" who, at King Saul's request, conjured up the ghost of Samuel.

Modern spiritualism had its origin at Hydesville, New York, in 1848. At the home of a Methodist minister named John Fox, strange rapping noises began to occur in the bedroom of Fox's daughters, eight-year-old Maggie and six-year-old Kate. They claimed the noises were communications from the departed spirit of a murdered peddler they called "Mr. Splitfoot." After a time, on the night of March 31, the girls' mother witnessed a remarkable demonstration (which she later described in a signed report).

Katie loudly addressed "Mr. Splitfoot" and said "do as I do," clapping her hands. Instantly there came the same number of mysterious raps. Next Maggie exclaimed, "Now do just as I do; count one, two, three, four," clapping her hands at each number. Four raps came in response. Said Mrs. Fox:

> I then thought I could put a test that no one in the place could answer. I asked the noises to rap my children's ages successively. Instantly each one of my children's ages was given correctly, pausing between them sufficiently long to individualize them until the seventh, at which a longer pause was made, and then three more emphatic raps were given, corresponding to the age

17

of the little one that died, which was my youngest child. I then
asked: "Is this a human being that answers my questions
correctly?" There was no rap. I asked: "Is it a spirit? If so,
make two raps," which were instantly given as soon as the
request was made. I then said: "If it is an injured spirit, make
two raps," which were instantly made, causing the house to
tremble. I asked: "Were you injured in this house?" The answer
was given as before. "Is the person living that injured you?"
Answer by raps in the same manner. I ascertained by the same
method that it was a man, aged thirty-one years; that he had
been murdered in this house; and that his remains were buried
in the cellar; that his family consisted of a wife and five children,
two sons and three daughters, all living at the time of his death,
but that his wife had since died.[1]

Soon neighbors were permitted to attend the phenomena
which always centered around the young girls. When they visited
their elder brother's home and later the Rochester home of their
elder sister, Mrs. Leah Fish, the ghostly spirit followed. According
to John Mulholland, in his book *Beware Familiar Spirits:*

Even on the canal boat going to Rochester the rappings followed
the girls. Sister Leah was most enthusiastic about the spirit
and his raps but her husband Calvin disliked the ghost most
thoroughly and expressed his opinion not only openly but
vociferously. Friendly as he was to Leah, Margaret and
Katherine, the spirit disliked Calvin and began, still always
during darkness, to throw slippers and other objects at him,
which still further annoyed him. Little by little the spirit became
more bold and during supper would shake the table, and once
when Calvin rose from his chair to reach for the water pitcher
the spirit slyly removed his chair, so that when he sat down
he fell on the floor and spilled the water all over himself. Calvin
began really to hate that ghost.[2]

News of the phenomena quickly spread across the city, and
newspapers around the United States began to report on the
"Rochester Rappings." The older sister, Leah, an enterprising sort,
began to charge an admission fee to attend the sessions, collecting
up to one hundred fifty dollars an evening. Attendees soon

discovered that the girls could conjure up not only the ghostly peddler but other obliging spirits as well. Explains Mulholland:

> And so the next big step in spiritism was reached. Those of the spirit world did not need to be unhappy to come back to earth, they did not need to have been murdered nor to have left omitted unrighted wrongs they had committed in their worldly existence. It was just as easy to call back Grandmother or Aunt Hattie. Naturally when a person's own dead could be brought back to him spiritism became of interest to every one.[3]

Soon Leah took Maggie and Katie to New York City, where their demonstrations received such attention that Leah originated a "spiritualistic" society. "Spiritualism" began to take on the trappings of a religion, with hymns being sung at the opening and close of a session (which they called a "séance"). Following their success in New York Leah took the girls on tour to towns and cities across the nation. Everywhere people were anxious to communicate—or so they thought—with the souls of their departed loved ones.

The tour lasted into 1853. Newspaperman Horace Greeley was so interested in the girls and their strange productions that he paid for Katie's education. A surgeon named Elisha Kane showed a less fatherly interest toward then thirteen-year-old Maggie. At first he arranged for her to be tutored and to be chaperoned by his aunt, but two years later he "married" Margaret by simply declaring the fact; there was neither a religious nor a civil ceremony. Unfortunately Dr. Kane died in 1857, and Margaret's common-law marriage yielded her only a handout from her husband's family.

Margaret returned to the spiritualistic circuit, and for nearly forty years eked out a living as a séance "medium." For her "sitters" she produced otherworldly "manifestations"—mostly rapped answers to their questions—although competitors soon appeared with more showy effects. Indeed, thousands cut in on her business, claiming they, too, had the power to conjure up spirits of the dead.

Indeed in 1854 some fifteen thousand spiritualists had sent

a petition to the U.S. Senate, calling for a government investigation because the dead were so anxious to contact those on
the mortal plane. The spiritualists' representative, James Shields
of Illinois, described how an "occult force" appeared to be "sliding,
raising, arresting, holding, suspending, and otherwise disturbing
ponderable bodies." He told how "lights of various forms and
colors, and of different degrees of intensity appear in dark rooms,"
and how "harmonious sounds as of human voices, and other
sounds resembling those of the fife, drum, trumpet, have been
produced without any visible agency." The senators jovially
responded by joking that the petition should be referred to the
Committee on Foreign Relations, and—to much laughter—the
spiritualists' plea was tabled.[4]

The spiritualists were not merely laughed at, however. Scientists and other rational-minded investigators came forth to
challenge their claims even in the early days in Rochester, where
University of Buffalo faculty members studied Maggie and Katie's
raps. Examiners excluded "spiritual causation" and asserted,
curiously, that the raps were "produced by the action of the will,
through voluntary action on the joints."[5]

Another investigation was held in 1857. A newspaper, the
Boston Courier, challenged Margaret to a test of her ability to
communicate with spirits. She was to get them to answer a question that was posed by the editor and which was unknown to
her. A committee adjudicated the challenge. Alas, the spirits failed
to provide a satisfactory answer, and Margaret failed to collect
the proffered reward of five hundred dollars. She claimed that
had she been well enough to conduct another sitting she could
have proved the committee's conclusion wrong.

A third investigation took place in 1884 when Margaret held
two sittings for the University of Pennsylvania's Seybert Commission. This time the "spirits" gave out erroneous information.
Furthermore, commission members caused the rapping sounds to
cease abruptly by controlling Margaret's feet. Margaret responded
by refusing to conduct further séances, and the commission stated
in its published report that the "so-called raps are confined wholly
to her person." Whether they were produced by her "voluntarily
or involuntarily," the scientists had not determined.[6]

A different form of attack came from religious fundamentalists. Instead of challenging the genuineness of the spirits, they accepted their reality but condemned those who sought communion with them. Ministers and others cited biblical prohibitions: "Regard not them that have familiar spirits" (Lev. 19:31); again, "And the soul that turneth after such as have familiar spirits, and after wizards, to go a-whoring after them, I will ever set my face against that soul and will cut him off from among his people" (Lev. 20:6).

In the meantime, Katie—now Mrs. Katherine Fox Jencken, an impoverished widow with two children to care for—had resumed practicing as a medium. Charges were soon brought against her by the Society for the Prevention of Cruelty to Children, charges she believed were instigated by rival mediums. Margaret, who also felt persecuted by them and who had turned to drink and then to the solace of Catholicism, wrote to the *New York Herald* to defend her younger sibling: "My sister's two beautiful boys referred to are her idols." She added, "Spiritualism is a curse," and—in a foreshadowing of further revelations about the cultish practice—equated mediums with "fraud."[7]

Some months later, in an interview in the *Herald*, Margaret followed up with a confession that the raps were not made by spirits at all; they were produced from childhood, she said, by "the manner in which the joints of the foot can be used." As proof she promised to hold a public demonstration "exposing Spiritualism from its very foundation."

A response came from one Henry J. Newton, president of the First Spiritual Society of New York, who stated: "The idea of claiming that unseen 'rappings' can be produced with joints of the feet! If she says this even with regard to her own manifestations, she lies! I and many other men of the truth and position have witnessed the manifestations of herself and her sisters many times under circumstances in which it was absolutely impossible for there to have been the least fraud."[8]

This time Katherine responded. She supported Margaret's statements and asserted: "Spiritualism is a humbug from beginning to end." Only two weeks later, on Sunday, October 21, 1888, the sisters appeared at the Academy of Music in New

York City. With Katherine sitting in a box and repeatedly nodding in agreement, while a number of spiritualists expressed their disapproval with groans and hisses, Margaret revealed all from the music hall stage.

Margaret explained how she had produced the rapping noises by slipping her foot from her shoe and snapping her toes. Placing her stockinged foot on a thin plank, she demonstrated the effect for the audience. As a newspaper reported the following day, "Mrs. Kane now locates the origin of Modern Spiritualism in her great toe."[9] Margaret went on to state:

> I think that it is about time that the truth of this miserable subject "Spiritualism" should be brought out. It is now widespread all over the world, and unless it is put down it will do great evil. I was the first in the field and I have the right to expose it.
>
> My sister Katie and myself were very young children when this horrible deception began. I was eight and just a year and a half older than she. We were very mischievous children and we wanted to terrify our dear mother, who was a very good woman and very easily frightened. At night when we were in bed, we used to tie an apple to a string and move it up and down, causing the apple to bump on the floor, or we would drop the apple on the floor, making a strange noise every time it would rebound. Mother listened to this for a time. She could not understand it and did not suspect us of being capable of a trick because we were so young.
>
> At last she could stand it no longer and she called the neighbors in and told them about it. It was this that set us to discover the means of making the raps.

Margaret continued:

> There were so many people coming to the house that we were not able to make use of the apple trick except when we were in bed and the room was dark. Even then we could hardly do it so that the only way was to rap on the bedstead with our hands.

After their older sister, Leah Fish, had taken them to Rochester, they learned different ways to produce the rapping sounds.

My sister Katie was the first one to discover that by swishing her fingers she could produce a certain noise with the knuckles and joints, and that the same effect could be made with the toes. Finding we could make raps with our feet—first with one foot and then with both—we practiced until we could do this easily when the room was dark.[10]

Mrs. Kane—Margaret—also stated that their older sister Leah knew that the spirit rappings were fake, and that when she traveled with the girls (on their first nationwide tour) it was she who signaled the answers to the various questions. (She probably chatted with sitters before the séance to obtain information; when that did not produce the requisite facts, the "spirits" no doubt spoke in the vague generalizations that are the mainstay of spiritualistic charlatans.)

Mrs. Kane repeated her exposé in other cities close to New York. However, explains John Mulholland, "It was expected that this would give her sufficient income to live but she shortly discovered that while many people will pay to be humbugged few will pay to be educated."[11]

Perhaps not surprisingly, then, Margaret returned to mediumship when she needed money again. After her death on March 8, 1895, thousands of spiritualist mourners attended her funeral.

Today, spiritualists characterize Margaret's exposé as bogus, attributing it to her need for money or the desire for revenge against her rivals or both. However, not only were her admissions fully corroborated by her sister, but she demonstrated to the audience that she could produce the mysterious raps just as she said. According to the *New York Sun*: "Doctors from the audience went upon the stage and felt the woman's foot as she made the motions by which she used to do the rapping. Then she stood in her stocking feet on a little pine platform six inches from the floor, and without the slightest perceptible movement of the person, made raps audible all over the theater." The *Sun* added: "She went into the audience, and there, resting her feet on another person's, showed how by the motion of the great toe the sound was produced."[12]

Finally, recall the investigations that Margaret earlier endured, especially that of the Seybert Commission in 1884. When her feet were adequately controlled (they were placed on tumblers), the rapping sounds were curtailed.

Clearly, the Fox Sisters, the very founders of spiritualism, were frauds. But what about other mediums who—often under controlled conditions—produced a range of spiritualistic phenomena that went far beyond the simple raps produced by Margaret and Katherine? Were all of these productions faked, or was it just possible that some spirit communication was genuine? Let us look then at some of the Fox Sisters' contemporaries and successors, some of whom were actually endorsed by men of science.

Séances

Soon after the Fox sisters had sparked the spiritualistic craze that spread across the United States, a variety of strange phenomena began to be produced at séances: "Spirits" not only rapped out messages but also rattled tambourines, spoke through trumpets, wrote messages on slates, and tilted tables. Many séances, which were held in dark or at best dimly lit rooms, yielded "materializations" in the form of disembodied hands or faces or even entire luminescent forms.

As indicated earlier, however, doubters not only refused to accept such apparent proof of the nether world but sought to detect and expose what they believed to be blatant fraud. Reporters, scientists, professional magicians, and others became the nemeses of the spiritualist mediums. For example, in the fall of 1876, Boston's "West End medium," a Mrs. Bennett, challenged the Herald to prove their claims that she employed trickery. The newspaper responded by dispatching a reporter to Mrs. Bennett's next séance. After she produced first the voice and then the materialized form of "Sunflower," her "Indian guide" through the spirit world, the reporter made a careful search of the room.

Suspecting a trapdoor, he ripped up several floor boards, whereupon he discovered Mrs. Bennett's thirty-year-old confederate
hiding in a recess.

In the same year, a Rochester, New York, newspaper published the confession of that city's best-known medium, a man
by the name of Jennings. "My accomplice," he explained, "used
false hair, wigs, beards, etc., and put flour on his hands to give
a ghostly appearance. For baby faces he had a piece of black
velveteen, with a small round hole cut out. This, placed over
the face, gave the appearance of the tiny features of a babe."
On one occasion Jennings employed a mask painted on a rolled-
up cloth fastened to a length of wire. "I poked it through the
screen, and then unrolled it by turning the wire. I also had a
piece of thick, dark worsted cloth which I used as a beard for
myself. . . . [T]wo faces appeared at once and almost threw the
meeting into ecstasies."[13]

While most mediums gave parlor demonstrations, the Davenport Brothers, Ira and William, gave stage performances. Traveling throughout the United States by river steamers and stage-
coaches beginning in the 1850s, the brothers convinced many
attendees that the spirits were indeed a reality. While the young
men were tied to chairs and placed in special "spirit cabinets"
on stage, the ghostly entities apparently strummed guitars and
rattled tambourines. Occasionally, in the near-darkness of the
performance halls, spectators would even glimpse a phantom
hand.

Later, while touring Europe for several years, the brothers
had several encounters with skeptics, notably professional stage
magicians. In one English parody of the Davenports' show, an
actor made up as their lecturer quipped: "Many sensible and intelligent individuals seem to think that the requirement of darkness seems to infer trickery. So it does. But I will strive to convince
you that it does not."[14]

In 1911, after many additional performances in their native
country, an elderly Ira Davenport showed magician/escape-artist
Harry Houdini how the brothers had been able to get out of
the ropes to produce the spirit phenomena, then slip back into
their bonds so as to appear to have been securely fastened all

the while. Houdini later used this knowledge to rout the Italian medium Nino Pecoraro. Pecoraro had amazed Sir Arthur Conan Doyle, the creator of Sherlock Holmes, with his spirit manifestations, apparently produced while the medium was securely tied to a chair. However, when Pecoraro was investigated by *Scientific American* magazine, Houdini took charge of tying the medium. As a result, the manifestations ceased completely.[15]

Some other elderly mediums taught Houdini their tricks also. One reformed spiritualist, Mrs. Benninghofen, demonstrated for Houdini how to gain the use of one hand in the dark, even though the sitter believed both hands were controlled. With her free hand, the medium caused a metal trumpet to appear to be levitating. Houdini learned other tricks from the aging Anna Eva Fay, once a leading medium in the United States and Europe.[16]

Fay had actually been exposed as early as 1876, when a former assistant began to give "anti-spiritualist" demonstrations in the northeastern states. Washington Irving Bishop had served for two years as a "floor walker" for the celebrated medium. It was his job to gather up the pads of paper after spectators had written and torn off their questions for the medium. Bishop went backstage where he developed the latent impressions that had been produced by waxed second sheets. He quickly copied the writings, then secretly relayed them to Miss Fay so she could astound the audience by revealing their very thoughts.

In his performances Bishop demonstrated a variety of tricks used by Anna Eva Fay and her fellow spiritualists. In response to his first public show, the *New York Times* editorialized: "The Spiritualists may as well give up." Bishop, said the *Times*, "has not only done all that the so-called spirits do, but he has beaten them at their own game. . . . This latest exposure leaves the spirits without a leg to stand on."[17] (Unfortunately, Bishop began to combine his exposé with demonstrations of his own alleged power of "mind reading," which he insisted was genuine. Eventually his tricks, too, were exposed, in England by the great magician John Nevil Maskelyne and in America by the city editor of the *Boston Globe*, Charles Howard Montagne.)

While most mediums tried to avoid investigators, the most celebrated Italian medium of her day, Eusapia Palladino, did not.

Instead, she confounded some of Europe's most distinguished men of science with her spiritualistic phenomena. She caused tables to float in the air and conjured up spirit hands, rapping noises, and a mysterious breeze (which supposedly emanated from a scar on her forehead). One professor, who desired to communicate with the departed spirit of his mother, said he felt something make the sign of the cross: "I distinctly felt the touch on my forehead, then on my breast, and then on each shoulder. . . . After that I distinctly felt a kiss on my lips, and after that two kisses on my right cheek."[18]

Some investigators were suspicious, noting that control of Palladino's hands and feet was of her own devising. Her left fingers touched the hand of the sitter to her left, while her right wrist was held by the sitter on her right. By slowly moving her hands close together she could eventually substitute her right fingers for her left. In the dark, the sitters would still be confident her hands were controlled, but, in fact, she would have a free left hand. Similarly, she could make one foot serve as two, thus enabling her to produce a wide variety of mysterious effects: raps were heard, breezes felt on sitters' faces, the table tilted, a nearby curtain billowed forward, and a stool behind the medium landed upside down atop the table.

At one American séance in 1909, a Harvard professor took advantage of the dim lighting to slip from his chair and lie on the floor behind the Italian medium. When he perceived the stool moving, he grabbed at whatever was propelling it: he had seized Palladino's left foot, causing her to scream. Releasing her, the professor secretly reclaimed his seat and only recounted the incident after he had returned from the séance.

At another series of séances, unknown to Palladino, the person on either side of her was a magician. As Milbourne Christopher says in his *ESP, Seers & Psychics*: "The two séances with the magicians in charge must have been the strangest Palladino ever gave. For long periods there were no manifestations; then the phenomena were produced as strongly as ever; then they ceased again."[19] The magicians had arranged for a third conspirator to signal, by coughing, for them to relax or tighten their control of the medium. Says Christopher: "During the relaxed period raps were heard, and the table tilted and floated. A cough terminated the activity as the magicians took firm grips on both her hands and feet. Not until another cough did they give her leeway to go into action again."[20]

Christopher continues:

Her greatest surprise must have been when she read that [the two magicians], clad in black from head to toe, had crawled into the room when the lights were dimmed and hidden under chairs occupied by two ladies. With their heads close to her feet they had seen her strike the table leg with her shoe to produce raps. They also saw her put her left foot under the left table leg as the table tilted to the right. When she lifted her foot, all four legs rose from the floor. She had pressed down with her left hand on the tabletop to clamp the table between hand and foot. With the table held by this pressure, it would go up when she lifted her foot, down when she lowered it.[21]

(Christopher himself demonstrated Palladino's technique on the "Tonight Show" with Johnny Carson, Ed McMahon, and Kay Ballard in attendance at the "séance."[22])

What about the cool breezes sitters felt on their faces? No doubt Palladino simply pursed her lips and blew noiselessly. Explains Christopher: "Most people believe human breath is warm and it is if you are very close, an inch or so away from the source. However, as it travels through the air it becomes cold." Christopher adds: "Palladino's great strength was that she required neither special equipment nor confederates to perform her most talked-about feats. She was a master of séance-room psychology. Even when intelligent men caught her cheating, she could usually convince them that the feats they had not detected were legitimate phenomena."[23]

Yet another medium, Daniel Dunglas Home (1833-1886), has been represented as "the medium who was never exposed." However, the claim needs clarifying. Home (pronounced Hume) took advantage of his credulous hosts, who lavished expensive gifts on him and allowed him to set the conditions under which he produced his seeming wonders.[24] Some, including poet Robert

Browning, did observe Home in a deception. At a séance in a dimly lit room, a "spirit" hand placed a wreath on the head of the poet's wife. Mrs. Browning was at first deceived, but later agreed with her husband that the hand had slipped from beneath the table and that Home had engaged in trickery. From then on, Browning referred to the medium with contempt. He set down his feelings in "Mr. Sludge 'the Medium.' "[25]

Home's greatest feat was to levitate, supposedly being borne aloft by spirit entities. On one occasion, at a London home in 1868, he allegedly floated out an upstairs window, then glided through another into an adjoining room. Although the rooms were dark, three men claimed they had observed the levitation by moonlight. Actually, an 1868 almanac proves that there would have been a new moon, which, according to historian Trevor Hall, "therefore could not even faintly have illuminated the room."

Moreover, the three witnesses gave different versions of what occurred that evening. None actually *saw* Home floating outside; they were merely *told* he exited one window and then he *appeared* to come in the other. Some researchers have suggested that, after noisily throwing open the first window, the medium slipped quietly in the dark to the other, which he then opened and pretended to enter. Under the conditions that prevailed, it would have been difficult to tell whether his dimly silhouetted body was outside or actually inside.

Regardless of what actually transpired, the dark room and other circumstances strongly indicate trickery. Home sternly instructed the witnesses to remain seated. "On no account leave your places," he insisted. What had he to fear from their moving about? Very likely he knew they might discover how his trick was done.[26]

Although Home sometimes communicated advice from the "spirits" to those suffering from various ailments, the entities were apparently unable to aid him: On June 21, 1886, at the age of fifty-three, he died of tuberculosis. His second wife attempted to enhance his memory through two books, but a much less favorable assessment came from Sir David Brewster, the famous Scotch physicist:

> Were Mr. Home to assume the character of Wizard of the West,
> I would enjoy his exhibition as much as that of other conjurers;
> but when he pretends to possess the power of introducing among
> the feet of his audience the spirits of the dead, bringing them
> into physical communication with their dearest relatives, and
> of revealing the secrets of the grave, he insults religion and
> common sense, and tampers with the most sacred feelings of
> his victims.[27]

The same may be said of others of Home's ilk, many of whom
practice spiritualistic chicanery today. For example, at the infamous Camp Chesterfield in Chesterfield, Indiana, in 1960,
infrared film—used to record images in the dark—revealed that
the "spirits" were using a secret door! Later, in 1976, M. Lamar
Keene, a former fraudulent medium at Camp Chesterfield, exposed
the "psychic sideshow" there and at other spiritualist camps in
the United States in his book The Psychic Mafia.[28]

Despite the exposés, spiritualism continues to be practiced at
the various camps and elsewhere. In recent years, spiritualism
has sometimes been recast in the form of "channeling"—the result
of a renewal of interest in spirit communication. This revival began
in the 1960s with several books of spiritual wisdom supposedly
dictated to their author by the spirit "Seth." In the 1980s, two
other "channels" (as the "New Age" mediums are now styled) came
into the limelight, in part due to the publicity given them by actress
Shirley MacLaine in her books Out on a Limb (1983) and Dancing
in the Light (1985). The two are J. Z. Knight, who claims to channel
a 35,000-year-old spirit named "Ramtha," and Kevin Ryerson, who
supposedly channels several different entities.[29]

An investigation I was involved in, through my membership
in the Kentucky Association of Science Educators and Skeptics
(KASES), gives an idea of just how valid the claims of channelers
are. KASES asked the distinguished linguist Sara Thomason, who
has extensively researched claims of past-life regression,[30] to
examine a tape recording of the alleged channeling of a centuries-
old Scotsman. Dr. Thomason's penetrating analysis demonstrated
that the Scotch dialect was bogus—nothing more than an ama-
teurish imitation.[31]

Spirit Pictures

Among the most intriguing of spiritualistic phenomena are photographs that supposedly depict the inhabitants of the spirit world. The first such productions occurred when a Boston engraver and amateur photographer named William H. Mumler discovered extra pictures on some photos he had taken of a fellow employee.

Mumler, however, realized the "extras" were actually due to the recycling of a used photographic glass-plate negative: because of insufficient cleaning, faint images had remained, sufficient to appear on the newly coated and exposed plate. This realization, coupled with the popularity of spiritualism at the time, prompted the opportunistic Mumler to go into business as a "spirit photographer." In 1862, Mumler came forth with what he maintained was "the first true photograph of a soul that has passed over." It depicted the photographer with the hazy form of a woman which, Mumler asserted, "I recognize as my cousin who passed away about twelve years hence."[32]

Almost overnight the spirit photographer was experiencing a thriving trade, regularly obtaining extra images on photographic portraits of his sitters. These "extras" were recognized as deceased celebrities, or as dead relatives or friends of the sitter. "In February of 1863, however," says John Mulholland, "recognition went too far—Doctor Gardner, a leading Boston Spiritualist, recognized some of the 'extras' as living Bostonians." Mumler's business declined as a result, but he relocated to New York in 1869. There he was prosecuted for swindling, but several of the spiritualist faithful testified that they recognized some of the spirit forms as their loved ones, and Mumler was eventually acquitted. He appears to have continued his work for a time but soon passed into obscurity and died in 1884.[33]

In the meantime, other unscrupulous photographers had followed Mumler's lead. One was a Parisian named Jean Buguet. His technique was to photograph his assistants, suitably dressed in a gauzelike shroud or similar attire, and then make a second exposure of the sitter. Eventually, needing more variety, Buguet began utilizing a dummy with interchangeable heads—all of which were soon seized by the police. During Buguet's trial, a man named Dessenon described the "spirit" picture of his dead wife as being "so like her that when I showed it to one of my relatives he exclaimed, 'It's my cousin.' " At this Judge Millet asked, "Was that chance, Buguet?" to which he replied: "Yes, pure chance. I had no photograph of Madame Dessenon."[34] Such is the will to believe.

Researcher Daniel Cohen, author of *The Encyclopedia of Ghosts,* observes that "most of the spirit photographs that were taken during that period look to the modern observer so obviously fake that one wonders how anyone but an idiot could be taken in by them."[35] Yet Fred Gettings, author of *Ghosts in Photographs,* rushes to defend Mumler, Buguet, and others (although he acknowledges that fraudulent practitioners existed). Gettings is impressed with the "superior artistic quality" and recognizability of some of the prints. He blithely refers to "Buguet's style" and of "a spirit pose characteristic of Mumler's work"[36] without apparently realizing the implicit argument therein: such differences in style from one photographer to another suggest their individualistic manipulation rather than the effect of some supernatural force (as they pretended) beyond their control.

In addition to the styles, the techniques of producing fake spirit photos varied—twenty-two methods by one 1921 count, "and more have been developed since," reports Mulholland.[37] A common technique was double exposure, used for example by Mrs. Ada Emma Deane in producing pictures of her "Spirit Controls," typically Egyptian princes or Indian chiefs. One of the latter, a chief in war bonnet and full regalia, was discovered to have been cut from the front cover of a popular magazine.[38]

Other pictures, notably those taken during séances, are obviously ordinary photos of dressed-up mediums, including those of the spirit "Katie King" who was allegedly summoned up by a winsome English girl named Florence Cook. Wearing a black dress, she would be tied into a spirit cabinet (like the Davenport Brothers, mentioned in the previous section). Soon, "Katie" would emerge into the dimly lit room, dressed in white. One observer who grabbed the ethereal figure discovered it was actually quite material and he believed it was Florence decked in a rumpled dress and tea towel. (On other occasions, the distinguished elderly scientist William Crookes drew attention "by falling for 'Katie' and embracing her rather too warmly and too often in the dimness of the séance-chamber."[39]) Photographs of the "materialized" Katie King taken in séances in London in 1873 and 1874 show that her features match those of Florence Cook.[40]

Not surprisingly, skeptics often played tricks on the trick photographers. Some of the latter—supposedly to "prove" their productions genuine—permitted sitters to bring their own plates. These would be surreptitiously exchanged for prepared ones, and the sitter even invited to use his own camera. But as Walter Gibson relates in his *Secrets of Magic*:

> One keen investigator used that opportunity to turn a plate upside down while putting it in the camera. The plate had already been switched, so the spirit faces appeared when it was developed, but not quite as expected. Instead of floating above the living person's head and peering benignly downward, they were all upside down at the bottom of the picture, looking up in surprise.[41]

In the course of my investigations I have encountered many pictures of spirits. One case featured a process called "spirit precipitation on silk," which involved having the spirits produce their self-portraits by using an open bottle of ink. Squares of apparently blank cloth were handed out by the glow of a photographer's safelight. After a suitable period of incantation, the medium took the red light from person to person, directing the cloths be turned over. Thereupon a few small portraits were seen on each.

A disgruntled sitter supplied me with her "precipitation" and I examined it in conjunction with professional photographer Robert H. van Outer and forensic analyst John F. Fischer. Visual examination revealed apparent anomalies: not only was one "spirit" wearing eyeglasses, but there was even a partial shadow area behind another figure as well as other indications the pictures were those of solid, material beings. Eventually argon laser light revealed solvent rings around each portrait, their presence not only being suggestive of a transfer process but being consistent with such a process described in M. Lamar Keene's exposé *The Psychic Mafia*. As he relates:

> The trick here was to prepare the silks in advance. I used to cut pictures out of old magazines or use snapshots of spirits known to the sitters if I had them, soak the picture in ammonia for thirty seconds, place it on bridal silk, put a handkerchief over it, and use a hot iron. The image impregnated the silk.[42]

Keene continues:

> Once at Camp Chesterfield, while doing precipitations, I got lazy or careless or both and caused a minor crisis. Sick of cutting out and ironing the damn things, I used any picture that was handy, one of a little girl on a recent cover of *Life* magazine. The woman who got the silk recognized the picture and went to Mamie Schultz Brown, the president of the camp that year. Mamie was very excitable; she almost fainted when the woman confronted her with the silk and the incriminating picture from *Life*.[43]

"However," Keene adds, "we smoothed it over by telling the woman that sometimes the spirits did mischievous things like that just to remind us they were still human and liked a joke."[44]

Using a variation on the Camp Chesterfield technique (the medium in our case was from Camp Chesterfield), we produced strikingly similar "spirit precipitations." With them and our other evidence, including affidavits from victims of the scam and a forensic report, I was able to obtain warrants for the medium's arrest on charges of "theft by deception."[45]

Two other cases included ghostly photos taken at "haunted" houses: Mackenzie House in Toronto, Canada, and Liberty Hall in Frankfort, Kentucky. In the former case, the photo depicts an alleged "warlock" with his hands extended above the keyboard of an antique piano in the historic house. There appears "a mysterious kind of mist between his hands and the keys," as Suzie Smith describes it in her book *Ghosts Around the House*.[46]

Actually a professional photographer's opinion confirms what is obvious: The camera's flash has been reflected by the white pages of music on the piano, thus washing out an area of the photograph.[47]

In the case of Liberty Hall, the photograph depicts an ethereal figure on the stairs, captured in a sequence of images that indicates the figure was in motion. This flash photo supposedly depicts the "Gray Lady" who is said to roam the old mansion. However, the original photograph and negative are suspiciously missing, and professional photographer Clint Robertson observes that "a ghost or a person would have to be moving faster than the speed of light to be represented several times in one normal flash exposure." After considering other possibilities and performing "several empirical tests to determine whether or not the photograph is a result of malfunction or darkroom manipulation," Robertson concluded: "It is my experienced and educated photographic opinion that the photograph is, at best, the result of an accident. I am certain for photographic and scientific reasons that the figure ascending the stairs definitely is a person and not an apparition." Robertson's experimental photos demonstrate how easy it is to create such an effect.[48]

Numerous other cases of "spirit" pictures are examined in my *Camera Clues* (1994). However, the foregoing should be sufficient to demonstrate that, far from constituting proof of the spirit realm, such photographs are invariably attributable to accident or hoax. Like spirit phenomena in general, spirit pictures have been debunked so often that few investigators take them seriously anymore.

Recommended Works

Christopher, Milbourne. *ESP, Seers & Psychics: What the Occult Really Is.* New York: Thomas Y. Crowell, 1970. A skeptical look at the "occult" world, including a penetrating analysis of spiritualism.

Gettings, Fred. *Ghosts in Photographs.* New York: Harmony Books, 1978. An attempt to portray spirit photography as a reality.

Gibson, Walter. *Secrets of Magic: Ancient and Modern.* New York:

Grosset & Dunlap, 1967. Reveals magicians' secrets as well as tricks used by séance mediums.

Keene, M. Lamar (as told to Allen Spraggett). *The Psychic Mafia*. New York: St. Martin, 1976. Exposé of spiritualist frauds by a former medium.

Mulholland, John. *Beware Familiar Spirits*. 1938; reprinted New York: Charles Scribner's Sons, 1979. An investigation of spiritualism and psychic phenomena by a professional magician.

Nickell, Joe. *Camera Clues: A Handbook for Photographic Investigation*. Lexington, Ky.: University Press of Kentucky, 1994. Discusses varied aspects of photo detective work, including investigations of "paranormal" photographs.

Notes

1. Report of Mrs. Margaret Fox, quoted in John Mulholland, *Beware Familiar Spirits* (1938; reprint, New York: Charles Scribner's Sons, 1979), pp. 30–31.

2. Ibid., p. 32.

3. Ibid., p. 33.

4. Milbourne Christopher, *ESP, Seers & Psychics* (New York: Thomas Y. Crowell, 1970), p. 175.

5. Mulholland, *Beware Familiar Spirits*, pp. 34–37.

6. Ibid., pp. 37–38.

7. Margaret Fox Kane, letter to editor of *New York Herald*, May 27, 1888, cited in ibid., p. 39.

8. Quoted in Mulholland, *Beware Familiar Spirits*, p. 40.

9. *The Evening Post*, quoted in Christopher, *ESP, Seers & Psychics*, p. 181.

10. Mrs. Margaret Fox Kane, October 21, 1888, quoted in Mulholland, *Beware Familiar Spirits*, pp. 41–42.

11. Mulholland, *Beware Familiar Spirits*, p. 43.

12. *New York Sun*, October 22, 1888, quoted in Christopher, *ESP, Seers & Psychics*, p. 181.

13. *Rochester Democrat and Chronicle*, quoted in Christopher, *ESP, Seers & Psychics*, p. 176.

14. Mulholland, *Beware Familiar Spirits*, pp. 49–70.

15. Milbourne Christopher, *Houdini: The Untold Story* (New York: Thomas Y. Crowell, 1969), pp. 167, 179–80.

16. Christopher, *Houdini,* pp. 207, 227-28, photo following p. 210.

17. Quoted in Christopher, *ESP, Seers & Psychics,* p. 59.

18. Ibid., pp. 188-92.

19. Ibid.

20. Ibid.

21. Ibid.

22. Ibid., pp. 194-99. For a more detailed discussion of spiritualists' tricks, see the text and illustrations of Walter Gibson, *Secrets of Magic: Ancient and Modern* (New York: Grosset & Dunlap, 1967), pp. 127-47.

23. Christopher, *ESP, Seers & Psychics,* pp. 203-204.

24. Ibid., pp. 174-87.

25. Joe Nickell, *Wonder-workers! How They Perform the Impossible* (Amherst, N.Y.: Prometheus Books, 1991), pp. 27-30; Christopher, *ESP, Seers & Psychics,* pp. 179-80.

26. Nickell, *Wonder-workers!,* pp. 31-32.

27. Quoted in ibid., p. 32.

28. M. Lamar Keene (as told to Allen Spraggett), *The Psychic Mafia* (New York: St. Martin, 1976).

29. Robert A. Baker and Joe Nickell, *Missing Pieces: How to Investigate Ghosts, UFOs, Psychics, and Other Mysteries* (Amherst, N.Y.: Prometheus Books, 1992), p. 59.

30. Sara S. Thomason, "Past Tongues Remembered," *Skeptical Inquirer* 11, no. 4 (1987): 367-75.

31. Sara S. Thomason and T. Kaufman, personal communication to KASES Chairman Robert A. Baker, January 16, 1989.

32. Mumler, quoted in Peter Haining, *Ghosts: The Illustrated History* (Secaucus, N.J.: Chartwell, 1987), p. 76.

33. Mulholland, *Beware Familiar Spirits,* p. 148; Fred Gettings, *Ghosts in Photographs* (New York: Harmony Books, 1978), pp. 23-25.

34. Gettings, *Ghosts in Photographs,* pp. 37-40; Daniel Cohen, *The Encyclopedia of Ghosts* (New York: Dorset Press, 1984), pp. 244-47.

35. Cohen, *The Encyclopedia of Ghosts,* p. 244.

36. Gettings, *Ghosts in Photographs,* pp. 35-37.

37. C. Vincent Patrick, cited by Mulholland, *Beware Familiar Spirits,* p. 149.

38. Haining, *Ghosts,* pp. 78-79; Mulholland, *Beware Familiar Spirits,* p. 152.

39. For the story of Florence Cook and William Crookes's apparent tryst, see Trevor H. Hall, *The Spiritualists* (New York: Helix Press, 1963).

40. Cohen, *The Encyclopedia of Ghosts*, pp. 22–29. Compare the photos of "Katie King" in Gettings (*Ghosts in Photographs*, pp. 46–48) with a portrait of Florence Cook (and another spirit picture of "Katie King") in Cohen (*The Encyclopedia of Ghosts*, p. 24).

41. Gibson, *Secrets of Magic*, p. 147.

42. Keene, *The Psychic Mafia*, pp. 110–11.

43. Ibid., p. 111.

44. Ibid.

45. Joe Nickell, *Secrets of the Supernatural* (Amherst, N.Y.: Prometheus Books, 1988), pp. 47–60. The medium could not be extradited, however, on what were multiple misdemeanor charges and he reportedly died some time ago.

46. Suzie Smith, *Ghosts Around the House* (New York: World Publishing Co., 1970), pp. 38–50.

47. Nickell, *Secrets of the Supernatural*, p. 22.

48. Joe Nickell, *Camera Clues: A Handbook for Photographic Investigation* (Lexington: University Press of Kentucky, 1994), p. 158.

2

Ghostly Habitations

Unlike the spirit manifestations we have discussed thus far, which mediums could purportedly call up on demand, many ordinary people report encounters with ghosts, earthbound spirits of the dead typically associated with a particular place such as a "haunted" house or graveyard.

People in all places and times have believed in ghosts. Dr. Samuel Johnson (1709-1784), the great English writer and lexicographer, once remarked to his biographer James Boswell that it was astonishing that since the creation of the world "it is undecided whether or not there has ever been an instance of the spirit of any person appearing after death. All argument is against it," said Johnson, "but belief is for it."[1]

To be sure, there have often been skeptics, such as the unflappable woman described by the Dutch scholar Erasmus (1466-1536). In an epistle, Erasmus told how the wealthy lady was assailed by a "ghost" who made "certaine rumblings and noyses in the ayre" in an attempt to frighten her to death. As it happened, the woman saw that the entity was actually a man covered in a white sheet, whereupon she beat him until he pleaded for mercy.[2]

This dichotomy of belief versus skepticism continues to characterize the study of hauntings, as the following discussion demonstrates. The discussion is divided into three parts: "Haunted Minds," "Case Motifs," and "Ghost Tour."

Haunted Minds

Psychoanalyst and psychic researcher Dr. Nandor Fodor wrote several books about his exorcisms of ghosts and poltergeists (poltergeist disturbances are the subject of the next chapter). In *Haunted People* (1951), *The Haunted Mind* (1959), and other books, Fodor detailed his use of psychotherapy in ridding people of ghosts, concepts that he wisely recognized in many instances as being inventions of the haunted person's own subconscious.

An excellent example that I am familiar with is a case investigated by my friend and fellow ghostbuster, Dr. Robert A. Baker, the nationally known psychologist and author of numerous books including *Hidden Memories*. Dr. Baker was contacted by a young married couple who were experiencing ghostly visitations. One day while the wife was home alone, she saw the apparition of a golden-haired little girl of about three or four. The child showed herself only briefly, then faded from view, but she returned on several occasions after that.

Investigating, Dr. Baker discovered that only the wife ever saw the ghost girl—not her husband or neighbors, even though the child often played in the yard. Although the entity never spoke or caused any disturbances, the woman's husband and friends were concerned, and the affair was proving more and more unsettling. After examining the house for any signs of paranormal activity, Dr. Baker talked at length with the woman. He eventually learned that she desperately wanted to have a baby but was unable to. Shifting easily from his role as ghostbuster to that of family counselor, Dr. Baker sagely recommended that the couple adopt a child. They accepted his advice, and the little ghost girl went away, never to return.[3]

Such a case gives evidence of the power of wishful thinking. It affects quite normal people, but may be particularly strong in what is known as a "fantasy-prone" personality. That is an otherwise normal person who has an unusual ability to fantasize. As a child, he or she may have an imaginary playmate and live much of the time in make-believe worlds. As an adult, the person continues to spend large amounts of time fantasizing, often reporting apparitions, as well as "out of body" experiences (a feeling of being outside one's physical self), "near-death" experiences (such as seeing a panoramic view of their life, visiting heaven, etc.), or other unusual or paranormal experiences. Fantasy-prone individuals may claim psychic powers, becoming self-styled mediums and psychics, or they may turn up as religious visionaries, UFO abductees, or other such types. They typically have vivid dreams and are particularly susceptible to suggestion, especially to hypnosis, which can unleash the wildest fantasies.[4]

Fantasy-prone individuals—or indeed anyone on occasion—may experience a type of dream that is particularly vivid and realistic. Technically termed *hypnogogic* or *hypnopompic* hallucinations (depending on whether they occur, respectively, while one is going to sleep or waking up), they are more popularly known as "waking dreams" or, in earlier times, as "night terrors." Because one is in the twilight between being asleep and awake, one experiences features of both: fantasy elements perceived as realistic occurrences. Consider, for instance, this description of a ghostly incident given by a caretaker's wife at Mackenzie House:

> One night I woke up at midnight to see a lady standing over my bed. She wasn't at the side, but at the head of the bed, leaning over me. There is no room for anyone to stand where she was. The bed is pushed against the wall. She was hanging down like a shadow but I could see her clearly. Something seemed to touch me on the shoulder to wake me up. She had long hair hanging down in front of her shoulder. . . . She had a long narrow face. Then she was gone.[5]

Clearly this lady, Mrs. Charles Edmunds, experienced a waking dream. As we shall see in other instances throughout this book, they are quite common.

Highly imaginative or fantasy-prone personalities appear to have been at the source of several hauntings I have investigated. For instance, the current owner of one central Kentucky house related to me how the previous owner, an emotional young man, had repeatedly heard mysterious noises, seen apparitions, and delighted in describing other ghostly occurrences during his tenancy. She, on the other hand, had never personally experienced anything in the house that she attributed to a ghost or other supernatural agency. Did she believe in ghosts? She most assuredly did not, she told me.[6] Comparative examples like this lead many investigators to conclude that "ghosts must be believed to be seen" (rather than the other way around).

Suggestion works in other ways also. One is by means of the psychological phenomenon called *folie à deux*, a French expression meaning "folly of two," in which one percipient convinces another of some occurrence. Take, for example, the case of an elderly couple in a Kentucky town who began to be tormented by ghostly goings on: there were gusts of cold air, strange banging noises, and voices that called their names while they were abed. It was the wife who first claimed to see and hear the spirit, while her husband remained unconvinced—that is, until one night he, too, heard his own name being called, after which he became a believer and frequent percipient. No one else, including the husband's sister who visited often, experienced anything out of the ordinary. It appears that the dominant personality—the wife, who was an imaginative person given to belief in ghosts—persuaded her less imaginative mate that a ghost was present. Very likely the voice that the husband heard calling his name was simply his wife's! Comments Dr. Baker, "We tend to see and hear those things we believe in."[7]

In some cases the second party may only pretend to believe in the alleged phenomenon in order to preserve marital harmony. For example, Dr. Baker and I once visited a "haunted" Indiana farmhouse where spooky noises were reportedly occurring upstairs and where the young mother had her four children huddling on sofas, cots, and other makeshift beds downstairs. She was highly interested in occult phenomena, telling us she had had a "psychic" visit the house and frequently watched the Fox network's "Sightings" program which promoted belief in ghosts and similar phenomena. There were several religious statues in the yard around the house.

At one point in discussing the ghost, the husband ventured, "Mostly my wife hears it," whereupon he received such a tongue-lashing from her that he never made another negative comment, but nodded in acquiescence thereafter. (In this case, by a variety of techniques—including counseling, having the husband sleep upstairs for a time armed with a flashlight, and the sprinkling of a white powder that Dr. Baker pretended was the "powdered bones of saints"—we succeeded in exorcising the "ghost.")

On a larger scale, suggestion can result in what is termed *contagion*—a type of influence that can perhaps best be described by a non-haunting example. In 1978 a small panda escaped from a zoo in Rotterdam, whereupon officials issued a media alert. Soon panda sightings—some one hundred in all—were reported across the Netherlands. Unfortunately a single animal could not have been in so many places in so short a time; indeed, as it turned out, *no one* had seen the panda, which had been killed by a train near the zoo. How do we explain the many panda sightings? The answer is, by contagion: people's anticipations led them to misinterpret what they had actually seen. For example, someone may have glimpsed a dog behind some bushes and thought it was a panda due to his or her own expectations. Others had similar illusory experiences. The publicity generated by the case may even have sparked some hoax calls.[8]

In hauntings, psychological contagion frequently plays a crucial role. For example, at Toronto's Mackenzie House the haunted caretakers' visiting grandchildren were soon claiming they had seen a ghost, and the local newspapers further hyped the story. There was also an exorcism. The following year, needed renovations brought workmen into the house who claimed that a sawhorse and dropsheets had been unaccountably moved at night. Caught up in the brouhaha, the men were obviously playing pranks on one another, with one worker encountering a hangman's noose that had been placed over the stairway.[9]

It turned out that a publicist for the nonprofit Mackenzie Homestead Foundation had helped promote the story, reports of which had prompted still other reports, creating a sort of bandwagon effect. Today, Mackenzie House's professional staff has taken a skeptical, even debunking stance regarding the matter, and this seems to have effectively laid the "ghost" to rest.

On an even larger cultural scale, people's perceptions of ghosts actually evolve over time, each period perceiving them in terms of its own cultural attitude. According to R. C. Finucane, in his *Appearances of the Dead: A Cultural History of Ghosts*:

Each epoch has perceived its specters according to specific sets of expectations; as these change so too do the specters. From this point of view it is clear that the suffering souls of purgatory in the days of Aquinas, the shade of a murdered mistress in Charles II's era, and the silent grey ladies of Victoria's reign represent not beings of that other world, but of this.[10]

Case Motifs

Whether they are the result of imagination or of other causes, ghostly phenomena are often related in terms of particularly striking *motifs* (or story elements). Some may involve illusions of various kinds, even outright hoaxes. Of course these may be augmented by individual or collective belief to produce vivid spectral phenomena. Motifs discussed here include the ghost at the bedside, strange specters, phantom footfalls, haunted rocking chair, ghostly door, light in the window, "spook lights," phantom hitchhiker, and other motifs.

   Ghost at the bedside. An example of this very common motif was given earlier in relating Mrs. Edmund's ghostly vision at Mackenzie House. As Dr. Baker states:

> People are easily haunted especially at night after retiring. One of the most common experiences occurs in the middle of the night when the sleeping person suddenly awakes and finds to his astonishment a ghostly figure standing by his or her bed. On many occasions this figure may be a vision of someone near and dear who has just died, or it may well be a vision of a monster or a demon or an alien spaceman. The person experiencing the vision is also startled to discover he is paralyzed, unable to move, and often experiences a floating sensation of moving across the room, out the door, through the walls, etc. Accompanying this experience is a feeling of calm and detachment as if the experience is happening to someone else. After the vision disappears or the experience is over, the percipient usually calmly goes back to sleep as if nothing happened.[11]

As mentioned earlier, such a vision is termed a "waking dream."

Such a dream and the power of suggestion may combine to create a ghost tradition in an ancestral home. There are many reported family legends relating to a haunted bed, for example, that of North Hill House in Colchester, England, described by Dr. Nandor Fodor. Supposedly the ghost haunted a large double bed in the house, "a glum-looking, rickety place." Some people only vaguely felt an air of depression in the room while others reported dreams of strangulation. Fodor amusingly relates his own experience at North Hill House—due apparently to the effect of the spooky environs and his own heightened expectations:

> I hoped that the strangler would pay me a visit while I was sleeping in the haunted bed. I fixed up a stereo camera on a tripod, covering the bed and the corner of a powder closet which was said to be the center of the disturbance. I used flash bulbs and infrared plates. The camera cord reached to my bed and I opened the camera after the light was put out.
>
> It was a glorious bed. I never felt so comfortable in all my life. In no time I was in sound sleep.
>
> I dreamed that the ghost, with a black doctor's bag and a very professional look, came to cure me of insomnia. He made passes over my head and when I refused to yield, he shook his head disapprovingly: "You are too tough, a radical cure is necessary. I regret to have to strangle you."
>
> As he threw himself on me, I awoke gasping. My hand tightened on the flash bulb lead. There was a blinding flare which must have frightened the ghost, if he was there, for the photograph showed no one but myself.[12]

I investigated a somewhat similar tradition at Liberty Hall in Frankfort, Kentucky, a historical site and the residence, supposedly, of an ethereal "Lady in Gray." The ghost is said to be that of a woman, an aunt of the original mistress of the house, who died in 1817. One source, citing "a very interesting tradition handed down in the family," asserts she died in an upstairs bedroom that is now called the "Ghost Room."

Interestingly, there is no recorded mention of the ghost from the time of the aunt's death until at least sixty-five years later.

Only one source describes the supposed first visitation of the ghost—i.e., the "origination of the expression 'Ghost Room.' " According to this source, Miss Mary Mason Scott, great-granddaughter of the original owners, was at the time "home from finishing school" and occupied the room in which her early relative had died. Then, "in the dead of night," she "ran screaming from the room exclaiming that she had seen a ghost"—a "Lady in Gray" as she described the apparition. Thus it appears that the ghostly tradition was launched by an impressionable and apparently quite emotional schoolgirl (who remained unmarried until her death in 1934 and who dabbled in fortunetelling and similar occult pursuits).[13]

Since the sighting occurred when the young lady was abed, there is every likelihood that she experienced an ordinary waking dream of the ghost-at-the-bedside variety. As to her reaction, Finucane writes of the Victorians that "some percipients became hysterical, others turned over and went back to sleep; both men and women ran the entire gamut of emotional responses."[14] As described, the ghost was just the type of image a young Victorian lady would have conjured up, since ethereal gray ladies represented the typical fashion in ghosts during Victoria's reign.[15]

Strange spectres. Many people see ghosts while fully awake and in bright light. One example comes from a small frame house in Lexington, Kentucky. Among other occurrences, when the mother was in her bedroom sewing, she would see a ghostly flash of white pass by her door. Investigation by Dr. Baker revealed: "When lights were on in the bath or the headlights from a passing car shown in the bathroom window, they were reflected off the mirror in the door, and when the door moved it was as if someone had flashed a searchlight across the bedroom door."[16]

Similarly, Milbourne Christopher explains how "a billowing curtain becomes a shrouded woman" and "a shadow becomes a menacing intruder to those with vivid imaginations."[17] Reflections, the misperception of movement seen out of the corner of the eye (a common illusion), and other effects of light and shadow can give rise to spectres.

An interesting case I investigated was that of the supposedly haunted La Fonda Inn in Santa Fe. At least one man lost his life there in 1857 when he was lynched in the hotel's back yard.[18] Reports of other hangings and shootings are part of the local tradition, as are stories of ghosts that supposedly roam the grounds. When I interviewed several of the inn's employees in late May of 1993, I found that while most had heard of the ghost and some knew of secondhand reports, almost no one had seen anything out of the ordinary. This was especially significant in the case of one man, who had been a bell captain there for forty-three years yet had never had any ghostly experiences.

A young female employee did say she had once seen an apparition, a ghostly figure in a white gown carrying a bouquet. This was supposedly the traditional ghost of a bride killed on her honeymoon (although one wonders at the incongruity of what was presumably a bridal bouquet being carried on such an occasion). Under questioning, the employee stated that she did not believe in ghosts, and she soon said she was "not convinced" that what she actually saw was a ghost. She admitted that what she saw "could have been a reflection from the dining room"— one presumably that she colored with her own imagination.[19]

I have done something of the sort. Some years ago while driving at night, I saw ahead of me a stooped old man standing by the roadside. A moment later, however, he had vanished! Fortunately, I just had time to see that what had looked like an old man had really been only a stump and some leaves seen from a particular angle. As the angle changed abruptly the illusion was lost.

Phantom footfalls. Another common motif is that of ghostly footfalls heard in a house when there is no one present to cause them. These can be an illusion caused by any of a number of sources, ranging from simply the odd noises produced by the settling of an old house to fruit-laden branches bumping a roof, or any of numerous other possibilities.[20]

One interesting case that some friends told me about involved a staircase in an old house that had a loose tread covering the steps. As one walked up or down the stairs, each depressed tread would pop back into place a moment later, giving the eerie illusion that someone was following whoever was on the stairs.

The most interesting example of the mysterious footsteps motif that I have investigated was at Mackenzie House. In 1960 Mr. and Mrs. Alex Dobban, who had succeeded the Edmundses as caretakers, told the *Toronto Telegram* about certain ghostly events in the house, including mysterious footsteps on the stairs late at night. Mrs. Dobban stated: "We hadn't been here long when I heard footsteps going up the stairs. I called to my husband, but he wasn't there. There was no one else in the house, but I definitely heard feet on the stairs." Subsequently Mrs. Edmunds came forward to reinforce the claim. She stated that what she had heard were "thumping footsteps like someone with heavy boots," adding, "This happened frequently where there was no one in the house but us, when we were sitting together upstairs."[21]

Some twelve years later, after the heavy-footed Mackenzie ghost had been immortalized in further articles and books, I investigated the site, learning almost immediately of a parallel staircase, made of iron, in a building next door, separated from Mackenzie House by only the narrowest of walkways! That this was the source of the phantom footsteps was corroborated by a tour guide in the historic house, who had heard the sounds herself and managed once to reach the stairs and hear the sounds coming from next door, and by the building superintendent next door, who had known the secret—obvious to him—for more than a decade. The latter said I was the first investigator to come next door, despite the proximity of the buildings. He had decided, bemusedly, to say nothing until asked. It had taken a dozen years.[22]

Haunted rocking chair. This is yet another extremely common motif. At Liberty Hall, for instance, a rocker was occasionally seen "going back and forth by itself." There are several possible explanations for such an event, including drafts. Milbourne Christopher states: "The strangest air-induced action I have seen was when a child's rocking chair moved back and forth by itself, until the slightly opened window directly behind it was closed. The chair was on an uncarpeted floor, and there was a heavy wind at the time."[23]

At one haunted historic house I saw an empty rocker move and was momentarily startled. Then I realized that a tour guide who had just walked by the chair without seeming to touch it had actually whacked it inadvertently with the hoop of her antebellum skirt.

One haunted rocker case I personally investigated was that of the historic Brown-Pusey House in Elizabethtown, Kentucky. Although I had heard the claim of the rocker's movement from a credible local source, to my surprise the house's long-time receptionist assured me it was news to her. In fact, she noted that her desk was immediately below the room where the rocker had been situated and that she would surely have heard it had it been active. The rocker was no longer in that room, but when I entered the chamber I immediately perceived the probable cause of the reported event: the floor was so rickety that walking on it caused even a dresser mirror to shake noticeably.[24]

There are other possible explanations for "haunted" rockers including deliberate pranks, a resident house cat or other pet, an overactive imagination, and other potential sources of "ghostly" activity.

Ghostly door. Like rocking chairs, doors may occasionally appear to move without human agency and be associated with ghosts. At the same time many of the forces that can animate a rocker—pets, rickety floors, pranksters, etc.—can also cause a door to move.

The recently retired curator of Liberty Hall, Mary Smith, told me of a rear door of the historic house that was usually kept ajar and that sometimes moved back and forth. However, unlike her predecessor who promoted the ghost as being good for business, Mrs. Smith is a skeptic who attributes the movement to the wind. During her tenure of more than fifteen years she did not experience any phenomena she attributed to the presence of a ghost.

Before Mrs. Smith's tenure, when ghost stories about the house were fostered and encouraged, once after a fire a fireman and newspaperman stayed in the building for three nights to prevent vandalism. They later told how doors shut behind them and candles were snuffed out "by sudden drafts of cool air."[25] However, drafts are common to old houses—no doubt especially so after a fire—and, together with wind that has found its way through cracked panes, slightly open windows, and other sources, has been responsible for many ghostly occurrences. Obviously the same drafts that snuffed out the candles could be responsible for closing the doors.

In 1978 I investigated the quite sensational claims of a haunted door that graced an abandoned eastern Kentucky farmhouse. According to local tradition, a child was crushed to death in a cane mill accident nearby late in the last century. The door was supposedly used to carry the child's mangled body which was later buried on a hill overlooking the farm. At the time of my investigation, the door was alleged to bang back and forth on occasion—or at least to produce such sounds. Workmen across the creek, who looked as the sounds continued briefly, were sure the door had not moved. A young hunter told me he had heard a banging sound "like someone stacking lumber" but checked and found no one there. Also, local residents told me, after a rain one could often see blood-like streaks running down the door!

Accompanied by the young hunter, my father and I visited the site. The house had been used in recent years as a makeshift barn for curing tobacco. Long two-by-four planks had been nailed up to serve as racks for hanging the tobacco. And a front room even had the side window enlarged into an open doorway for easy access. It was while we were standing in this room that the "ghost" manifested itself. Bam! Bam-bam-bam-bam. We looked at each other and the young man had a sheepish look. The door to the room, located immediately behind the "haunted" front door, had been opened against one of the two-by-fours, and a momentary gentle breeze had drifted up the branch, through the side opening, rattling the door against the plank. The gust spent, the noise ceased.

As our companion agreed, this noise would account for the sounds both he and the workmen had heard. Of course the front door had not moved at all, yet it had seemed the source of the noise. As to the "blood," it proved only to be dark streaks of water-borne substances, possibly tar, decaying leaves, dirt, etc., washing down from the roof. Later forensic tests proved no blood was present.[26]

Light in the window. This motif is widely reported, one instance being a mysterious light seen one evening by two security officers looking up at the third-storey tower window of White Hall, the central Kentucky home of Cassius Marcellus Clay (1810–1903), the politician and abolitionist. Investigating, the officers found no one in the tower and were unable to explain the strange occurrence.

Such events, however, often turn out to be reflections from the moon or other light source on the window, an effect I have witnessed on more than one occasion. It can look exactly like a light *inside* the house. Milbourne Christopher relates the following interesting case study:

> Edward Saint, who was Mrs. Harry Houdini's manager during her last years in Hollywood, was intrigued by the tale that a specter had been observed moving from room to room in a deserted suburban house; the lantern it carried was visible through the windows. The ghost always walked one route from a room at the right end of the house to the left; it never went in the opposite direction. Saint discovered that the moving light so many people had reported was not in the house. It was the reflection from the headlights of an automobile as it approached the house. As a car came up the road the reflected beams went, as the car progressed, from window to window—the path the ghost always traveled.[27]

"Spook lights." In many locales across the United States there are reports of "spook lights," ghostly illuminations that are steeped in folklore. Among the most famous of such phenomena is the intermittent Brown Mountain Light located in the western North Carolina mountains. As is the case with many such mysterious lights, the Brown Mountain phenomenon may have more than one cause. For example, in 1913 the United States Geological Survey investigated the light and concluded it was merely reflections of the head lamps of trains at the base of the mountain. However, since the phenomenon has been reported since 1771, other explanations have been proffered, including St. Elmo's Fire (a type of electrical discharge), so-called "earthquake lights" (an as yet little-understood phenomenon that is associated with seismic disturbances), and other possible sources. Less likely is the folkloric explanation that the light is the moon's reflection from a great gem located somewhere on the face of the mountain.[28]

Another famous phenomenon of this type is that of the Marfa lights near Marfa, Texas. While not ruling out other possibilities, one investigation demonstrated that what are usually seen were automobile headlights merged into a single light due to the viewing distance of about thirty miles. Because of the distance, the light does not appear to be moving, but it does wink on and off as the car goes out of sight behind a cut or other obstruction.[29]

More relevant to our discussion are ghost lights that appear over a graveyard just outside the town of Silver Cliff, Colorado. Again, various theories are offered, but some people insist that the phenomenon is merely the result of lights from nearby towns being reflected from tombstones.[30]

A small hillside cemetery in eastern Kentucky is the source of another ghost light that supposedly shines from the grave of a nine-year-old girl. In fact, the light is a "rectangular halo around the front of the headstone" and is visible only from a particular spot on the bank of the nearby creek. These details suggest the light is a reflection and, indeed, the owner of a grocery near the spot believes the source may be a nearby security light. In any event, when crowds of up to two hundred sightseers continued to gather at the spot, the mother of the dead child abruptly covered the granite tombstone with a blanket. The light ceased.[31]

Phantom hitchhiker. In his book *The Encyclopedia of Ghosts,* Daniel Cohen terms this "unquestionably the most popular and widespread ghostly legend in the United States."[32] Briefly stated, the typical version of the tale has a young man driving along a lonely road one rainy night when he stops for a hitchhiker, a teenage girl wearing a party dress. He gives the shivering girl his jacket, but when he arrives at her stated destination in the next city, she has disappeared! Knocking at the door, the young man learns she was killed ten years ago in an automobile accident on the very road where he encountered her. Later, when he looks for his jacket, it, too, has disappeared. Next day he locates the family plot in the cemetery, whereupon, neatly folded atop the girl's tombstone, is the missing jacket!

There are many versions of the proliferating legend, but no one appears to know just when and where it originated. For our purposes, perhaps, it is enough to know that it is a century-old tale that well illustrates the human desire for legend making, especially concerning the spine-tingling realm of the unrequited dead.[33]

Other motifs. The foregoing is only a beginning. Numerous other motifs in the form of mysterious sights and sounds could easily be given. However, perhaps those we have discussed thus far are sufficient to make clear the role the human imagination plays in cases of alleged haunting. As Dr. Baker says, "We tend to see and hear those things we believe in."[34] The examples should also point to the necessity of investigating claims on a case-by-case basis and demonstrate a panoply of potential sources for many supposedly ghostly occurrences.

Ghost Tour

Of the numerous "haunted" houses I have investigated since 1972, I was able to visit several during a vacation trip to the northeastern United States that I took with my mother in 1993. Again and again I found myself following in the footsteps of so-called "ghosthunters" whose techniques of "investigation" clearly left much to be desired. Our trip focused primarily on three states: Pennsylvania, New Jersey, and Connecticut. (In addition to the alleged haunting sites, we also investigated a previous "poltergeist" disturbance at Bridgeport, Connecticut, and two "demonic" attacks, one at Southington, Connecticut, and the other at Amityville, New York. These will be discussed in the following two chapters.)

The present "ghost tour" begins in Pennsylvania with a search for the resident spirit of Farnsworth House in downtown Gettysburg. After a brief stop at the Gettysburg battlefield, we proceed to Altoona, Pennsylvania, where we encounter a strangely animated wedding dress. In New Jersey, we tour the house and nearby graveyard of historic Ringwood Manor, then dine at a "haunted restaurant" in Morristown. Finally, in Connecticut, we venture to the ruins of the "haunted village" called Dudleytown, before ending our tour at Easton's Union Cemetery, the subject of a 1992 book, *Graveyard: True Hauntings from an Old New England Cemetery*.[35]

The Ghost at Farnsworth House. In downtown Gettysburg, Pennsylvania, at 401 Baltimore Street, stands the historic Farnsworth House Inn. Originally built in 1810, then expanded into the present brick structure in 1833, the house was occupied by the Sweeney family during the famous Battle of Gettysburg. That transpired on the first, second, and third days of July 1863. Confederate sharpshooters occupied the house whose south side—pockmarked with more than a hundred bullet holes—still bears silent witness to the intensity of the battle that swept through the town. After the Northern army was victorious, the Sweeney house became a temporary Union headquarters. In the early years of the twentieth century, the George E. Black family operated it as a lodging house.

In 1972 the Loring H. Schultz family began restoration of the house—now named in honor of Brigadier General Elton John Farnsworth (1837–1863). (Farnsworth received his battlefield promotion on the eve of the historic struggle. On July 3, following the failure of Pickett's charge, Farnsworth's regiments were ordered to attack the right flank of Lt. General James Longstreet's position, but in the ill-fated assault Farnsworth was killed along with sixty-five of his troops.)

Today the historic house is a charming bed-and-breakfast inn featuring an authentically restored dining room with period fare that includes pumpkin fritters, peanut soup, and game pie. To add to the historical flavor, living history tours begin in the basement, where cases mounted on the stone walls display Civil War artifacts, and conclude in the garret with its conspicuous window that the Rebel sharpshooters employed. The atmosphere seems perfect for phantoms of the past, and the house's advertising brochure confides that "some believe a ghostly visitor still walks the corridors at night."[36]

As a promotional gimmick the house even sponsors "Ghost Stories: Hauntings of Gettysburg," as the entertainment period is styled in the brochure. Beneath the photograph of a shrouded lady holding a candelabrum is the caption: "Descend the staircase into the darkness of the stone cellar. Hear, by candlelight, tales of phantom spectres whom [sic] are still believed to haunt the town and its battlefield." The stories are told on Friday and Saturday evenings, at nightfall, during the tourist season.

These storybook ghosts may be the only ones to inhabit Farnsworth House. The owner, Loring H. Shultz, who once lived upstairs in the house, stated emphatically to me, "I don't believe in that stuff!" He said he had never seen a ghost—there or anywhere else—and would only believe in their existence if he personally encountered one. However, Mr. Shultz said we should talk to his daughter, Patty O'Day, whom he described as *not* being skeptical of ghosts.[37]

In fact, Ms. O'Day, who graciously gave us a special tour of the house, stated that she had never personally seen a ghost but had "felt" a "presence." Of course this is a subjective response that anyone might feel. Others, she stated, had had similar feelings, and some had even thought they had glimpsed a ghost, especially after attending the story sessions. On one occasion a ghost was reportedly seen by one individual but not by others who were also present. She thought this could indicate that the percipient had a heightened sensitivity but agreed with me there was no way to tell whether the one person was instead simply more imaginative or more suggestible than the others.

Ms. O'Day went on to say that at least one woman who had been an overnight guest at the inn described a spectral figure that had visited her after she had gone to bed. After I explained the phenomenon of "waking dreams," Mrs. O'Day agreed that that seemed to explain the woman's experience.

The only other evidence for spiritual entities there came from a self-styled "psychic" who had visited the house. That the visit had been part of a television production for Halloween provided a measure of the credibility—or rather the lack thereof—that the event deserved. Although the psychic told some colorful stories that she had purportedly conjured up from the spirit realm, Ms. O'Day conceded she had not found time to check them out.[38] Indeed, if such people and incidents were verifiable from the historical record, how would one know that the psychic had simply not previously researched the facts? (Invariably psychics decline scientifically controlled tests that are designed to determine the genuineness of their alleged powers, or they take the tests but demonstrate no psychic ability.[39])

In short, there appears to be no credible evidence that the

Farnsworth House is haunted. Skeptics do not have ghostly encounters there, and those who do seem merely to be responding to the active promotion of ghosts that takes place there.

Gettysburg Battlefield. To those who believe in spirits of the dead, Gettysburg, which claimed thousands of American lives in three days, should have them in profusion. And if not ghosts, ghost *stories* abound. States ghost-story collector Mark Nesbitt:

> [A]s far as finding an event that should supply America with innumerable stories—explained or inexplicable—there cannot be one more ripe than the Civil War, the greatest of all American spiritual calamities, the horrible, monstrous manifestation of Cain and Abel right from Genesis, where the two sections of the country tore at each other's entrails until we were fortunate that either side remained.[40]

Nesbitt's statement could be that of a skeptic, explaining why Gettysburg would stimulate people's imaginations to conjure up visions of the dead. But he is instead a credulous advocate of the reality of ghosts, having thus far produced two slender volumes, *Ghosts of Gettysburg* and *More Ghosts of Gettysburg,* that offer support for his beliefs. In his introductions he faults skeptics and attempts to invoke science, but he would have done better to offer into evidence something more than a dubious collection of tales.

Not only do many of the narratives sound like ghost yarns spun around a campfire, but some seem to have been collected in practically such a fashion. Speaking of certain dead soldiers, he states:

> Countless others as well, unready, perhaps unwilling, left their mortal shadows behind them on the boulder-strewn mountain, to begin from there, the Great Journey. It cannot be surprising then, that one of the older park rangers, engaged in conversation about ghost stories of the battlefield, reluctantly told his own— although he claims he was not the only one to see the apparition.
>
> Now, on particularly sultry moonlit summer nights on the battlefield, when the mists hang low in what is appropriately known as the Valley of Death between Little Round Top and

Devil's Den, there can be seen, slowly picking his way down
the rocky western slope of the much-fought-over hill, a lone
horseman, replete in the finery of a Civil War officer.[41]

Or so unnamed informants allegedly claim. (According to one
local source, some of the nighttime battlefield sightings of "ghosts"
are believed to be pranks played by reenactment soldiers.[42])

Nesbitt was assisted in collecting tales by other less-than-
objective sources. One is a lady friend and park ranger who is
described as a "collector of odd and unexplainable stories of
Gettysburg." She once employed a "psychic" to give a paranormal
"tour" of the battlefield. (We are told the psychic "is renowned"
and has been "called in numerous times by the FBI and CIA
to help find clues undetected by the forensic scientists in cases
stalled in their progress." Yet we are never given this amazing
psychic's name![43] In fact, the FBI does not employ psychics in
its investigative work.[44]) As is usually the case with psychics
performing for credulous spectators, this one made some dubious
pronouncements while the eager listeners sought to interpret
them, somehow, as uncanny revelations. For example, Nesbitt
writes:

> The medium saw and spoke of a black man carrying a casket
> through the Wheatfield. Odd, since no black troops were used
> in the Battle of Gettysburg. Odd, until one realizes that the
> Timbers' Farm, located just south of the Wheatfield, was occu-
> pied by a black family.[45]

Note the *implication* that the historic fact confirms the psychic's
evocative image, whereas it does nothing of the sort. In fact,
the psychic might only have shrewdly supposed that at least
one family had sent a black worker to retrieve a loved one's
body sometime after the battle.

Moreover, Nesbitt's friend even joined with some other
rangers to hold a Ouija-board séance at the Devil's Den. That
is a great array of boulders that was defended during the battle
by Union troops from several states and was attacked, notably,
by a brigade of Texans. The rangers gathered after dark and

invoked the spirits that supposedly manipulate the board. "And what did it keep spelling, over and over?" asks Nesbitt. "T . . . E . . . X . . . A . . . S. Of course."[46]

In fact, the operation of the Ouija board is well understood and has nothing whatever to do with ghosts. As the Ouija phenomenon was described in the original patent application, "A question is asked and *by the involuntary muscular actions of the players,* or through some other agency, the frame will commence to move across the table" (emphasis added). That participants are supplying the answers can be easily shown, as Milbourne Christopher has observed: When the board is out of sight and the alphabet scrambled, only gibberish is spelled out.[47] Obviously, someone in the group of rangers was, consciously or unconsciously, manipulating the board's planchette to spell out what was an admittedly obvious answer in any case.

Another of Nesbitt's tales illustrates his tendency to dismiss an obvious explanation in favor of a supernatural one. He is describing a group of women who lived in one of the historic— and supposedly haunted—Gettysburg houses:

> One of the women was napping in the afternoon. The shades were drawn and the room was in semidarkness. She awoke to see what she described as a lady sitting in her rocking chair at the foot of her bed wearing a long, outdated dress with long sleeves and either short hair or hair done up in a bun. Though thoroughly frightened and confused at the appearance of a woman from apparently another century in her room, she gathered enough courage and found her voice long enough to ask the stranger a couple questions [sic]. "If there is anyone in here besides myself, knock twice for yes and once for no." Incredibly, from somewhere in the room she heard two knocks. "If you are friendly, knock twice for yes and once for no." No response. Growing frightened at the lack of an answer to whether the apparition was friendly, she repeated the first question and got the same response of silence. Suddenly, the image disappeared.
>
> She sprinted downstairs, as her housemates described it, in hysterics.[48]

Although Nesbitt obtained the account from a skeptical college researcher who presumed the woman was experiencing a waking dream, Nesbitt asks: "Couldn't sleep—'death's counterfeit' as Shakespeare so poetically described it—be but one of the many windows to glimpses into the other world?"

Whether or not there are ghosts at Gettysburg—and I can only say that during the day I spent there I saw no evidence of them—certainly we must ask for better evidence than that provided by raconteurs and players of Ouija boards.

Haunted wedding dress. Travelers on the Pennsylvania Turnpike who stop at a visitors' center may see, among the proliferation of advertising brochures there, one headed: "*See the Haunted Wedding Gown* featured in *Life* magazine. Visit . . . Baker Mansion Museum, Altoona, PA." Altoona is located in the central part of the state, about thirty-five miles north of the turnpike on US 220.

The Baker mansion, considered one of central Pennsylvania's finest examples of Greek Revival architecture, was commissioned by a wealthy nineteenth-century ironmaster, Elias Baker, in 1844 and completed in 1848. Baker, together with his business partner (his nephew Roland Diller), owned and operated the Allegheny Furnace. Located just down the road from the mansion, it was the second iron furnace established in Blair County. By utilizing the Pennsylvania Canal and the Allegheny Portage Railroad, Baker transported iron and other materials throughout the United States, amassing a fortune that enabled him to acquire a 3,373-acre tract and build upon it his thirty-five-room mansion. The Baker family continued to live in the mansion until 1914. Since 1941 it has served as the home of the Blair County Historical Society.[49]

Well worth seeing for its collections of period furniture, Abraham Lincoln material, and other artifacts and treasures, the Baker Mansion is best known for its publicity ploy of the ghostly gown. A photograph of the display appeared in a 1980 issue of *Life* with the explanation that Elias Baker had forbidden his daughter Anna to marry one of his workmen. Anna, so the romantic tale continues, vowed never to marry anyone else and so remained unmarried in the home until her death in 1914.[50]

Several years ago an old wedding dress was mounted in a

display case in Anna Baker's winter bedroom. Subsequently, on several occasions, the dress was reportedly seen to sway on its hanger. As well, the satin slippers beneath the gown have allegedly moved to new positions. "Sometimes," adds the *Life* account, "the resentful Anna rests during the night in her summer bedroom, where the bedcover, with the impression of a human form, is found rumpled the following morning."[51]

As deliciously spine-tingling as this ghost story is, the present staff and management are skeptical of it, despite the advertising brochure (which I am told is to be replaced) and despite the fact that Baker Mansion has repeatedly hosted a program, "Ghost Stories" (performed by Allegheny Storytellers of Pennsylvania). Indeed, I was told (not for attribution) that a former curator probably "started the whole ghost business," that it was she who had witnessed the swaying dress and the indentations in the bed, heard mysterious footsteps, and otherwise repeatedly "experienced" the ghostly phenomena.

Others, however, have also reportedly seen the swaying dress, notably a group of young students a few years ago. But according to our tour guide, Jim Kennedy, there are simple enough explanations for the gown's movements. The display case rests on rather loose boards and a heavy person or group of persons walking in front of it can cause the dress to rustle. Kennedy stated that people who did not notice a tour guide accidentally bump the case (their attention being focused on the dress) had been frightened by the sudden animation of the "haunted" artifact.

Kennedy added that if you stare at the dress you can soon *convince* yourself that it sways even though, objectively, it does not. (A similar explanation debunked the "miraculous" swaying statue of the Virgin Mary at Ballinspittle, Ireland in 1985. Although a group of scientists also "saw" the statue sway, a motion-picture sequence proved no such movement had actually occurred. The scientists discovered that an expectant viewer may sway unconsciously, deceiving himself or herself that it is really the statue that moves.[52])

Kennedy, who said he had worked in the house since 1990, has never personally experienced anything he would attribute to a ghost. "I don't believe the place is haunted at all," he states.[53]

Kennedy did relate a mysterious occurrence there a few years ago: Strange voices were unmistakably heard throughout the house. Eventually the source was discovered: a radio station broadcasting from a nearby hill. The radio waves were being picked up by the lead strips that are inserted between the house's limestone blocks. When the radio station reoriented its broadcast, the voices ceased.[54]

Ringwood Manor and cemetery. Hans Holzer, self-styled "ghost hunter" and author of numerous books that promote belief in hauntings, terms Ringwood Manor "one of the most interesting haunted houses I ever visited."[55]

Haunted or not, the stately mansion is a showpiece of Ringwood State Park, located near the town of Ringwood in northern New Jersey. It is among that state's significant historical houses and has been designated a National Historic Landmark. An earlier house had been built on the property in 1762 and eventually acquired by Robert Erskine (1735–1780), a member of the Continental army and surveyor general to George Washington. Erskine, known as "the Forgotten General," provided Washington with the military maps needed to help win the Revolutionary War. His grave is located in a small cemetery on the property.

In 1807 Martin Ryerson tore down the original old house and erected a portion of the present structure. In 1854 it was acquired by U.S. manufacturer and later New York mayor Abram Hewitt (1822–1903). Mrs. Hewitt converted it into the present-day mansion of fifty-one rooms, outfitted in early Victorian style. It remained in the Hewitt family until 1936, when Erskine Hewitt bequeathed the estate to New Jersey.[56]

In his book *America's Haunted Houses*, Hans Holzer tells of his "investigation" of Ringwood Manor. Holzer's method is to bring along a "reputable medium" who, after supposedly going into a trance, invariably claims to substantiate the haunting. Holzer arrived at Ringwood with Ethel Johnson Meyers in tow, a dubious choice given that she plied her alleged psychic powers in the "Amityville Horror" case (discussed in chapter 4) without realizing it was a hoax. At Ringwood she supposedly made contact with the spirits of two former servants but without proof that either had ever existed. One was said to be responsible for ghostly footsteps in the house, while the other, "Jeremiah," "complained bitterly about his mistress," Mrs. Erskine. Of the latter, Holzer states: "The ghost lady whose manor we were visiting was not too pleased with our presence. Through the mouth of the medium in trance, she told us several times to get off her property! She may still be there," Holzer adds glibly, "for all I know."[57]

The curator of Ringwood Manor, Elbertus Prol, is annoyed with Holzer's account. As a Senior Historic Preservation Specialist who has been at Ringwood for a quarter of a century, Prol discounts claims that the house is haunted. He has never seen anything of a paranormal nature about the house and insists, "I don't believe in ghosts." (He does speak of the house's "presence" but explains it in the subjective sense of "ambiance," of the house having its own personality, not as anything supernatural, and not as the spirit of a deceased person.)

He emphatically discounts the Meyers/Holzer claim that Mrs. Erskine mistreated a servant—whether named "Jeremiah" or not. He observes that the present house was never seen by Mrs. Erskine. In fact, he adds, "the area of the house isn't even near the location of the original house!"[58] Thus when Holzer writes, "The center of the hauntings seems to be what was once the area of Mrs. Erskine's bedroom,"[59] he betrays an utter lack of historical credibility.

As to the alleged footsteps, the Meyers/Holzer version is at odds with the traditional ghost story. This concerns not a servant but the son of a former resident who had been out drinking with friends:

> He asked them to take him home, which they did. Farther down the road, their coach crashed and all were killed. People have reported hearing the sounds of a coach pulling up to the house and a person emerging, entering the house and climbing the stairs to the second floor.[60]

Of course the concept of ghostly footfalls is a contradiction in terms since, being nonmaterial, a ghost would walk noiselessly. Prol suggests that if people report hearing footsteps it may simply be their imagination or the creaking sounds of an old house.[61]

Another traditional legend concerns the ghost of Robert Erskine. According to one version:

> Robert didn't seem to be content to stay put. His ghost must have been pushing and pulling on the walls of the vault in which his body was interred, for one night, to everyone's surprise (maybe even Robert's), one of the bricks from which the walls of the vault were constructed gave way. It popped out of its place, falling to the ground with a plop. The ghost of Robert Erskine followed, and it's been cavorting around the area ever since.
>
> Many of the curious who've visited the cemetery when the moon is full have been disappointed, but many of those brave enough to venture there when the moon is dark and the night inky black have encountered the ghost of Robert Erskine sitting on top of the vault, swinging a lantern in one hand. Some of these visitors have even reported that Robert Erskine, ever the gentleman, has escorted them down the dark road to the old bridge that led them out of the cemetery.[62]

Even Holzer is skeptical of this tale, stating "there is no evidence to substantiate this legend."[63]

Holzer is right on that point, but then again—Ethel Johnson Meyer's "psychic" revelations notwithstanding—there is no evidence to substantiate *any* ghostly occurrences at Ringwood Manor.

Haunted restaurant. Arthur Meyers, in his book *The Ghostly Register,* dares to ask the question: "Is this restaurant haunted?" He is referring to the Society Hill Restaurant in central Morristown, New Jersey.

An investigator's first task in attempting to answer that question, as I learned, was to discover the new identity of the place: Argyle's All American Restaurant and Bar, still located at 217 South Street.

Originally the structure was a house built by John Sayre in 1749. The Sayre family resided there for several generations, followed by other families, until it became a restaurant in 1946. Originally styled the Wedgwood Inn, it has had various names and owners since then. In 1957 it suffered a devastating fire and required extensive renovation, at which time additions were also made.

According to Meyers, the ghostly manifestations "purportedly spring from a triple murder that took place in the house in 1833." Continues Meyers:

> At this time, the owner of the place was Samuel Sayre, who lived there with his wife Elizabeth and a servant girl, Phoebe. Sayre hired a sailor from the West Indies, who was unemployed in New York City, by the name of Antoine LeBlanc. There was an immediate misunderstanding. LeBlanc thought he was coming to Morristown as superintendent of a sizable operation, whereas Sayre wanted him as a farmhand. He stayed on but became more and more frustrated and isolated. He couldn't speak English and became very much a loner. Finally he decided to go back to New York, if possible in style. He thought the Sayres had a great deal of money secreted in the house, so one day he killed man, wife, and servant girl. He found some money and took off for New York, but a posse caught up with him. He was tried, found guilty, and hanged on Morristown Green. To pay for the trial and to celebrate the festive occasion, the skin was stripped from his body and made into purses and wallets. Some Morristown residents still have them.[64]

In light of such allegedly gruesome events, the ghostly goings-on at the Society Hill Restaurant were meager indeed. Says Meyers: ". . . nothing truly malevolent seems to have happened, at least in living memory—just the usual pranks and mischief."[65] Reported phenomena included cold spots, ghostly touchings, and lights that went on and off. Indeed, these are the types of occurrences that are easily explained by imagination and the pranks of staff which result from contagion. (Recall the workers' pranks at Mackenzie House, discussed earlier in this chapter.) I have been involved in two cases of alleged haunting in which lights were being turned off and on, and in both instances this was human mischief by a prankster who confessed; one was even an employee in a restaurant.[66]

There was in fact a climate conducive to contagion at the restaurant. The previous owner stated: "It had a reputation for having ghosts. It was good conversation for the kind of business we're in. I never tried to dissuade anyone."[67] The subsequent owners went even further, using ghost stories in their promotional material and on the back page of the menu, and establishing a Ouija Board Night in their lounge. As one of them explained: "Over a week we'd give out Ouija boards. We were playing up the fact that the house was haunted."[68] The mix of ghost hype, Ouija boards, and alcohol proved volatile and exploded into a full-blown case of "haunting."

Actually it was a punch bowl that exploded. According to one of the owners: "On our grand opening party . . . a punch bowl for no apparent reason just cracked and exploded. It was sitting on a table and punch was being put into it, and all of a sudden it just broke, and the punch went all over the place."[69] Ordinarily, one would think, this would not seem at all mysterious: if the bowl had become cracked, the outward pressure of the liquid filling it could easily cause breakage. It would seem odd to attribute the event to a ghost unless one were seeking publicity (it was, after all, the grand opening) or unless one were caught up in haunting hysteria. In any event, the restaurant owners decided to bring in "expert" help.[70]

Enter the Warrens. Ed and Lorraine Warren of Monroe, Connecticut, have made a business of spirits—particularly sinister ones. According to a satirical profile on the couple in the *Chicago Tribune*, at which time they were helping to promote the movie *Amityville II*:

> Evil spirits stalk the land, portending demons, infestations, possessions . . . and selling movie tickets. They have appeared before, in many guises, on many talk shows, in many films.
> These days they are revealing themselves through a Monroe, Conn., couple name of Ed and Lorraine Warren. . . .[71]

The couple operate something they call the New England Society for Psychic Research with Ed as director. A burly man in his late sixties, Ed has a business card that bills him as a "Demonologist." Lorraine, a year younger and sporting a bouffant hairdo, claims to be a "clairvoyant."[72] They have been called other things, ranging from "passionate and religious people" and "ghost-hunters" to "scaremongers" and other appellations.[73] One skeptic

stated, "I consider them to be total charlatans." As he explained:
"They are dealing in a subject that doesn't exist. They might
as well be pursuing Santa Claus or the Easter Bunny."[74]

Arriving at the restaurant, Lorraine Warren allegedly used
her mediumistic powers to "communicate" with the spirit of the
murderer, whom she identified as the ghost "who had made his
presence known in different ways throughout the building."[75] (She
thus differed from the popular view that the ghost was Phoebe,
the murdered servant girl.)

The Warrens responded by urging that a Roman Catholic
priest conduct an exorcism. (The Warrens are themselves Catholic.[76]) This is typical of their approach, to convert a case that
involved only harmless "pranks and mischief" into one of a sinister aspect, involving evil spirits or demons. To critics, such
as a Catholic scholar who decries exorcisms as an embarrassing
carry-over from the Middle Ages,[77] exorcism proponents might
point to the apparent successes in some cases. But as one expert
on exorcism acknowledges, "The suggestion itself may do the
healing."[78]

Lorraine Warren says the exorcism was successful. Whether
or not that is so, she and her husband took another action that
may have had a more practical effect: they recommended dis-
continuing the Ouija Board Night.[79] The self-styled demonologists
hold that dabbling in the occult can prove dangerous, and skeptics
may agree—but for different reasons. Instead of believing that
evil spirits are a reality that may imperil one's soul, rational
thinkers are simply aware of the power that suggestion plays
in episodes of "haunting."

In my own investigation of the matter, I observed that
knowledge of the restaurant's allegedly haunted past was still
common to staff members and some customers, and so individual
incidents of imagined encounters could still occur. However, ghost
lore is no longer hyped by the management, so spirit manifestations there seem to be on the decline. I interviewed several
staff members. A food and beverage manager had had only a
single experience that he thought might be suggestive: feeling
a chill late one evening outside the room supposed to have been
Phoebe's. On the other hand, a hostess and another employee

said they had never experienced anything they would attribute
to a ghost, and the overall air was of employees who had more
serious things to do than engage in foolishness.[80]

Haunted village. In northwestern Connecticut, at the end of
a winding mountain road, lie the ruins of a forgotten village.
We often call such a place a "ghost town," but if some people
are correct the term is more than figurative: they insist
Dudleytown is haunted.

Located near the town of Cornwall Bridge, some forty miles
due west of Torrington, stands Dudleytown Hill, with an elevation
of 1,520 feet. Accessible to the adventurous, it is known locally
as the "the curse-stricken hill."[81]

According to volume two of *Folk Tales of Connecticut* by
Glenn E. White:

> The Curse of the Dudleys goes back at least as far as when
> John Dudley, Duke of Northumberland, was beheaded by order
> of King Henry VIII in 1533. So was his son, Robert Dudley.
> A third scheming Dudley, the Earl of Leicester, narrowly escaped
> being beheaded by Queen Elizabeth's command. Trouble and
> misfortune followed all the Dudleys.
>
> In 1747, Abriel and Barzillai Dudley returned from the third
> French and Indian War, King George's War, and settled in the
> Dudleytown area, principally because there was good hunting
> in the region. Joined soon by the Jones, Patterson, Carter, Tanner,
> Dibble, and Porter families, the timber was cleared and grain
> was planted. A congenial village grew rapidly.[82]

Before long, however, some of the families "seemed cursed
and haunted." Raconteurs give a litany of people supposedly
afflicted by the "Curse of Dudleytown." For example, old Abriel
became feeble-minded, dying a pauper at the age of ninety. Some
families suffered epidemics; one man was murdered; lightning
killed the wife of a General Swift, "leaving the General only
half sane." One family who moved to New York State were
massacred by Indians, except for two girls who were subsequently
ransomed, "one crazed and the other ill for the rest of her life."[83]

As White adds:

Probably the brilliant editor Horace Greeley, married to a Dudleytown girl, felt that the curse had reached him too, when though he was nominated for the presidency of the United States by both Liberal Republicans and by the Democratic Party in 1872, he was defeated by General Grant. Samuel Jones Tilden, of the Dudleytown Joneses, won the majority of popular votes in the 1876 election for president, but was defeated 185–184 in the electoral college, thus losing the contested election.[84]

Some even say that Greeley's wife eventually went mad—a victim of the "curse."

Of course, this is a familiar ploy, one used for example by those who tout "King Tut's Curse" (actually a journalistic hoax[85]). In fact, if we focus on virtually any place and count only misfortunes, we can easily compile a similar list. Dudleytown's real problems were quite down to earth—literally. The hilly site resulted in erosion of topsoil. Although residents built myriad stone walls in an attempt to retard the loss, the problem contributed to the village's decline.[86] No doubt there were other factors, including a blight that fell on the surrounding woodlands.[87]

Throughout the nineteenth century people began to leave Dudleytown. By the 1880s only decaying buildings remained. Finally, an Irishman by the name of Brophy sought to work an abandoned farm there. However, his wife reportedly died of consumption and his two sons "became outlaws." Finally, says White: "On one wild night in 1901 his house burned and he disappeared. No trace was ever found of him."[88] Today only stone foundations remain of the homes, school, and church that once comprised a thriving village.

Not surprisingly, perhaps, Ed and Lorraine Warren have been attracted to Dudleytown, which they discuss in their book *Ghost Hunters*. Unfortunately, they distort historical facts and make sensational claims for which no documentation whatsoever is provided. For example, they say of the unfortunate Irishman: "One night Brophy stumbled into an inn in the adjacent township, muttering madly of creatures with cloven hooves." And Lorraine Warren has somehow learned: "A few years ago a motorcycle gang started going to the mountain above [sic] Dudleytown and performing Satanic rituals there. So by this time the place has been infested [by demonic forces] for sure."[89]

My investigation included a visit to the lonely site. I can agree with Lorraine Warren that the place is a quiet one, but her statements that "there's a strange silence to the place" and that "you've never heard a place so quiet"[90] are exaggerations. Lonely, deserted mountain tops typically are quiet places.

On my visit to the area I spoke with eighty-nine-year-old resident Walter Kilham who built a weekend home at the lower outskirts of Dudleytown in 1938—his home being situated upon one of the old cellar holes—and he has thus had more than half a century of experience with the place. Far from having been driven mad by Dudleytown, he has an alertness and wit that many younger people should envy.

He recalled a visit made to the site some years ago by a "parapsychologist" who claimed to "feel spirits." Mr. Kilham said the man came with a bus tour group and had managed to get the people "worked up." He added that the local historical society has been trying to discourage stories of ghosts because they do not like to see history distorted and false stories perpetuated. He said, for example, that the story about Horace Greeley's wife having been driven mad at Dudleytown was fundamentally untrue, that whatever the state of her mind Dudleytown "had nothing to do with it."[91]

Mr. Kilham insisted that no ghosts have ever bothered him. His voice taking on a lighter tone, he did recall once a rather mysterious event: on the lonely hillside near his place, he discovered the unlikely but unmistakable tracks of a cow! He thought it amusing to speculate about a "ghost cow" of Dudleytown, but he soon discovered that an area farmer had had just such an animal missing at the time.

Tourists who visit Dudleytown have invariably heard tales about the "haunted" site and ask Mr. Kilham for his opinion. His response is a refreshing antidote to the nonsensical approach of people like the Warrens. "If you believe in ghosts," he tells people, "the town is full of them; if you don't, there aren't any!"[92]

Union Cemetery. If the spirits of dead people truly survive the grave, what better place to seek them out than a cemetery?

Certainly, folklore brings us many tales of haunted graveyards, and there are contemporary accounts as well. Typically, though, ghosts in cemeteries prove as elusive as those in haunted houses: here is a dubious tale, there a questionable photograph, elsewhere what proves to have been the merest illusion.

However, Ed and Lorraine Warren (and their New England Society for Psychic Research) have taken the concept of graveyard hauntings into astonishing new realms of silliness. In their book *Graveyard: True Hauntings from an Old New England Cemetery* (which, like their other books, was written for them by a professional writer), the Warrens are once again serving up outlandish claims without offering anything resembling proof (let alone documentation of sources).

For instance, their very first chapter, sensationally titled "A Case of Lust and Murder," describes events that happened a vague "several decades ago" and, since the account is bereft of any newspaper or other documentation, may be one of the tales covered by the book's prefatory disclaimer: "Names and particulars have been changed in some of the following stories to protect the reputations of both the living and the dead." A central element of the story, an apparition of "a dark man-shape" that haunted the hapless murderer, has admittedly "never been verified" (although it was allegedly confided to fellow prisoners—unnamed of course and, for all we know, entirely fictitious).[93]

The book is supposed to feature hauntings from a particular graveyard—the Union Cemetery at Easton, Connecticut—yet the foregoing apparition appears to be nonexistent. Without it, the only connection with the alleged haunting site is that the murdered man's body was allegedly buried "in a sinkhole not far from the cemetery."[94]

The book goes downhill from there. A later chapter, "The Haunted Monastery," discusses the ruins of a cloister that is "in the region of" the graveyard. The apparent point of the short chapter is as vague as it is brief:

> In the later 1800s a group of people traveled through this area and stayed for nearly a month, living in primitive conditions. There was trouble with some townspeople and trouble with

the law. There were also rumors of strange activities at night. After the people had left, the clean bones of many dead animals were found in a sandy pit, and several satanic symbols were later discovered carved into many trees. Many of these people camped where the monastery was eventually to be built.[95]

Then follows the blithe admission that, although the Warrens feel the account is true, "today there is no record of these people having been here."[96]

Still another chapter features anecdotal accounts, mostly unattributed, of alleged sightings of Union Cemetery's legendary spectre. For example:

There are many tales of the White Lady, perhaps the oddest being of the man who went to the cemetery late one night to speak with his recently buried wife. Just by kneeling at his wife's grave, the man felt as if she were with him again.

This particular night, however, as he knelt there in the chill autumn night, dead leaves scraping across the gravestones surrounding him, a great sorrow filled him . . . and as he looked up from his wife's grave, he saw the White Lady standing there, watching him.

"I wish my husband would have loved me as much as you love your wife," she said.

And then she was gone, leaving him alone in the midnight graveyard, and to his own grief and loss.[97]

Or so an alleged source reportedly said, on some occasion, it was rumored.

For utter silliness, there are Ed Warren's claims regarding staining seen on the surface of old gravestones. Warren says that, just as one sees pictures in clouds or in ink blots, the gravestone patterns "are really the faces and costumes of the people who are buried there." He adds: "Over the years, we've learned that spirits project their images on to gravestones and help us take their photographs. Many spirits want to communicate with the living."[98] Is he serious? Sadly, apparently, yes.

Ed Warren considers photographing the patterns a type of "psychic photography." He also claims to have videotaped the

White Lady, the footage having turned out "incredibly well" and offering "incontrovertible proof to any doubters." Alas, the Warrens do not provide a single image from the tape in their book's photo section. Instead they merely show one or another nighttime photo taken near a "grave sight" [sic] that depicts "spirit energy" as spherical blobs or mistlike forms. The mist may be merely that, of course, and the small bright dots are easily explained: with nighttime flash pictures "tiny particles of dust or raindrops in front of the camera may appear on the picture like brilliant balls of light."[99]

Graveyard continues in this vein, but so scant is the information on Union Cemetery that nearly two-thirds of the book (pp. 69–194) is padded with "Incidents at Other Graveyards." These are not even firsthand investigations by the Warrens but are "other stories submitted to the New England Society for Psychic Research."[100]

When I visited Union Cemetery I found only a well-groomed, New England churchyard burying ground, with quaint headstones dating back to the mid-eighteenth century. The Easton Baptist Church, a white frame building with a louvered spire, stood primly in the background. My photographs failed to depict a single spectre, unless that free-form lichen shape in one close-up shot of a gravestone is—could it really be?—Casper the Friendly Ghost!

Perhaps that is the right note on which to end our ghost tour. The following chapter, however, will look at quite a different type of spirit phenomenon: so-called poltergeist disturbances, which in some cases—particularly as outbreaks of fire—can prove quite dangerous.

Recommended Works

Baker, Robert A., and Joe Nickell. *Missing Pieces: How to Investigate Ghosts, UFOs, Psychics, and Other Mysteries.* Amherst, N.Y.: Prometheus Books, 1992. A complete manual for investigating paranormal occurrences with extensive material on ghosts.

Christopher, Milbourne. "Haunted Houses," chapter 12 in *ESP, Seers*

& *Psychics: What the Occult Really Is.* New York: Thomas Y. Crowell, 1970. Concise skeptical look at hauntings by a professional magician.

Cohen, Daniel. *The Encyclopedia of Ghosts.* New York: Dorset Press, 1984. Balanced look at ghostly phenomena with entries on most famous cases.

Finucane, R. C. *Appearances of the Dead: A Cultural History of Ghosts.* Amherst, N.Y.: Prometheus Books, 1984. Demonstration of how each historical period perceives ghosts according to its own particular expectations.

Fodor, Nandor. *The Haunted Mind: A Psychoanalyst Looks at the Supernatural.* 1959; reprint, New York: Signet Mystic Books, 1968. A look at mediumship, hauntings, telepathy, reincarnation, etc., by a sometime skeptic who attempts to separate the psychological from the supposedly psychical.

Holzer, Hans. *America's Haunted Houses: Public and Private.* Stamford, Conn.: Longmeadow Press, 1991. Credulous look at alleged hauntings by a ghost hunter who "investigates" via a trance medium.

Warren, Ed, and Lorraine Warren, with Robert David Chase. *Graveyard: True Hauntings from a New England Cemetery.* New York: St. Martin's Press, 1992. Recommended only as an example of bizarre, undocumented claims by a self-styled "demonologist" and a "clairvoyant."

Notes

1. Samuel Johnson, quoted in Peter Haining, *Ghosts: The Illustrated History* (Secaucus, N. J.: Chartwell Books, 1987), p. 8.

2. Erasmus, quoted in *ibid.*, p. 22.

3. See chapter 2, "The Ghost Girl," in Joe Nickell, *The Magic Detectives* (Amherst, N.Y.: Prometheus Books, 1989), pp. 13–15, 109; See also Robert A. Baker and Joe Nickell, *Missing Pieces: How to Investigate Ghosts, UFOs, Psychics, and Other Mysteries* (Amherst, N.Y.: Prometheus Books, 1992), pp. 133–34.

4. Baker and Nickell, *Missing Pieces*, pp. 221–26.

5. Quoted in Susy Smith, "Turbulence in Toronto," chapter 2 in *Ghosts Around the House* (New York: World, 1970), p. 44.

6. Author's case file.

7. Baker and Nickell, *Missing Pieces*, p. 129.

8. Joe Nickell with John F. Fischer, *Secrets of the Supernatural* (Amherst, N.Y.: Prometheus Books, 1988), p. 21.

9. Ibid.

10. R. C. Finucane, *Appearances of the Dead: A Cultural History of Ghosts* (Amherst, N.Y.: Prometheus Books, 1984), p. 223.

11. Baker and Nickell, *Missing Pieces*, p. 130.

12. Nandor Fodor, *The Haunted Mind* (1959; reprint, New York: Signet Mystic Books, 1968), p. 36.

13. For a full account of the Liberty Hall ghost, see Joe Nickell, *Mysterious Realms: Probing Paranormal, Historical, and Forensic Enigmas* (Amherst, N.Y.: Prometheus Books, 1992), pp. 19–33.

14. Finucane, *Appearances of the Dead*, p. 211.

15. Ibid., p. 223.

16. Baker and Nickell, *Missing Pieces*, p. 127.

17. Milbourne Christopher, *ESP, Seers & Psychics* (New York: Thomas Y. Crowell, 1970), p. 172.

18. "The History of La Fonda," advertising brochure, n.d.

19. Author's case file.

20. Christopher, *ESP, Seers & Psychics*, p. 169.

21. Quoted in Nickell with Fischer, *Secrets of the Supernatural*, p. 23.

22. Ibid., pp. 24–27.

23. Christopher, *ESP, Seers & Psychics*, p. 169.

24. Author's case file.

25. Arthur Myers, *Ghostly Register* (Chicago: Contemporary Books, 1986), p. 131.

26. Nickell with Fischer, *Secrets of the Supernatural*, pp. 120–28.

27. Christopher, *ESP, Seers & Psychics*, pp. 172–73.

28. E. Randall Floyd, *Ghost Lights and Other Encounters with the Unknown* (Little Rock, Ark.: August House, 1993), pp. 56–58.

29. Herbert Lindee, "Ghost Lights of Texas," *Skeptical Inquirer* 16, no. 4 (Summer 1992): 400–406.

30. Daniel Cohen, *The Encyclopedia of Ghosts* (New York: Dorset Press, 1984), pp. 251–52.

31. Lee Mueller, "Mysterious Light Shines from Grave of Girl, 9," *Lexington Herald-Leader* (Lexington, Ky.), May 21, 1994; "Grave's Glow Mysterious, Intriguing," *Paintsville Herald* (Paintsville, Ky.), May 25, 1994.

32. Cohen, *Encyclopedia of Ghosts*, p. 291.

33. Ibid., pp. 291–93.

34. Baker and Nickell, *Missing Pieces*, p. 129.

35. The "tour" sites are not given in the same order as the author's visits.

36. "The Historic Farnsworth House Inn: Showplace of the Civil War," advertising brochure, n.d.

37. Loring H. Schultz, interview with author, June 8, 1993.

38. Patty O'Day, interview with author, June 8, 1993.

39. Joe Nickell, ed., *Psychic Sleuths: ESP and Sensational Cases* (Amherst, N.Y.: Prometheus Books, 1994), pp. 12–14, 55, 80–81.

40. Mark Nesbitt, *Ghosts of Gettysburg: Spirits, Apparitions and Haunted Places of the Battlefield* (Gettysburg, Pa.: Thomas Publications, 1991), p. 11.

41. Ibid., p. 60.

42. Patty O'Day, interview with author, June 8, 1993.

43. Ibid., pp. 63–64.

44. Nickell, *Psychic Sleuths*, p. 69.

45. Nesbitt, *Ghosts of Gettysburg*, p. 64.

46. Ibid., pp. 17–18, 65.

47. Christopher, *ESP, Seers & Psychics*, p. 131.

48. Mark Nesbitt, *More Ghosts of Gettysburg* (Gettysburg, Pa.: Thomas Publications, 1992), pp. 20–21.

49. Baker Mansion Museum, advertising brochure, n.d.

50. "Baker Mansion," excerpt from *Life* magazine, November 1980: 154 (supplied by museum staff).

51. Ibid.

52. "Those Who Sway Together Pray Together," *Discover*, October 1985: 19.

53. Jim Kennedy, interview with author, June 13, 1993.

54. Ibid.

55. Hans Holzer, "The Ghostly Servants of Ringwood Manor," chapter 36 in *America's Haunted Houses* (Stamford, Conn.: Longmeadow Press, 1991), p. 124.

56. Ibid., pp. 124–25; Joan Bingham and Dolores Riccio, *More Haunted Houses* (New York: Pocket Books, 1991), p. 215; Kathy Shwiff, "Ghost Stories that Go 'Boo!' in the Night," *Today* (North Jersey Newspapers), October 28, 1992: 27.

57. Holzer, *America's Haunted Houses*, p. 125.

58. Elbertus Prol, interview with author, June 12, 1993.

59. Holzer, *America's Haunted Houses*, p. 125.

60. Shwiff, "Ghost Stories that Go 'Boo!,' " p. 27.

61. Elbertus Prol, interview with author, June 12, 1993.

62. Bingham and Riccio, *More Haunted Houses*, pp. 215–16.

63. Holzer, *America's Haunted Houses*, p. 125.

64. Meyers, *Ghostly Register*, pp. 227–29.

65. Ibid., pp. 227–28.

66. One case is reported in Baker and Nickell, *Missing Pieces*, pp. 128–29; the other is in my case file: " 'Haunted' Japanese Restaurant—Rome, Georgia" (1993).

67. William McCausland, quoted in Meyers, *Ghostly Register*, p. 228.

68. David DeGraff, quoted in ibid., pp. 230–31.

69. Ibid., p. 228.

70. Ibid., p. 230.

71. Clarence Peterson, "Demonologists Hellbent on Selling 'Amityville II,' " *Chicago Tribune*, September 23, 1982.

72. Ibid.; Bill Richards, "And You Thought 'Ghostbusters' Was Just a Movie Farce?" *Wall Street Journal*, October 31, 1989.

73. Jodi Duckett, *The Morning Call* (Allentown, Pa.), November 5, 1991.

74. Ibid.

75. Lorraine Warren, quoted in Myers, *Ghostly Register*, p. 230.

76. Myers, *Ghostly Register*, p. 230.

77. An interview with Rev. Richard McBrien, on ABC's "Nightline," April 5, 1991.

78. Rev. Alphonsus Trabold, theology professor and expert on exorcism at St. Bonaventure University, quoted in Richards, "And You Thought 'Ghostbusters' Was Just a Movie Farce?" *Wall Street Journal*, October 31, 1989.

79. Myers, *Ghostly Register*, pp. 230–31.

80. Interviews with Joe Nickell, June 12, 1993.

81. Glenn E. White, comp. and ed., *Folk Tales of Connecticut*, vol. 2 (Meriden, Conn.: The Journal Press, 1981), p. 47.

82. Ibid., p. 45.

83. Ibid., pp. 45–46.

84. Ibid., p. 46.

85. See Kendrick Frazier, "Mummy's Curse Tut-tutted," *Skeptical Inquirer* 5, no. 1 (Fall 1980): 13.

86. Walter Kilham, interview with author, June 10, 1993.

87. White, *Folk Tales of Connecticut*, p. 46.

88. Ibid., pp. 46–47. Cf. Ed and Lorraine Warren with Robert David Chase, *Ghost Hunters* (New York: St. Martin's Paperbacks, 1989), pp. 173–77.

89. Warren and Warren with Chase, *Ghost Hunters*, pp. 176–77, 182.

90. Ibid., p. 182.

91. Walter Kilham, interview with author, June 10, 1993.

92. Ibid.

93. Ed and Lorraine Warren, with Robert David Chase, *Graveyard: True Hauntings from an Old New England Cemetery* (New York: St. Martin's Press, 1992), pp. 16–28.

94. Ibid., p. 21.

95. Ibid., p. 40.

96. Ibid.

97. Ibid., p. 51.

98. Ibid., pp. 9–10.

99. Gerald Mosbleck, quoted in Joe Nickell, *Camera Clues: A Handbook for Photographic Investigation* (Lexington: University Press of Kentucky, 1994), p. 159.

100. Warren and Warren with Chase, *Graveyard*, p. 69.

3

Poltergeist Disturbances

"Noisy Spirits"

Certain types of disturbance, usually of a purely mischievous nature, and for which there is no apparent cause, are popularly attributed to "poltergeists," after the German word for a "noisy" (*poltern*) "spirit" (*geist*).[1] Apparently it was Martin Luther who coined the term in the fifteenth century; four centuries later, the word was adopted into English, being used to indicate the phenomenon of the "merry ghost."[2] Given this meaning—although some sources equate the poltergeist with demons or, in at least one instance, with the vampire[3]—I have chosen to render this discussion of poltergeists as a separate chapter of Part One.

Most investigators would probably agree with Rossell H. Robbins's list of manifestations that characterize poltergeist phenomena:

1. Noise or knockings without apparent natural origin
2. Uncontrolled movement (telekinesis) of small objects, such as dishes or bric-a-brac
3. Disappearance of small objects and their subsequent recovery in unexpected places
4. Occasional major disasters such as arson[4]

An example of what would today be termed poltergeist activity was reported as early as the sixth century B.C. The case, recounted by the Roman historian Livy, involved a shower of stones.[5] Another such disturbance occurred in A.D. 355, with stones bombarding a house and loud pounding noises emanating from its walls. Jaffe cited a case in his *Bibliotheca Rerum Germanicarum* which occurred ca. 760 and was characterized by mysterious fires, disappearing objects, and the reported hurling of an infant into a fire.[6] In 858, near the German town of Bingen, came more showers of stones and loud knocking sounds. In 1184, at the home of a Welshman named William Nott, an unseen force threw clods of earth and ripped up clothing.[7] The poltergeist appeared in America at least as early as 1682, at which time Richard Chamberlin, Secretary of the Province of New Hampshire, studied an outbreak caused by a "stone-throwing devil."[8]

What causes such attacks? Investigators generally concede that most such disturbances center around a disturbed person, usually a child. Believers often attribute the phenomenon to repressed hostilities of the pubescent child, that is, that it is "a sidetracking of the sexual energies in a maturing body" (as Fodor said) which somehow manifest themselves as kinetic energy.[9] Skeptics have a simpler explanation, attributing the effects to the cunning pranks of a naughty youth or disturbed adult.[10] Those holding to the latter view might accept Fodor's term "poltergeist psychosis"[11] but only as it applies to the mental state that causes a person to engage in such behavior, not to any psychic force.

In eighteenth-century England came a poltergeist case in which the cause was eventually learned. The account was given in a contemporary pamphlet as involving "the most surprising and unaccountable Events that Ever happened."[12] In early January of 1772, in Stockton, Surrey, strange happenings began in the home of an elderly widow named Mary Golding. Mrs. Golding heard a loud clatter, whereupon her young maid claimed a row of plates had unaccountably fallen from a kitchen shelf. While the widow looked at the broken crockery, dishes from another shelf crashed to the floor. Soon a clock and then a lantern fell, a platter of beef crashed, and mirrors were broken.

Mrs. Golding's niece, Mrs. Mary Pain, insisted her aunt leave the house and spend the remainder of the day and night with her and her family. They were joined by the young maid, and soon thereafter an egg sailed across the kitchen and broke on a cat's head. A side of bacon and two hams fell from their hooks by the chimney. In the cellar a cask of beer was found overturned. Elsewhere in the Pains' house a wooden box was broken, and a coal scuttle and table were overturned. Goblets, bottles, and chinaware crashed, and water in a pail away from the kitchen stove began boiling.

Finally, Mr. Pain pointed out that only when the maid was present did the phenomena occur; Mrs. Golding took his advice and dismissed the girl. The disturbances ceased abruptly. Not until almost a half-century had passed, however, was the public to learn the solution to the mystery.

William Hone, editor of *The Every-Day Book*, reported the details as they had been given by the maid, Ann Robinson, to the Reverend J. Brayfield. As magician Milbourne Christopher explains in his *ESP, Seers and Psychics*:

> Ann Robinson had confessed to the clergyman that she had thrown some of the objects whose movements were attributed to "an unseen agency." She had pelted the cat with an egg, hung the hams and bacon so they would fall when their weight caused the hooks to tear through their skins. She had dropped a chemical in the pail of water to make it bubble. Rows of plates were dislodged when she yanked a wire she had earlier arranged behind them. Long horsehairs were attached to other objects to give them sudden life. They seemed to jump or fall when she pulled the ends.[13]

Similar trickery was behind the poltergeist-like disturbances that characterized some of the early spirit manifestations of the Fox Sisters, as we saw in chapter 1. Recall the noises they produced by bumping the floor with an apple on a string and by knocking on the bedstead. Then there was the mischief that transpired after the "spirit" decided it did not like the girls' brother-in-law: the children secretly threw slippers at him, shook the dinner table, and displaced his chair so that as he attempted to sit down he fell on the floor. As Margaret confessed some forty years later, she and Katie were "very mischievous children" who began their shenanigans "to terrify our dear mother, who was a very good woman and very easily frightened. . . . She

... did not suspect us of being capable of a trick because we were so young."[14]

Another practitioner of the supposedly paranormal who began her career as the focus of a "poltergeist" was teenager Lulu Hurst. Performing as the "Georgia Magnet" for two years in the 1880s, she packed lecture halls and opera houses in Atlanta, New York, Chicago, Milwaukee, and elsewhere. One of her feats was to repel two strong men pressing against a stick she held, using a supposedly magical power. Actually, as she confessed publicly before giving up her act to become a housewife, Lulu simply employed well-known principles of force deflection.[15]

But it is the *origins* of Lulu Hurst's powers that concern us here. In 1883 at the Hurst family home at Cedarville, Georgia, there were mysterious disturbances that transpired in the presence of the fifteen-year-old girl. Small objects moved, crockery was smashed, popping sounds were heard, and other activity transpired that today would be termed poltergeist phenomena.

In her statement explaining that she was leaving the stage in part because she had "become burdened with the idea of the vast amount of superstition and delusion in the public mind concerning the 'power,'" she also explained how she had accomplished her wonders, including the original poltergeist-type effects. Those, she explained, were simply a girl's tricks; for example, like Margaret Fox, she discovered she was able to make rapping noises with her toes.[16]

As we shall see in the following section, poltergeist cases that have been competently investigated and the cause of the disturbances clearly indicated invariably turn out to be due to human agency, i.e., pranks like those played by Ann Robinson, Maggie and Katie Fox, and Lulu Hurst.

Modern Attacks

The historical poltergeist cases mentioned thus far are quite similar to numerous ones of much more recent vintage. For example, consider this case, related by Milbourne Christopher as an example of how media coverage can increase the frenzy of an attack by so-called poltergeists:

> Sunday, December 30, 1951, boxes, bottle caps, and Christmas cards began acting oddly in one room in the Henry Thatchers' home in Louisville, Kentucky. Neither he, his wife, nor the three Saunders girls who lived with them could explain why or how the objects whirled over their heads. Until then, it had been a sad Christmas season for the children. They were wards of the county Children's Home, which paid their board with the Thatchers. Their mother was in a hospital, suffering the ravages of cancer. Their father long before had deserted her. Joyce Saunders, an eleven-year-old student in the fifth grade, gave visitors to the house, in the days that followed, a vivid word picture of the phenomena. Sometimes objects flew when newspaper reporters were present, though they were always in flight by the time they were noticed. Joyce and her sisters posed for cameramen and appeared on television. Nothing so exciting had ever happened to them.[17]

However, Christopher adds:

> Joyce, two policemen noticed, was the magnet that seemed to attract soaring pins, cans, and table knives. She finally confessed to officers Russell McDaniel and Jack Fischer that she had caused the disturbances to attract attention. Not all the phenomena reported had actually occurred. The child admitted: "I didn't throw all those things. People just imagined some of them."[18]

The year 1957 saw a number of poltergeist outbreaks including stones that showered on a small frame house in Clayton, California. For three weeks, the family was terrified by additional disturbances. Stones even fell inside the house, apparently dropping from the ceiling. As well, dishes and bottles, pots and pans, even onions and a fountain pen became airborne inside the Portuguese family's home. As often happens, the events ran their course and eventually ceased, with results that, while not conclusive, are nonetheless suggestive. Outsiders hinted that the trouble was caused by the retired workman's two grandsons, ages ten and thirteen, and the phenomena ceased after a parapsychologist spent four days in the home intent on observing the cause. It is certainly a possibility, some would say a probability, that the youths were responsible and quit either because they tired of the pranks or because they feared being caught by the observant outsider.

A similarly inconclusive but even more suggestive denouement characterized another case that year. Furniture was toppled, people were pelted with fruit, and other disturbances occurred in the home of the Wall family in an Illinois town with the ironic name of Resthaven. Revealingly, however,

> When fourteen-year-old Susan Wall was not in the farmhouse, all was quiet. If, however, she crossed the road to visit her grandparents, the Mikuleckys, the poltergeist seemed to follow her. Bangs and squeaks were heard in unoccupied rooms, and there were rumbling noises in the walls.
>
> Deputy Sheriff Chester Moberly was satisfied that there was nothing supernatural about the things that happened when Susan was around. He told the Walls flatly that if he heard one more report about weird events in their vicinity he would subject them all to a lie-detector test. Nothing more was heard about poltergeists in Resthaven.[19]

More definitive results came from a case that occurred that summer in Hartsville, Missouri. Nine-year-old Betty Ward was the focus of a series of poltergeist attacks which included a comb that took flight, buckets of water that were spilled, laundry baskets that shook wildly, and other odd events. Betty told reporters that she was terrified by the strange happenings, but a magician who visited the house to investigate the case thought otherwise: he actually observed a can opener as it fell from its place of concealment under the girl's arm![20]

Despite such evidence, the late D. Scott Rogo, a psychical researcher and author, continued to believe there were genuine poltergeist occurrences. Frequently, in his The Poltergeist Experience, Rogo argued that one could not conclude that all the events in a given case were the result of trickery simply because someone was caught red-handed on an occasion or two.[21]

Typical of this approach is one investigator who describes a case investigated by Hans Bender: "The incidents centered around Brigitte, a thirteen-year-old daughter. As in other poltergeist cases which seemed to include genuine effects, when these began to wane, the focal person, Brigitte, was discovered to cheat. Bender found the girl's fingerprints on a dish which she claimed the poltergeist had thrown out the window."[22] Note the unwillingness to draw the obvious conclusion from the evidence. Clearly, such a position unfairly favors belief in poltergeist phenomena since, as magicians and other trained observers can attest, it may be impossible to catch someone faking every event. In the typical case, if one watches the suspected "poltergeist" too closely he or she will simply refrain from pranks; if on the other hand, one lets up on the monitoring so as to provide an opportunity for trickery, one risks being unable to catch the mischief maker in the act.

Milbourne Christopher analyzes one "unsolved" case of 1958, noting that the father would not allow a magician in the house or the use of lie-detector tests on family members. Christopher points out that police and psychical researcher J. Gaither Pratt from Duke University, who thought the phenomena genuine, accepted without question the statements of one child, twelve-year-old Jimmy, who was often the only one to witness one of the events. All that is necessary to see the case in quite a different light, he says, is to "suppose that what the boy said was not true, that he was in one room when he said he was in another in some instances. Also let us suppose that what people thought they saw and what actually happened were not precisely the same."[23] Not only ordinary people but even supposedly "reliable witnesses" are capable of misperception. Numerous factors plague eyewitness reporting, as has been well established.[24] As Christopher illustrates in the case at hand:

Take the single instance where an outsider, Miss Murtha, saw a statuette take off and land. A television set was on at the time. It is logical to suppose her attention was there. A quick movement by the occupant of the sofa could have jarred the small end table with enough impact to send the upright figurine falling to the floor the mere two feet away.

Jimmy spoke to Miss Murtha, as Pratt's interview with her indicates, just before she saw the figurine move. She turned in his direction to answer. At *that* moment the falling motion began.[25]

Christopher concludes, "That is the *only* time anyone saw the takeoff of a flying object." In every other instance, he observes, Jimmy could simply have thrown the object.[26]

Of course, as indicated earlier, there are many cases in which the child confesses. In one such case that occurred in Alabama in 1959, a series of household blazes that caused a fire chief to wonder about spontaneous combustion and a father to consult a local "witch" ended with the confession of the nine-year-old son. His motive had been to cause his family to return to the city from which they had moved.[27] In 1974, a spate of flying-object incidents ceased after a thirteen-year-old girl with "deep hostilities" was seen to "deliberately kick an object and then claim that the poltergeist had done it."[28]

Quite often the confessions can provide lessons in perception and useful aids for investigating future cases. Take for example the case of a "bewitched" one-room schoolhouse in Stark County, North Dakota, in the spring of 1944. Strange sounds seemed to emanate from a coal bucket; then the bucket turned over and lumps of smoldering coal bombarded the walls. Smoke and flame soon burst from window shades, curtains, a bookcase, and a wall map. The big classroom dictionary moved eerily as though pushed or pulled by an unseen hand. The twenty-two-year-old school-teacher, Mrs. Pauline Rebel, sought outside help.

The local fire marshal stated his intention of sending some of the lumps of coal, the bucket, and dictionary to the FBI for analysis. "At first we were convinced that the whole thing was a hoax and suspected arson," he told a reporter, "but after we used the lie detector with negative results we are of the opinion that witnesses were telling the truth. To put it mildly, we are puzzled." Many townsfolk ascribed supernatural forces to the mysterious events, but the school board clerk, J. F. Hoff, thought otherwise. Recalling some threatening notes posted on the schoolhouse door that warned the teacher to leave town, Hoff stated: "I think we'll find that the whole thing was caused by a crank who threatened the life of Mrs. Rebel."[29]

But in only three more days the mystery was solved. In the presence of the fire marshal, a special assistant attorney general, and their own parents, four of the pupils confessed how they and other children had tormented the hapless teacher. For example:

> When Mrs. Rebel was not wearing her glasses, or when she was out of the room, they had used long rulers and blackboard pointers to stir up the coal and tip the scuttle. While their teacher was not looking their way, they had hurled the coal at the walls, and they had used matches to ignite the lumps, set fire to the blinds, curtains, wall map, the bookcase, and papers on their desks. They had thrown the coal with underhand tosses so that no arm movements would be seen if the teacher happened to glance their way. They had shoved the dictionary so that it appeared to move on its own. Two of the older girls—one twelve, the other fifteen—had written the harassing, and at times obscene, notes that they then fastened to the door.[30]

The children admitted that the gullibility of their teacher and townsfolk had been tempting, and they enjoyed all the attention their mischief had yielded.[31]

Where confessions are not forthcoming, certain investigatory techniques may prove effective. One is the use of dye powder, a substance used by police and private investigators to catch thieves and other criminals literally "red-handed." In a poltergeist case that transpired in Tulsa, Oklahoma, in 1957, investigators set a trap for the potential poltergeist, the twelve-year-old adopted daughter of the plagued couple. Tracer powder was dusted on certain objects in the house. After the next bout of disturbances telltale traces were discovered on the girl's hands, whereupon she then confessed that she had been responsible for the troubling events.[32]

Cameras represent another way of catching a pseudo poltergeist. On one of the television programs of "Arthur C. Clarke's Mysterious World" featuring poltergeist phenomena, there was a revealing bit of film footage: It showed a little girl in bed; looking about, she slipped across the room, seized an object from a table and smashed it, then scampered back under the covers; after a moment, she yelled to her mother about what the poltergeist had just done![33]

Cameras *inadvertently* captured the tricks of a poltergeist impostor in a Columbus, Ohio, case in 1984. The home of John and Joan Resch was assailed in the classical way: Furniture was overturned, picture frames and glass objects were smashed, and a telephone handset was thrown from its cradle. The Resches' fourteen-year-old adopted daughter, Tina, described as "hyperactive and emotionally disturbed," was suspected of the events, which typically occurred when witnesses were looking away from the teenager. Although family members, some reporters, and two parapsychologists were apparently duped, at least for a time, some photographs and television newstapes captured the girl in the act—toppling a lamp, for instance—and a TV technician saw her surreptitiously move a table with her foot. As to motive, the noted magician and paranormal investigator James Randi states: "She was admittedly under stress and had good reason to want to attract media exposure: she wanted to trace her true parents, against the wishes of the Resches. And her 'best friend' . . . had a fight with her and broke off their relationship two days before the phenomena began."[34] (Years later Tina Resch Boyer at age twenty-three was awaiting trial in Georgia along with her former boyfriend, for the murder of her three-year-old daughter. The child had been badly bruised and died of injuries to the head.[35])

Two other modern poltergeist cases that have been written about extensively are worth discussing, the "Enfield Poltergeist" and the so-called "Lindley Street Infestation." Both have been "investigated" by Ed and Lorraine Warren, so it seems needless to point out that the poltergeist hijinks have been blown into accounts of "demonic possession."

The Enfield case, which takes its name from that of a northern suburb of London, England, began in August 1977. The outbreak reportedly featured furniture that was overturned, that even "levitated," and a softball-sized rock that "manifested out of thin air in the middle of the living room and slammed to the floor with a thud!" The phenomena inspired a popular book on the "poltergeist" and, more recently, a chapter on the "possession" aspects of the case in *The Demonologist: The True Story of Ed and Lorraine Warren, the World-Famous Exorcism Team* by Gerald Brittle.[36]

Unfortunately, further investigation by Anita Gregory, reported in the *Journal of the Society for Psychical Research,* suggested that the case had been overrated. She described several episodes of behavior concerning the two girls in the family (ages eleven and thirteen) that were clearly suspicious. Gregory concluded that the children were *nonpsychically* responsible for many of the incidents that were attributed to "poltergeist" phenomena. Although she believes the outbreak *may* have originated paranormally (Gregory is a British parapsychologist who is inclined to believe in paranormal phenomena), she thinks it quickly turned into a farcical performance for the benefit of overly credulous investigators as well as for reporters seeking a sensational story. In addition, skeptical investigator Melvin Harris has cast doubt on some of the photographs that purportedly depict the Enfield phenomena and has demonstrated how they could easily have been faked.[37] Magician Milbourne Christopher, who was in England at the time of the Enfield case and became involved in it, concluded that the poltergeist-like antics were those of "a little girl who wanted to cause trouble and who was very, very clever."[38]

The "Lindley Street Infestation," named after the site of the 1974 outbreak in Bridgeport, Connecticut, has a similar development and outcome. The Warrens term it "perhaps the most widely reported case involving a poltergeist in the past few decades."[39]

The events in the home of Mr. and Mrs. Gerald Goodin actually began two years earlier, and were reported to police at the time. Mr. Goodin, described as a "devout Catholic," stated that the family had heard noises—like the house was being pelted with stones—each night. No one was in the house at the time but the Goodins and their then eight-year-old daughter Marcia. Marcia, a Five Nations Indian from Canada, had been adopted by the Goodins two years previously, following the death of their young son.[40]

In late November 1974, however, the disturbances escalated. They apparently began on the evening of Saturday, November 23, but continued all day Sunday. "Under mysterious circumstances, furniture began moving and toppling over onto the floor, dishes rattled, a TV set turned over and a child sitting in a chair [Marcia, now ten] was slammed against a wall," stated the Monday *Telegram*, adding cautiously, "it was reported."[41] By then police and firemen were at the scene along with Ed Warren.

Warren claimed that "a malevolent force here, a demon of some sort" was responsible and that it was speaking audibly through the "medium" of the family cat! The feline, named Sam, was described as "a six-month-old, white-yellow alley cat that sat for minutes on this reporter's lap purring."[42] The claim that the cat could talk seemed, ironically, to come in response to a glib statement in a photo caption in the previous day's newspaper: "If this cat . . . could talk, it might solve the mystery. . . ."[43] Could the cat actually speak? A policeman and a fireman, according to the *Telegram*, said Sam only "talked" when held by Marcia "as her teeth were clenched Edgar Bergen-style."[44]

Not surprisingly, Marcia seemed to be the focal point of the phenomena. Although some claimed an object fell or was moved when no one was near it, we have seen that people often do not make good witnesses to such events, reporting what they *think* happened or what they believe they saw rather than what may actually have occurred. Trickery, of course, is intended to deceive. In fact, three investigators from the Psychical Research Foundation stated that several events which occurred in their presence were "all things that happened when our backs were turned or when our attention was drawn to something else," as one of the three, Boyce Batey, later told the *Bridgeport Post*. Skeptical investigators usually see such evidence of a "shyness factor" on the part of a phenomenon as being suggestive of hoaxing.

Indeed, the researchers stated that there had definitely been "fraudulent" events at the Goodin bungalow, but they believed these were mixed with genuine ones. "There was a melding of the two," said Batey, "which is quite common in such cases." However, Batey conceded that the "genuine" events could have been "simulated." For example, speaking of two plaster-of-paris cherubs that fell from the wall with a crash, Batey stated: "I have no way of knowing how these cherubs fell on the floor. Perhaps they had been taken off the wall by Marcia and thrown across the room." He added, "I did not notice the two cherubs before the incidents occurred."[45]

Batey went on to concede: "The Goodin case has characteristics that are found in many incidents in the history of psychical research: different people with different orientations had different views and reached different conclusions based on their observations of similar events."[46]

As it turned out, the police soon closed the case on the grounds that it was a hoax, stating specifically that the young girl had confessed. Police Superintendent Joseph A. Walsh, who had earlier told newsmen, "There are no ghosts in Bridgeport," made the announcement. Walsh said that under questioning by police, Marcia admitted "she had been the one who had done the banging on the walls and floors, knocked a crucifix to the floor, threw pictures down and caused other unusual things to happen."[47] The girl was to be "taken in [sic] a mental hospital, probably today [Nov. 27] for examination, police reported."[48]

For his part, Ed Warren charged that the police labeled the affair a hoax only "to get things quieted down." "If the whole thing is a hoax, it's one of the biggest hoaxes I've ever seen," Warren huffed.[49]

Eventually, after psychical researchers, priests, and demonologists had left,[50] the events subsided. (Batey said: "Events occurred frequently when a psychological change was introduced into the house by people arriving or leaving the house either in person or psychologically by telephone."[51]) Over a year later the Goodins, who had attempted to sell their house, were still living in it. The house had been given a new coat of white paint, and neighbors reported Marcia was doing fine at school. Wisely, the Goodins had obtained an unlisted telephone number, and when a reporter came calling in person Mrs. Goodin "slammed the door in his face."[52]

My visit to Bridgetown in 1993 turned up little additional information. The happenings of almost two decades before were still recalled, but details were sketchy. About all I learned from a trip to the police station was that, according to a public relations officer, Sgt. W. Chapman, one policeman was recalled as having been genuinely frightened by events at the Lindley Street address. As for himself, Chapman said laughingly that, to be a believer, he would have had to have witnessed paranormal events for himself.[53]

Lest it be thought that all "poltergeist" cases are hoaxes, it should be pointed out that some disturbances may have a mundane explanation. Ghosthunter Dr. Robert A. Baker investigated a case of this kind. He calls it "the poltergeist that wasn't." Although there was a variety of reported events—a bedroom door slamming, a telephone flying off its table, a vacuum cleaner restarting itself, etc.—Dr. Baker thought that the events did not seem to fit the usual poltergeist pattern, but appeared more like random events. On a visit to the home he discovered simple explanations for each occurrence: When the kitchen door was opened quickly, air pressure caused the bedroom door to shut; when a chair leg was placed inside the phone cord on the floor and the chair scooted forward, the telephone was yanked off its table; and when the vacuum cleaner was bumped (the family had a dog) it came to life. States Dr. Baker, "The most fascinating aspect of this case is just how clearly it demonstrates the power of expectation and how our attitudes and mental sets can influence our perceptions and beliefs."[54]

House of Blood

If it was not a poltergeist, then what was the nature of the phenomenon that could cause the floors and walls of a suburban Atlanta house to bleed? That is the question many are asking in the wake of the strange occurrence that has come to be known as the House of Blood Mystery.

The story begins shortly before midnight on Tuesday, September 8, 1987, at 1114 Fountain Drive in southwest Atlanta, the home of an elderly black couple, seventy-seven-year-old Minnie Clyde Winston and her husband William, age seventy-nine. Mrs. Winston was just stepping out of the bathtub when she saw blood spurting, as she reportedly said, "like a sprinkler," from the bathroom floor.[55] Discovering blood on the lower walls and floors of other rooms of the house, Mrs. Winston phoned the Atlanta police. According to the police "Offense Report," the call was received at 0001 hours (a minute past midnight) on the ninth, and the police arrived just nine minutes later (at 0010 hours).[56]

Detective Steve C. Cartwright of the homicide division, noting there were no bodies at the scene, said of the blood: "There must be some sort of natural explanation for it. Even though it sounds pretty mysterious right now, once we get through the facts it will be demystified."[57] Cartwright took photos of the blood and collected samples for analysis. Later, forensic serologist Ted Staples arrived from the Georgia Bureau of Investigation (GBI) Division of Forensic Services (the state crime lab), and took additional samples.

The story was carried nationally by CNN television and by AP and UPI news services. A spokesperson for Atlanta's WVEE radio said, "We got lots and lots of calls. Several were from psychics saying they could get the blood out of the house." As well, Mrs. Winston said her phone "rang all night" and she announced she was "fed up with all this." She added: "If anybody comes here today, I'm not going to open my door." The police too were "swamped with calls," according to police spokesperson Charles Cook. "This place is a madhouse. Some people wanted to know if the radio stations were joking. Now they know it isn't a joke."[58]

Serological tests soon confirmed the substance was human blood, type 0, whereas the Winstons both had type A. As the *Atlanta Journal* reported: "Initially, police had considered the possibility that the source of the mysterious blood . . . was Winston because he is a dialysis patient."[59] Despite unanswered questions, police signalled an early closure to the case when homicide commander Lt. Horace Walker, revealing police frustration with what amounted to only a nuisance, stated: "We will continue a routine investigation and if we find that no crime was committed, we're through with it. As we see it now, there has been no crime."[60]

There the matter ended for a time. As much as a year later there had been no follow-up story from the Atlanta newspapers or other news media. And since there were no indications of foul play, investigating officer C. R. Price officially recorded the case as closed.[61]

Before long, however, the mystery-mongering promoters of superstition had seized on the "unexplained" case. It appeared in the hyper-credulous book by Janet and Colin Bord, *Unexplained Mysteries of the 20th Century,* which exaggerated that the bathroom floor was "covered with blood" and suggested the case was one of poltergeist activity.[62] By 1993, it had made *The Book of Lists* as one of "The 15 Strangest Stories" to appear in the *Fortean Times,* "The Journal of Strange Phenomena." Headed "House Sweats Blood," the entry was number twelve in the list which began with the report of a "lizard man" in South Carolina.[63] Repeating the claim that the floor was "oozing blood 'like a sprinkler,' " the brief account showed the story was on its way to becoming a minor paranormal classic, destined to show up again and again to taunt "orthodox scientists" whom forteans (after Charles Fort, 1874–1932) love to despise. (Fort made a career of challenging scientists to explain what today would be classed as "paranormal" claims.)

In 1991, after an invitation to give a talk in Atlanta and following a query about the case from Gordon Stein, who was then editing the *Encyclopedia of Hoaxes,* I decided to investigate the matter. Becky Long of the Georgia Skeptics showed an interest in the case and made an appointment for us to meet with Lt. Walker, who was still commander of the homicide division, accompanied by Larry Johnson and Rick Moen. We went over the case with Lt. Walker both on and off the record, and examined the official crime-scene photographs taken throughout the Winston home.[64] Later, thanks to Ms. Long's persistent efforts, we were able to secure original duplicates of some of the color prints. Still later, I was able to secure a copy of the GBI's file on the case from Ted Staples. This file included crime-scene sketches and various serological worksheets and official reports pertaining to the case.[65]

One of the things our investigation did was clarify the amount of blood involved. None of the floors was "covered with blood" as the Bords had exaggerated. Neither was it true, however, as one skeptical source stated (citing a police detective) that only "two small sprays of human blood had been found on one wall. . . ."[66] There were blood sprays throughout the house: in each of three bedrooms, the living room, hall, bath, kitchen, dining room, and basement.[67]

Although investigators had determined at the time that the blood did not appear to emanate from the walls but rather to have been "apparently squirted from a syringe," an appearance with which I concurred, I nevertheless sought to obtain an expert forensic opinion. I put the photos and files in the hands of Judith L. Bunker, the nationally known crime-scene reconstruction expert and blood-pattern analyst. According to her detailed report:

1. Blood was clearly applied to the walls and floors. This was accomplished primarily by projecting the blood in some manner, such as forcing it through tubing or a syringe. There is no continuity to the patterns to suggest medical explanation such as a breached artery.

2. All "spurt" patterns appear to originate low to the floor. The ellipse of individual stains indicate heights ranging from 14″ to 24″ above the floor. Triangulation of some patterns allowed me to approximate the distance between the blood source and the stains.

3. There is contamination observed in many areas. At least two "spurt" patterns are associated with alteration of the stains immediately following the issuance of the blood. This object moved through the blood, swiping or smearing the still wet stains. It is interesting to note that this seems to occur only to the right of the pattern. Other areas on the floor represent the presence of some object making contact with the floor, altering the wet stains. There is also evidence of transference of a blood-stained source to floor surfaces. This is commonly caused

by tracking of shoes or feet that have been previously stained with blood.

NOTE: Certainly this "contamination" could occur when or if the residents of the house moved across the floor immediately following the bloodshed. The transfer patterns could be consistent with such an occurrence; however, the swiping motion to the right of the "spurt" patterns in two separate locations would be too coincidental and strongly suggest that their occurrence relates to the source issuing the blood. This could represent a foot, a shoe, a cloth, etc. Better photographs of these areas would be necessary in order to clarify the source.

4. There is a strong suggestion of repositioning of objects prior to the taking of photographs. A trash can lid appears to have been moved. The area rug noted near the hamper has obviously been moved and possibly stepped on. Of course, we have no idea what might have occurred prior to the arrival of the photographer.[68]

She also added these observations:

These "spurt" patterns are unusual and have no continuity. They go in many different directions. They all originate low to the floor with some created by a blood source close to the walls, others by a source located a foot or so away. None of the bloodshed was directed upward, nor did it occur from a standing position. The origins do not suggest the work of a child, since a child tends to shoot liquids upward. Instead it suggests the intent to deliver the blood in a similar manner, for as long as the blood lasts. I cannot estimate the volume of blood used, but based on the photographs, I wouldn't be surprised if the volume is less than ½ pint.[69]

As this expert analysis indicates, clearly the blood was squirted by a hoaxer. That person's identity is unknown, but if Mr. Winston was correct in asserting that prior to blood being discovered in the house he had locked all the doors and even activated a security system, and that "there was nobody in this house but me and my wife,"[70] the list of suspects is greatly narrowed. Other factors to be considered are whether Mrs. Winston actually claimed to see blood spurting "like a sprinkler" from the bathroom floor (which she could not have done), and the fact that blood was found in the basement in places that would presumably have been difficult for the ailing Mr. Winston to reach.[71] One police investigator would only say cryptically, "Some adults will act like children just to get attention."[72]

Newberry Demon

We have now studied a sufficient number of cases to prepare us to try our hand at solving a historic mystery, one that at the time was attributed to a demonic spirit but which we easily recognize as a classic "poltergeist" case. We find it in the writings of Increase Mather (1639–1723), the American minister, author, and statesman, who was the father of Cotton Mather (1663–1728). (The younger Mather wrote *Memorable Providences Relating to Witchcraft and Possessions*, which helped to spark the witchcraft delusion of 1692, as we discuss in the next chapter.)

Despite all the praise justifiably heaped upon the memory of Increase Mather, who has been called (in the subtitle of a biography) "The Foremost American Puritan,"[73] it is with emotions ranging from embarrassment to virtual anger that some commentators have approached his perhaps most notable work, *An Essay for the Recording of Illustrious Providences* (1684). Mather's modern biographer, Mason I. Lowance, Jr.,[74] discusses the work in a chapter titled "Science and Pseudoscience," having cautioned apologetically in his preface that we should not be too critical of some of Mather's views without attempting to understand the times in which he lived. Justin Winsor, on the other hand, in his 1896 *Literature of Witchcraft*, described *An Essay* harshly as a premium on "invention and exaggeration."[75]

Chapter 5, "Concerning things preternatural which have hapnd in New-England," has seemed to be especially problemmatical, particularly such of its entries as "An account of the House in Newberry lately troubled with a Daemon."[76] The point, one supposes, is that modern, enlightened readers do not believe in such superstitious nonsense; therefore, the sophisticated critic feels he must apologize or condemn—but he must do *something* with the unruly demon that has gotten into the great man's book and will not go hence. Actually, such attitudes are unnecessary—even unfair—at least in this particular instance; what is truly problematical about the Newberry demon affair is that some moderns seem to know less what to make of it than did Mather himself.

As I hope to demonstrate, insofar as this account from *An Essay* is concerned, Mather probably exaggerated very little if at all. In fact, from clues he is careful to record (one of which Lowance suggests is a fabrication either by Mather or by his source), we are able to compare the case with analogous, documented occurrences to arrive at a probable explanation and to more accurately assess Mather's handling of it.

As Mather relates, "In the Year 1679, the House of *William Morse* in *Newberry* in *New England,* was strangely disquieted by a *Daemon.*" The events, which began on December 3 and continued until at least early February of the following year, are catalogued in considerable detail over several pages. For example, Mather says:

> People were sometimes Barricado'd out of doors, when as yet there was nobody to do it: and a Chest was removed from place to place, no hand touching it. Their keys being tied together, one was taken from the rest, & the remaining two would fly about making a loud noise by knocking against each other. But the greatest part of this *Devils* feats were his mischievous ones, wherein indeed he was sometimes Antick enough too, and therein the chief sufferers were, the Man and his Wife, and his Grand-Son. The Man especially had his share in these *Diabolical* Molestations. For one while they could not eat their Suppers quietly, but had the Ashes on the Hearth before their eyes thrown into their Victuals; yea, and upon their heads and Clothes, insomuch that they were forced up into their Chamber, and yet they had no rest there; for one of the Man's Shoes being left below, 'twas filled With Ashes and Coals, and thrown up after them. [p. 40]

The boy slept with his grandparents in their bed. Frequently one or all would be pricked as they lay in the dark. On searching, on one occasion they found an awl and on another "found in the Bed a Bodkin, a knitting Needle, and two sticks picked [sic] at both ends."

At other times sticks, bricks, and stones were hurled through an open window; the grandfather's inkhorn was "taken away" while he was writing; and objects were frequently thrown at him or his wife. On the twenty-eighth of December,

> frozen clods of Cow-dung were divers times thrown at the man out of the house in which they were; his Wife went to milk the Cow, and received a blow on her head, and sitting down at her Milking-work, had Cow-dung divers times thrown into her pail. . . . On that night ashes were thrown into the porridge which they had made ready for their Supper, so as that they could not eat it. [p. 41]

The grandfather, an iron hammer "flying at him," was struck on the back. His wife,

> going into the Cellar for Beer, a great iron Peel flew and fell after her through the trap-door of the Cellar; and going afterwards on the same Errand to the same place, the door shut down upon her, and the Table came and lay upon the door, and the man was forced to remove it e'er his Wife could be released. [p. 41]

As to the boy, Mather writes,

> there remains much to be said concerning him, and a principal sufferer in these afflictions: For on the 18. of *December,* he sitting by his Grandfather, was hurried into great motions and the Man thereupon took him, and made him stand between his Legs, but the Chair [in which the grandfather sat] danced up and down, and had like to have cast both Man and Boy into the fire. [p. 41]

On another occasion, Mather says of the boy:

He barked like a Dog, and clock't like a Hen, and after long distraining to speak, said, there's *Powel*, I am pinched; his Tongue likewise hung out of his mouth, so as that it could by no means be forced in till his Fit was over, and then he said " 'twas forced out by *Powel*." [p. 42]

When the lad was taken to the home of a doctor, the disturbances ceased, only to resume when he returned home that evening. He was found to be "best at a Neighbors house."

What are we to make of all this? Certainly Lowance's guess that the child's "fits" were "probably epileptic seizures combined with other forms of psychological disorders" must be wide of the mark: Epileptic seizures that happened only a few times in the space of three months, and then ceased forever, would be remarkable indeed. That they did cease, together with all other disturbing phenomena, Mather makes quite clear. He states that a seaman who often visited at Morse's home told him that his wife was not guilty of witchcraft, as some had suspected, and that, if he could have the child for a single day, he would put an end to the troubles. Morse agreed and the seaman fulfilled his promise. Mather considers the possibility that a witch or "Conjurer" had been responsible for the disturbances, but he adds: "Or it may be some other thing as yet kept hid in the secrets of providence might be the true original of all this Trouble."

It is indeed some other thing, what we today would readily classify as an example of so-called poltergeist phenomena. The particulars in this account are extremely similar to those in case after case we have examined thus far. Of course, imagination may have played some part in the Morse case, but if so, it was probably less in the imagining of whole incidents than in Morse and his wife's subtle, unconscious coloring of them. (For example, if one turns suddenly to see a thrown object—a bottle, say, that usually stood on a shelf—flying through the air, one could easily imagine he saw the object actually propel itself from its resting place.) In Mather's account there is little that is not readily explained by the hypothesis that the grandson contrived the mischief. In fact, on one occasion when he was taken to an aunt's home, he boldly "threw a great stone at a Maid in the house."

Obviously the child had psychological problems, possibly stemming from what seems to have been a broken home (since he lived with his grandparents).

Seen in light of similar cases then, the details in Mather's narrative coalesce into what appears to be a credible account of rather "typical" poltergeist activity. Lowance, therefore, seems most unfair when he says:

> Perhaps the most telling aspect of this episode is the way it ends. Mather (or the original narrative account) introduces a *deus ex machina* in the form of a seaman, who is miraculously able to cure the boy of his illness.[77]

Unless one accuses Mather of outright lying, it is obvious that Mather presented the incident of the seaman simply because it was mentioned in the original narrative taken from Morse who, states Mather, "does moreover affirm" the fact. The detail rings true: "Having a talk" with the mischief-maker has proved successful in ending many poltergeist outbreaks, whether it took the form of a "grilling" by police or a sympathetic discussion about family problems by counselors familiar with such cases.[78]

In fact, a case related in *Arthur C. Clarke's Chronicles of the Strange and Mysterious* (by John Fairley and Simon Welfare) provides just such an example. A poltergeist outbreak occurred in Sri Lanka in 1965. For nearly three months a family was terrified by flying stones and bottles and plagued by sand and dirt in their food. Money, keys, even a pair of false teeth went missing. Eventually the family sought the help of Sri Lanka's "ghostbuster," Dr. Abraham Kovoor. He questioned everyone in the family and soon zeroed in on a suspect.[79] As he wrote:

> The fifth person to be questioned was the 13-year-old Devanayaki. Unlike the others who were questioned earlier, I adopted a different technique in dealing with her. I started with the assurance that I was in the know of what had happened in the house, and that I knew who was responsible for them. Without any hesitation, and with a smile on her face, Devanayaki

explained to me in answer to my questions all that she had
done during the previous two and a half months.[80]

Dr. Kovoor explained that the girl's facial expressions had given
her away, as had the fact that the incidents never occurred while
she was at school. She had been jealous of her younger sister
and was angered by the lack of attention she herself received.
(As it turned out, she was not responsible for the missing false
teeth. Those had been placed on a stone beside a well, and the
"poltergeist" in that instance was thought to have been "a passing
crow"!) Dr. Kovoor recommended hypnotherapy for the teenager
coupled with an extra dose of love and understanding. The result
was that the "poltergeist" vanished, leaving behind "a model
schoolgirl."[81]

The Sri Lankan story sheds light on what probably happened
in the Morse case, the wise seaman spending a day counseling
the troubled grandchild. Contrary to Lowance's suggestion, the
ending of the Newberry narrative could not be more credible,
and we may confidently conclude that the historic case is solved.

In fairness to Lowance, it must be acknowledged that his
treatment of Mather is, overall, most sympathetic. And he is
certainly correct in insisting that, essentially, Mather's

concern with nature was focused on the employment of nature
as a source for corroborating the evidences and truths already
revealed to him through Scripture. But the modern reader should
not be too cynical in his approach to Mather as a scientific
thinker; for his time, Increase Mather was progressive and
advanced rather than wholly conservative and backward-
looking.[82]

Lowance observes that throughout *An Essay for the Recording
of Illustrious Providences*, Mather indicates his familiarity with
scientific thinking of the time. If this did not include an understanding of poltergeist phenomena, then Mather can scarcely be
blamed. (In fact, it is probable that the demon motif was not
imposed by Mather, or even, directly, by Morse, since it is known
that "poltergeists often reflect the cultural climate and beliefs

of the day," often acting "in such a way as to conform to the expectations and beliefs of the observers."[83])

Even today scientists can be baffled by such outbreaks, and we have our psychoanalysts and parapsychologists who postulate "psychokinesis" (or "mind over matter") as an explanation for them.[84] Sometime in the future, commentators will no doubt be telling their readers that they must consider the times in which these theorists lived. And Increase Mather's vague suggestions of demons, tempered with frank confession of ultimate puzzlement and an obvious desire to report facts as he knew them, may seem relatively scientific after all.

Recommended Works

Christopher, Milbourne. "Poltergeists," chapter 11 of *ESP, Seers & Psychics: What the Occult Really Is.* New York: Thomas Y. Crowell, 1970, pp. 142–63. Excellent skeptical look at alleged poltergeist phenomena, illustrated with case studies in which children's mischief is the usual cause.

Nickell, Joe. "Poltergeist Hoaxes," in *Encyclopedia of Hoaxes,* ed. Gordon Stein. Detroit: Gale Research, 1993, p. 201. Concise argument that when nonnaturalistic explanations have been eliminated, poltergeist cases invariably prove to be hoaxes.

Randi, James. "The Columbus Poltergeist Case," *Skeptical Inquirer* 9, no. 3 (Spring 1985): 221–35. An exposé of the Tina Resch case by a noted conjurer and challenger of paranormal claims.

Rogo, D. Scott. *The Poltergeist Experience.* New York: Penguin Books, 1979. Informed, if overly credulous, view of poltergeist activity by a well-known psychical researcher.

Warren, Ed, with Lorraine Warren and Robert David Chase. "Case File: A Poltergeist Explosion," in *Ghost Hunters: True Stories from the World's Most Famous Demonologists.* New York: St. Martin's Paperbacks, 1989, pp. 195–211. Sensationalized claims of "poltergeist" activity with typical Warren overtones of the demonic, including a "talking" cat. Recommended for contrast with the Bridgetown, Conn., police statement that the affair was a hoax and that the ten-year-old girl confessed.

Notes

1. Richard Cavendish, ed., *Encyclopedia of the Unexplained* (London: Routledge & Kegan Paul, 1974), p. 196.

2. Owen S. Rachleff, *The Occult Conceit* (Chicago: Cowles, 1971), p. 198. *The Oxford English Dictionary (OED)*, compact edition, 1971, gives the earliest reference as 1871.

3. *OED*, compact edition.

4. Rossell H. Robbins, cited in Rachleff, *The Occult Conceit*, p. 198.

5. Rossell H. Robbins, cited in ibid.

6. These cases are cited in D. Scott Rogo, *The Poltergeist Experience* (New York: Penguin Books, 1979), pp. 41–42.

7. Cavendish, *Encyclopedia of the Unexplained*, p. 196.

8. Ibid.

9. Nandor Fodor, *The Haunted Mind* (1959; reprint, New York: Signet Mystic Books, 1968), p. 51.

10. Milbourne Christopher, *ESP, Seers & Psychics* (New York: Thomas Y. Crowell, 1970), pp. 142–63.

11. Fodor, *The Haunted Mind*, p. 51.

12. Christopher, *ESP, Seers & Psychics*, p. 160.

13. Ibid., p. 163.

14. John Mulholland, *Beware Familiar Spirits* (1938; reprint, New York: Charles Scribner's Sons, 1979), pp. 30–31, 41–42.

15. Joe Nickell, "The Human Magnet: Lulu Hurst," chapter 4 of *Wonder-workers! How They Perform the Impossible* (Amherst, N.Y.: Prometheus Books, 1991), pp. 38–39.

16. Ibid., pp. 35–40.

17. Christopher, *ESP, Seers & Psychics*, p. 149.

18. Ibid.

19. Ibid., pp. 144–45.

20. Ibid., p. 145.

21. Rogo, *Poltergeist Experience*, passim.

22. W. G. Roll, "Poltergeist," in *Encyclopedia of the Unexplained*, ed. Richard Cavendish (London: Routledge & Kegan Paul, 1974), p. 198.

23. See Christopher, *ESP, Seers & Psychics* pp. 149-60, for a complete discussion of this case.

24. See G. Wells and Elizabeth Loftus, eds., *Eyewitness Testimony: Psychological Perspectives* (New York: Cambridge University Press, 1984).

25. Quoted in Christopher, *ESP, Seers & Psychics*, p. 158.

26. Ibid.

27. Rogo, *Poltergeist Experience*, pp. 164–67.

28. Ibid., pp. 112–22.

29. Quoted in Christopher, *ESP, Seers & Psychics*, pp. 147–48.

30. Ibid., pp. 146–49.

31. Ibid.

32. Ibid., p. 146.

33. Joe Nickell, "Poltergeist Hoaxes," in *Encyclopedia of Hoaxes*, ed. Gordon Stein (Detroit: Gale Research, 1993), p. 200.

34. James Randi, "The Columbus Poltergeist Case," *Skeptical Inquirer* 9, no. 3 (Spring 1985): 221–35.

35. Greg Land, "The Trouble with Tina," *Creative Loafing* (Atlanta weekly) 22, no. 3 (June 12, 1993): 20–30.

36. Gerald Brittle, *The Demonologist: The True Story of Ed and Lorraine Warren, the World-Famous Exorcism Team* (1980; reprint, New York: St. Martin's Paperbacks, 1991), pp. 219–37.

37. Jerome Clark, "Update . . . ," *Fate*, July 1981: 94.

38. Milbourne Christopher, in "A Final Interview with Milbourne Christopher," *Skeptical Inquirer* 9, no. 2 (Winter 1984–85): 161.

39. Ed and Lorraine Warren with Robert David Chase, *Ghost Hunters* (New York: St. Martin's Paperbacks, 1989), p. 195.

40. Juan O. Tamayo, "UPI Reports 'Father Bill' 'Exorcist,' Not Church-Sent," *Bridgeport Telegram*, November 26, 1974. (This source gives the child's name as "Meredith." Also, apparently the events of two years ago occurred at an earlier residence.)

41. Pete Mastronardi, "Things Move Mysteriously in House Here, It's Said," *Bridgeport Telegram*, November 25, 1974.

42. John Sopko, " 'Man of the House' Tense and Worried," *Bridgeport Telegram*, November 26, 1974.

43. *Bridegeport Post/Telegram* clipping, n.d. [November 25, 1974], in vertical file of Bridgeport Public Library.

44. Tamayo, "UPI Reports 'Father Bill' 'Exorcist.' "

45. Herbert F. Geller, "All's Quiet with Goodins on Lindley Street But Who Knows?" *Bridgeport Sunday Post*, January 18, 1976. (This source quotes from a letter to the *Post* by Boyce Batey.)

46. Ibid.

47. Pete Mastronardi, "Case is Closed. Or Is It?" *Bridgeport Telegram*, November 27, 1974; " 'House of Happenings' Here Put Up for Sale by Goodins," *Bridgeport Post*, January 14, 1975.

48. Mastronardi, "Case Is Closed."

49. Ibid.

50. The events seem to have abated after the girl's confession, but resumed briefly for the end-of-the-year visit of the three investigators mentioned earlier; then they apparently ceased completely.

51. Geller, "All's Quiet with Goodins."

52. Ibid.

53. Sgt. W. Chapman, Bridgetown, Conn., Police, interview with author, June 11, 1993.

54. Robert A. Baker and Joe Nickell, *Missing Pieces* (Amherst, N.Y.: Prometheus Books, 1992), pp. 135–39.

55. "Bleeding House Mystifies Atlanta Police," *Detroit News* (based on AP and UPI reports), September 10, 1987.

56. City of Atlanta Bureau of Police Services Offense Report by Det. S.C. Cartwright, Complaint No. 70917758, September 9, 1987.

57. "Bleeding House Mystifies . . . ," *Detroit News*, September 10, 1987.

58. Walter W. Miller, "Blood Found at Atlanta House Stirs Hulabaloo," *Atlanta Journal*, September 10, 1987.

59. Walter W. Miller, "Second Person's Blood Ruled Out at 'Bleeding House,' " *Atlanta Journal*, September 11, 1987.

60. Homicide commander Lt. Horace Walker, quoted in ibid.

61. Bob Grove, "Atlanta's Infamous 'House of Blood': Case Closed," *Skeptical Inquirer* 13 (Spring 1989): 248–49.

62. Janet and Colin Bord, *Unexplained Mysteries of the 20th Century* (Chicago: Contemporary Books, 1989), p. 22.

63. David Wallechinsky and Amy Wallace, *The Book of Lists* (New York: Little, Brown and Co., 1993), pp. 448, 450.

64. Lt. Horace Walker, interview with author, July 22, 1991.

65. GBI Division of Forensic Sciences, case file no. 87-18731.

66. Grove, "Atlanta's Infamous 'House of Blood.' "

67. See notes 53, 61, 62.

68. Judith L. Bunker, J. L. Bunker & Associates, letter report to author, April 28, 1994.

69. Ibid.

70. "Bleeding House Mystifies Atlanta Police."

71. Miller, "Blood Found."

72. Grove, "Atlanta's Infamous 'House of Blood.' "

73. Kenneth B. Murdock, *Increase Mather: The Foremost American Puritan* (Cambridge, Mass.: Harvard University Press, 1925).

74. Mason I. Lowance, Jr., *Increase Mather* (New York: Twayne Publishers, 1974).

75. Quoted in Thomas James Holmes, *Increase Mather: A Bibliography of His Works* (Cleveland, Ohio: Printed at the Harvard University Press for William Gwinn Mather, 1931), p. 246.

76. I have relied on the excerpt from Mather's text in *The Literature of America*, vol. 1, eds. Arthur Hobson Quinn et al. (New York: Scribner's 1938), pp. 38–43.

77. Lowance, *Increase Mather*, p. 96.

78. For instances of this, see Rogo, nn. 25 and 26 above.

79. John Fairley and Simon Welfare, *Arthur C. Clarke's Chronicles of the Strange and Mysterious* (London: Collins, 1987), pp. 148–49.

80. Quoted in ibid., p. 148.

81. Ibid., p. 149.

82. Lowance, *Increase Mather*, p. 81.

83. Rogo, *The Poltergeist Experience*, p. 43.

84. Rogo, ibid., follows this approach, and he cites many such theorists.

Part Two
Theological Beings

4

Demonic Attacks

Devils, Demons, and Witches

The forces of evil are reputedly carried out by a variety of supernatural entities, many of which have benevolent counterparts (for example, there are supposedly "good" demons and "white" witches). It is the former we are concerned with here, however.

Although the entities we will discuss—devils, demons, and witches—are variously defined and characterized, perhaps we can agree on a few simple (if admittedly somewhat oversimplified) definitions. *Satan*, or *the Devil*, is the "evil one," who in Christian doctrine is a fallen angel who established the netherworld kingdom of hell. *Demons* are spirits which in Christianity are associated exclusively with evil and thus are seen as the Devil's agents. *Witches*, considered malevolent in most cultures, are those who practice the black arts, who are therefore in league with, and who worship, the Devil.[1] Let us look at each in turn.

Devils. The term being generic, a devil is any spirit of evil, whereas *the* Devil is the chief such spirit. As the Prince of Darkness, the Devil or Satan represents all that is evil. Explains Gerald Larue in his *The Supernatural, the Occult, and the Bible*: "It is he and his fellow demonic angels who tempt humans and bring evil and sickness and disruption into society. He is God's cosmic antagonist."[2] He has domain over hell, which is a place where the wicked are tormented by eternal fire (Matt. 13:41; Mark 9:42; Luke 16:23–24), an idea that may stem from the fact

111

(observable from volcanic activity) that the earth has a molten core.[3]

While the concept has roots in even more ancient theologies, belief in the Devil has been fostered largely through Judaic and Christian monotheism, primarily as expressed in the Bible as well as in such biblically related sources as the Koran (and still more recently in the Book of Mormon, and the writings of Christian Scientists, Jehovah's Witnesses, and Seventh-day Adventists).[4]

By the medieval period, the Devil had become "the god of a new and closely organized religion: the anti-Christian but nonetheless dualistic religion of Satanism,"[5] although the extent to which such a force existed has been disputed. Richard Cavendish declares it unlikely that there were satanic groups of any significant size before the seventeenth century. Noting that in the Middle Ages certain groups such as the Cathars were condemned as satanists by the Church, Cavendish explains:

> It seems likely that Satanism, far from being of Cathar origin, actually had its roots in the bad theology of a minority of Roman Catholic priests. Exactly what the doctrines of the early Church were concerning the Mass—the sacramental consumption of bread and wine—is uncertain, but by A.D. 700 a belief in the Real Presence of Christ in the sacramental elements, approximating to the later scholastic doctrine of transubstantiation, was widespread in western Europe. Once it was accepted that any priest, however ignorant, however unworthy, had the power to transform bread and wine into the Body and Blood of Christ by the words of institution, it was only a step to believing that both the priest and the Mass were possessed of inherent magical powers. Theologians, naturally, did not share this belief, and saw a vast gulf between the sacramental gifts of the Holy Ghost and any form of magic, but the distinction went unperceived by many ordinary people and many of the frequently illiterate secular clergy.[6]

Continues Cavendish:

> As a result, some priests were prepared to turn their supposed magical powers to evil ends: as early as the seventh century,

the Council of Toledo prohibited the performance of Requiem Masses sung, not for souls in purgatory, but for living men with the intention of killing them. Belief in the effectiveness of such practices survived among simple Catholics into the nineteenth century and Frazer recorded it in *The Golden Bough* as current Breton folklore, under the name of "the Mass of St. Secaire." The evocative term "Black Mass" probably originated with this practice, for until comparatively recently Black Mass was an unusual but perfectly respectable alternative term for a Requiem Mass.[7]

Of course Satanism could exist only so long as belief in Satan continued. Although modern, educated Christians would agree with theologian A. E. Garvie, who states that "belief in Satan is not now generally regarded as an essential article of the Christian faith, nor is it found to be an indispensable element of Christian experience,"[8] many would disagree. Certainly, to Pentecostals and other charismatic and fundamentalist Protestants, as well as their counterparts in the Catholic and Episcopal churches, Satan is still very much alive and is seen in traditional terms.

To those who believe, Satan is not merely a personification, but the very embodiment of evil. Frequently he is depicted as a serpent (signifying his lowly position and his cunning, poisonous ways) or, alternately, he is portrayed as a goatlike figure (apparently after pre-Christian goat deities like Pan), complete with whiskers, horns, cloven hooves, and a tail.[9] (Recall from chapter 1 the Fox sisters' claim to have been in contact with a spirit they dubbed "Mr. Splitfoot.")

From time to time evidence is brought forth that supposedly confirms the existence of the goatlike Satan. For example, there were the cloven-hooved tracks allegedly discovered outside the Long Island house that featured in "the Amityville Horror" tale— a hoax, however, as we shall see later in this chapter.

A more interesting example is the nineteenth-century case of "the Devil's hoofprints" that reportedly appeared overnight in the county of Devon, England. One morning in early February 1858, residents of some eighteen towns and villages around the Exe estuary awoke to discover the snow marked with strange tracks: cloven footprints that the superstitious rural folk were quick to believe had been caused by the Devil. Some tracks supposedly led to walls where they ended abruptly, while others were reportedly discovered on the roofs of houses; in another place they allegedly passed through a six-inch drain.

These different locations, however, must be considered in light of varying descriptions of the tracks. For example, some said they resembled those of a small donkey, while others noted claw marks within the "hooves"; the famous zoologist Richard Owen thought they resembled the tracks of badgers. One minister attributed them to a kangaroo that had escaped not long before from a Sidemouth zoo, while a farmer suggested they were prints of cats' paws which had been distorted by thawing and had then been refrozen. The most likely explanation of the mystery is *contagion* (explained in chapter 2 and illustrated by the one hundred mistaken sightings of a ubiquitous panda). That is, the tracks were probably from a variety of different sources, and some of them—especially those which appeared after the original "outbreak"—may well have been those of pranksters.[10]

My own closest encounter with a "devil" featured a supposedly mummified creature I came across in the window of a curio shop in Toronto, Canada, in 1971. It had budding horns, fans, clawlike nails, a long tail, and realistic hooves: a devil-baby mummy! Apparently I showed too much curiosity (or skepticism) about the small creature, because the owner snapped at me that it was not for sale and that I should not interest myself in it. I did wrest from him the statement that he had bought it from an Irish museum twelve years before. Later the figure was moved to the rear of the store, but a photographer I commissioned obtained a photo by shooting through the window with a long-range lens.

Still later, I sent a friend to the store. Using a wad of cash to get the proprietor's attention, my friend received an offer to sell the sinister creature for a five-figure sum. Before leaving, he was able to get a close look at the curio, observing that the hair had been glued on.[11]

Subsequently, in a book titled *Vampires, Zombies, and Monster Men,* I discovered a photograph of a similar creature—

or rather a pair of them, with arms folded in the repose of death. Headed "Clahuchu and his Bride," a sign mounted in the creatures' coffin stated: "These shrunken mummified figures were found in a crude tomblike cave on the island of Haiti in 1740 by a party of French marines. They are supposed to be the remains of a lost tribe of 'Ju-Ju' or Devil Men—who, after death followed a custom of shrinking & mummifying their dead." The sign concluded: "Are they real? We don't know, but . . . X-*Rays showed skin, horn, & hooves human!*" There was, astonishingly, however, no mention of a skeleton. Painted beneath the sign were these mumbo-jumbo words: "YENOH M'I DLOC!"[12] Reading each word backward in turn, I discovered, yields the prankish message, "Honey I'm Cold!"—presumably an indication of the seriousness with which we should approach the "devil" figures.

Still another such creature was once in the possession of a cult leader who claimed it was his satanic offspring, which was stillborn. As described by John Anderson in his *Psychic Phenomena Unveiled: Confessions of a New Age Warlock*, it had "the shape of a small petrified body. The skin was very dark, almost black. Its feet were those of a goat. The body appeared to be half human, half animal, the face long, with a pointed chin." Later, Anderson heard from a former cult member who had managed to sneak a closer look at the figure in the daylight. He said: "Impressive all right. An impressive papier-mâché and plaster of paris job . . . not the remains of some mutant offspring of Satan."[13]

The existence of such "satanic" cults is largely exaggerated. As law enforcement specialist/criminal justice analyst Robert D. Hicks has shown, much of what is popularly believed to be widespread criminal activity by satanic cults is in reality simply a loose collection of crimes, including teenagers' malicious mischief, together with "a pastiche of claims, exaggerations, or suppositions." For example, such juvenile delinquency as toppling gravestones is often attributed to satanic activity, whereas Satanists rarely commit such acts. Again, a rash of cattle mutilations in the western United States during the 1970s was once attributed to Satanists, whereas more careful investigation showed it was probably the work of predators and scavengers.[14]

As Hicks explains:

Fundamentalist Christianity drives the occult-crime model. Cult-crime officers invariably communicate fundamentalist Christian concepts at seminars. They employ fundamentalist rhetoric, distribute literature that emanates from fundamentalist authorities and sometimes offer bibliographies giving many fundamentalist publications, and they sometimes team up with clergy to give seminars on satanism. The most notable circular among cult-crime investigators, *File 18 Newsletter*, follows a Christian world-view in which police officers who claim to separate their religious views from their professional duties nevertheless maintain that salvation through Jesus Christ is the only sure antidote to satanic involvement, whether criminal or noncriminal, and point out that no police officer can honorably and properly do his or her duty without reference to Christian standards.[15]

Hicks concludes: "Law enforcers who meld cult-crime theories with their professional world-views have transformed their legal duties into a moral confrontation between good and evil."[16]

Much of the evidence for the existence of the devil, however, comes not from dubious creatures, nor from the alleged worship and ritual activities of Satanists, but rather from reputed demonic activity and spiritual possession—claims we take up in the following discussion.

Demons. The term "demon" is derived from the Greek *daimon,* "divine power." To the Greek mind a daimon was an intermediary, advisory spirit. However, in Christian belief and superstitious lore demons are solely evil. "As agents of the Devil," states one source, "demons devote themselves to leading humans astray, tormenting them, assaulting them sexually, and in some cases possessing them."[17]

In Europe in the Middle Ages, evil demons were believed often to attack people in their sleep. Nightmares were caused by a demon (the Germanic *mara*) that supposedly squatted on a sleeping person's chest, thus giving him or her a feeling of being suffocated, and also causing terrible dreams. The Latin term for "nightmare" was *incubo,* and a demon called an incubus appeared in male form and lay with women, sometimes fathering a child. Twins or a deformed child could be attributed to such unnatural coupling. If the demon took a female form and lay with a man, it was known as a succubus.[18]

According to Richard Cavendish:

> In the background of the incubus and succubus were earlier beliefs about unions between spiritual beings and humans. In Genesis there was the story of the angels, or 'sons of God,' who saw that the daughters of men were fair and begot children on them. There were numerous Greek and Roman tales of the loves of mortals with gods and goddesses, nymphs and satyrs and other spirits. One of them, Faunus, a Roman forest god identified with the Greek Pan, was also identified with Incubo, the nightmare. There were similar beliefs in northern Europe, as St. Augustine noted.[19]

Today we recognize attacks by incubi and succubi as indeed nightmares, but in the modern sense of the term, as representing a type of dream. We would see the obvious similarity between such attacks and the type of experience we discussed in chapter 2 that represents what are called "waking dreams" or "night terrors." Whether it is the demon of the Middle Ages, the ghost of a later period, or an alien spaceman of today, the bedside visitor is obviously a product of the human imagination. The feeling of being weighted down, so common to reports of incubi/succubi, is quite similar to the reports of paralysis or at least a difficulty of moving that is a common feature of waking dreams.[20] In contrast to such occasional nightmares are cases of alleged possession: "The taking over of a person's mind, body, and soul by an external force perceived to be a deity, spirit, demon, entity, or separate personality."[21] According to *Harper's Encyclopedia of Mystical & Paranormal Experience*:

> Possession generally is unwanted and troublesome. It has been recognized since antiquity, and has been blamed for virtually every conceivable problem of luck, health, wealth, love, and sanity. Some types of possession, such as by gods or the Holy Spirit, are desirable and voluntary. Some types of mediumship, such as direct voice and channeling, are forms of temporary possession by spirits of the dead or nonphysical entities. The

cure for unwanted possession is exorcism, performed according to a specified ritual. Voluntary possession, on the other hand, terminates at the end of a religious ceremony, healing ritual, or sitting.[22]

Belief in spirit or demon possession takes root in societies where there is ignorance about mental states. Such societies include relatively primitive cultures like those that may be found in the villages of India or Ethiopia, or among the voodoo practitioners of the Caribbean. The medieval Church held that demons were able to take over an individual and control that person's behavior. By the sixteenth century, demonic manifestations had become rather stereotyped: they included convulsions, together with unusual strength, temporary blindness or deafness, insensitivity to pain, and such other abnormal characteristics as clairvoyance.

There have been various theories about possession. Some early notions may have been fomented by three brain syndromes: epilepsy, Tourette's syndrome, and migraine.[23] Psychiatric historians, on the other hand, have long attributed the behavior to aberrant mental conditions like schizophrenia and hysteria, noting that as mental illness began to be recognized as such after the seventeenth century, demonic superstitions declined.[24]

A different view has been provided by Nicholas Spanos, the noted expert in abnormal psychology. Spanos rejected the interpretation of demonic possession as mental illness, instead seeing it as a learned role that fulfills certain important functions for those claiming it. Agreeing with Spanos, Robert A. Baker explains in his book *Hidden Memories*:

In France, for example, during the sixteenth and seventeenth centuries the most celebrated possession cases occurred among the nuns. Becoming a nun wasn't usually highly desired, and families would place their adolescent daughters in convents to avoid the financial burden involved in providing a dowry. Unless one was truly devout, being a nun left a lot to be desired. The life was hard, dull, filled with chores, frequent prayer, rigid rules, loneliness, no men, boredom, and monotony. The unwilling nun had no means of protesting against her predicament. If she adopted the demoniac role—and the script for this role was well known by all of the nuns—this was a relatively safe way to protest. The nun could take out her frustrations on her family, her superiors, and the Church, and act out her sexual frustrations on the exorcist and other males and blame it all on the nasty, possessing demon! Other advantages of being possessed included escape from unpleasant duties and responsibilities, being the center of attention, flaunting constrictive rules and regulations, as well as getting sympathetic attention from the higher ups, priests, physicians, and others. Moreover, the possessed nun instantly became a seer who possessed strange, magical powers—one who was due awe and respect. Once a nun was possessed, and her advantages were made apparent to other nuns—epidemics of possession would often sweep across the convents. Adoption of the possession role frequently led to a dramatic rise in social status. Moreover, the demonically possessed, despite their invective against God and Church, were more the unwitting servants of the clerical establishment than they were rebels against it.[25]

That demonic possession is childishly simple to fake was shown by a case which was the subject of a televised "exorcism" in 1991. ABC's "20/20" program broadcast the segment, which featured a sixteen-year-old girl whose family claimed that she was possessed by no fewer than ten demons. I watched the program with a group of magicians, psychologists, and other skeptics. Exhibiting what looked to us like poor acting, the girl could be seen stealing glances at the camera before affecting "convulsions" and other supposedly demonic behavior. When a priest claimed that were she not being held down she would be levitating, several of the magicians in our group gleefully encouraged, "Let her go! Let her go!" The girl's speaking in tongues was even less impressive; she merely chanted: "Sanka dali. Booga, booga."

Although she was reportedly much improved after the exorcism and had resumed attending school, it was also reported that the teenager continued to be "on medication."[26] What was most astonishing in this case was not the girl's behavior but instead the credulity and foolishness of the adult men and women who participated in the farce. One Catholic scholar subsequently denounced the entire affair as an embarrassing carry-over from the Middle Ages, decrying such Catholic "fundamentalists." He said that exorcism—and by inference a belief in demon possession—"holds the faith up to ridicule."[27]

Gerald Larue has observed that many who are allegedly possessed by demons are puberty-age children, who may feel alienated and misunderstood. States Larue: "Just as poltergeist activity has been demonstrated to be the action of children in this same age range, so demon possession requiring exorcism is often associated with adolescent behavior."[28]

Witches. Witchcraft, a type of sorcery, is considered malevolent by most cultures.[29] "Historically," observes Owen Rachleff,

> witchcraft is Satanic, and the "white witch" is a misnomer. . . . The non-Satanic witches, rather than being called "white," or benign, would probably be best defined as the library book variety, those who pick and choose among the many books concerning occult subjects in order to create for themselves a respectable, yet secretive, beneficent yet potent form of self-centered religion. . . . Unfortunately this creation usually turns out to be a confusing hybrid of paganism, sorcery, wicca herbology, Zen Buddhism, and drug cultism, replete with the messages of love, faith, and back-to-nature simplicity.[30]

Whatever its form, since it was practiced by pagans, Christianity equated it with Devil-worship, and by the mid-fifteenth century (under the general concept of sorcery) witchcraft was branded a heresy by papal decree. Christian demonologists issued tracts accusing witches of such abominations as worshipping the Devil in obscene sexual rites, killing their neighbors, eating children, and destroying people's crops. According to *Harper's Encyclopedia of Mystical & Paranormal Experience:*

> Over about 250 years, an estimated 150,000 to 200,000 people were executed for witchcraft. Some were burned alive at the stake; others were strangled first and then burned; others were hung. Most of the executions took place in Europe, especially in Germany. In England, which escaped the Inquisition, witch-

craft was prosecuted largely as a civil crime rather than as heresy. In America the worst case was the Salem witch trials in 1692 and 1693, in which 141 people were falsely arrested on the basis of accusations by hysterical children; nineteen were hung and one was pressed to death.[31]

Among the victims were those who were reputed to have any magical power, such as the ability to heal, as well as virtually anyone *accused* of witchcraft. (The Salem hysteria began with the accusations of several young girls who claimed that a West Indian slave and two elderly women had bewitched them.) Often victims were tortured into making confessions and then executed; if they refused to confess, they frequently died as a result of the torture.[32] No wonder authorities like Owen Rachleff say, "Witchhunting is as much a recourse to delusion as is witchcraft itself."[33]

For witchcraft is indeed a delusion. Only in fairy tales or in their own minds or the minds of the credulous can witches fly, conjure up demons, influence the elements, predict the future, cast spells, or accomplish any of the myriad other supernatural feats attributed to them. Says Rachleff:

A little logic would help. White or black, frivolous or serious, witchcraft remains a complicated delusion, a deception that attempts to answer life's inconsistencies in terms of the greater inconsistencies of a medieval concept of the universe. . . . Followers of this concept in their disaffection for and alienation from the Christian God, turn for salvation to the Christian devil. At best this is a "cop out," at worst a menacing perversion.[34]

To sum up, the same may be said of those who believe in devils and demons, as we shall see presently in the case studies that follow.

The Amityville Horror

On December 18, 1975, the Lutz family—George (twenty-eight), Kathy (thirty), and their three children (ages five, seven, and nine)—moved into their "dream house": a six-bedroom Dutch Colonial at 112 Ocean Avenue, Amityville, New York, a community on Long Island. The big two-and-a-half story house, a frame affair with white trim, featured an enclosed porch, backyard pool, and paved driveway, at the end of which was a lamppost sporting a small sign, "High Hopes."[35]

After only twenty-eight days, the Lutzes fled the house, reportedly leaving behind their possessions except for a few changes of clothes. They claimed they had been driven from their home by sinister forces that ripped open a two-hundred-fifty-pound door, leaving it hanging from one hinge; threw open windows, bending their locks, and wrenched a bannister from its fastenings; caused green slime to ooze from a ceiling; slid drawers rapidly back and forth; flipped a crucifix upside down; caused Kathy to levitate off the bed and turned her, briefly, into a wrinkled, toothless, drooling ninety-year-old crone; peered into the house at night with red eyes and left cloven-hooved tracks in the snow outside; infested a room in mid-winter with hundreds of houseflies; moved a four-foot ceramic statue of a lion about the house; produced cold spots and stenches; and produced other ostensibly paranormal phenomena, including speaking in a masculine voice, "Get out!"[36]

A priest who had come to bless the house experienced some of the phenomena, and later was afflicted with inexplicable, painful blisters on his hands. A policeman called to investigate on January 2 saw a wrecked garage door and the cloven hoofprints "still visible in the frozen snow," but he was unable to do more than suggest they call a priest. Something seemed to be effecting "a collective personality change" on the family, turning the children into "misbehaved monsters," and giving George "the look of a man possessed." Soon, he had been to the Amityville Library and checked out a book "on witches and demons," then "sat alone in the living room, deep in the subject of the Devil and his works."[37]

Some three weeks after moving out of 112 Ocean Avenue,

George and Kathy Lutz appeared on a local TV news broadcast, on New York's Channel 5. By this time they had already consulted "a psychic research group." Several days later the couple held a press conference in the office of their new attorney, William Weber. As it happened, Weber was more than familiar with the house: He was the lawyer for former resident Ronald DeFeo who more than a year before, on November 13, 1974, had shot to death his parents, two sisters, and two brothers. Despite the plea for insanity Weber entered for his client, who claimed he had heard voices in the house instructing him to kill, DeFeo received a sentence of six consecutive life terms. Now, with the evidence provided by the Lutzes that some force influenced the behavior of people who lived in the house, Webster felt he might be able to win a new trial for his client.[38]

On February 18, Channel 5 decided to further "investigate" the reports concerning the "cursed home." Their notion of investigating involved bringing in alleged psychics together with "demonologist" Ed Warren and his wife, Lorraine, the professed "clairvoyant." The group held a series of séances in the house, and to "provoke" the evil forces they placed on the dining room table some blessed candles and a crucifix. Soon, one of the psychics claimed to be ill and left the room saying that "in the back of everything there seems to be some kind of black shadow that forms a head, and it moves. And as it moves, I feel personally threatened."[39]

Another psychic, "in a mediumistic trance," began to gasp. "It's upstairs in the bedroom. What's here makes your heart speed up." At this point Ed Warren suggested ending the séance, but the psychic "quickly came out of her trance and back to normal consciousness." Next a "psychic researcher" became ill, and an "observer" from a local radio station said he felt a chill. Finally, Lorraine Warren spoke: "Whatever is here is, in my estimation, most definitely of a negative nature. It has nothing to do with anyone who had once walked the earth in human form. It is right from the bowels of the earth," she added, leaving little doubt that she referred to the domain of the Devil himself. A further séance was unproductive, but the various psychics agreed the house held a "demonic spirit," one that could be removed only by an exorcist."[40]

Soon a book was in the offing. A professional writer named Jay Anson was commissioned to turn the Lutzes' story into a book by Prentice-Hall. *The Amityville Horror,* boldly subtitled *A True Story,* came out in September 1977 and promptly went through thirteen printings by March 1978; the following August, Bantam books issued a paperback edition, which promptly went through numerous additional printings to become "one of the biggest publishing successes of the year." The Lutzes shared in the profits garnered by the "phenomenal best seller," since they shared the copyright with Anson.[41]

Anson stated in an afterword:

> To the extent that I can verify them, all the events in this book are true. George Lee and Kathleen Lutz undertook the exhaustive and frequently painful task of reconstructing their twenty-eight days in the house in Amityville on a tape recorder, refreshing each other's memories so that the final oral "diary" would be as complete as possible. Not only did George and Kathy agree on virtually every detail they had both experienced, many of their impressions and reports were later substantiated by the testimony of independent witnesses such as Father Mancuso and local police officials. But perhaps the most telling evidence in support of their story is circumstantial—it takes more than imagination or a case of "nerves" to drive a normal, healthy family of five to the drastic step of suddenly abandoning a desirable three-story house, complete with finished basement, swimming pool, and boathouse, without even pausing to take along their personal household belongings.[42]

As we shall see presently, however, there would soon be reasons to doubt these assertions.

Anson also claimed:

> Before they had moved into their new home, the Lutzes were far from being experts on the subject of psychic phenomena. As far as they can recall, the only books they'd read that might be even remotely considered "occult" were a few popular works on Transcendental Meditation. But as I've since discovered by talking with those familiar with parapsychology, almost every

one of their claims bears a strong parallel to other reports of hauntings, psychic "invasions" and the like that have been published over the years in a wide variety of sources.[43]

Yet during their stay in the house, George Lutz—by his own admission, as we have already seen—read at least one book about "how these witches and demons work."[44]

Anson further asserted, "There is simply too much independent corroboration of their narrative to support the speculation that they either imagined or fabricated these events." He did concede:

> There is no evidence that any strange events occurred at 112 Ocean Avenue after the period of time reported in this book, but this, too, makes sense; more than one parapsychologist has noted that occult manifestations—especially those with poltergeist overtones—very often end as suddenly as they began, never to reoccur. And even traditional ghost-hunters assure their clients that structural changes in a house, even a simple rearrangement of furniture, such as would be effected by a new tenant, will bring a speedy end to reports of the abnormal.[45]

In fact, the man who later lived in the house at 112 Ocean Avenue for a period of eight months (at the time the movie version of the story revived interest in the alleged happenings there) said he had experienced nothing more horrible than the incessant gawkers and sightseers who tramped onto the property. "I have never heard sounds of ghosts, ghouls, or the supernatural," stated the thirty-two-year-old resident, Frank Burch. "The only sound you can ever hear in this house is a bump when I sometimes fall out of bed."[46]

Similarly, the couple who purchased the house after it was given up by the Lutzes, James and Barbara Cromarty, poured ice water on the hellish tale. When I visited Amityville as a consultant to the "In Search of . . ." television series, Barbara Cromarty told me not only that her family had experienced no supernatural occurrences in the house, but that she had evidence the whole affair was a hoax.[47] We shall return to the Cromartys presently, but in the meantime let us consider the work of other investigators who were examining the Lutzes' claims following publication of Anson's book.

One thing most experienced investigators had noted, myself included, was the uncharacteristic mixture of phenomena reported in the Lutz-Anson story: It was part traditional haunting, part poltergeist disturbance, part demon possession, with some elements that were curiously similar to those from the movie The Exorcist thrown in for good measure. Researchers Rick Moran and Peter Jordan were suspicious of the admixture, feeling that the atypical, hybrid features were more suggestive of a hoax than of a genuine (at least honestly reported) paranormal case.

Moran and Jordan went to Amityville to check out details of the events the Lutzes had related to Anson. Searching newspaper files they discovered that the earliest news accounts of the alleged events, although quoting George Lutz, made no mention of any damage to the house: no ripped-off doors or bannisters, no twisted door or window hardware, nor other damage so colorfully reported in The Amityville Horror.[48]

Moran and Jordan further discovered that, despite claims that a priest who had blessed the house had experienced certain sinister phenomena, no such events had occurred: the priest neither attempted to exorcise demons from the house using holy water nor did he have a mysterious car accident or an affliction of blisters. These and other incidents were completely fictitious; indeed, the priest never even set foot inside the Amityville home.

The investigators also debunked claims that police were called to the 112 Ocean Avenue address. The police—whose officer, "Detective Sergeant Lou Zammataro," supposedly made an on-site inspection—denied that they had ever been to the scene.[49] Thus, sources that Anson claimed corroborated the Lutzes' version of events actually did no such thing; indeed, they thoroughly discredited them.

Furthermore, when investigators checked weather reports in comparison with events reported in the book, the results were illuminating. For example, the Lutz-Anson account describes a torrential rainfall that allegedly occurred on January 13, forcing the family to remain in the house an extra night and adding a dramatic element to the narrative. Referring to the "storm of hurricane strength," the book claimed: "It was as though all the water in the world was being dumped on top of 112 Ocean Avenue." However, actual weather records examined by Robert L. Morris showed mild conditions with a mere 0.01 inches of rainfall during that day (7 A.M. to 7 P.M.) and just 0.39 inches throughout the night (7 P.M. to 7 A.M. the following day).

Furthermore, weather reports thoroughly debunked one of the book's central demonic claims. On the day that George Lutz reportedly saw the cloven hoofprints in the snow, records established that there had actually been no snowfall at that time.[50]

Additional, clear evidence that major events in *The Amityville Horror* were untrue—and could not be explained away as misperceptions or other errors—came from Barbara Cromarty, whom I talked with on three occasions. Recalling the extensive damage to doors and windows detailed in the book, she noted that they still had their old hardware (hinges, locks, doorknob, etc.). Upon close inspection, one could easily see that disturbances in the paint and varnish that would have resulted from any subsequent repair were totally absent.[51] In addition, Moran and Jordan searched the Amityville area for locksmiths and other repairmen who might have been called to the house during the Lutzes' residency. They found none.[52]

When the then-forthcoming television series "That's Incredible" called to ask my advice about filming inside the house for its premier episode, I recommended having Mrs. Cromarty take the TV camera on a tour of the house, pointing out such discrepancies for a close-up view. Thus the program took a debunking stance. (Unfortunately the program's producers were reportedly flooded with letters afterward decrying the skepticism— something the viewers emphatically did not want—and that was the last I heard from the staff of that popular and dishonest show.)

By the time the movie had opened (on July 27, 1979) the Lutzes' attorney, William Weber, was revealing that the elaborate tale was a hoax. Weber thus, according to science writer and *Skeptical Inquirer* editor Kendrick Frazier, "confirmed the suspicions of virtually everyone who had examined the story with even a modicum of skepticism."[53]

Weber said the Lutzes had come to him after leaving the house, and he told them their "experiences" could be useful to him in preparing a book about the Ronald DeFeo trial. "We created this horror story over many bottles of wine that George Lutz was drinking," Weber told the Associated Press. "We were really playing with each other. We were creating something the public wanted to hear about." Weber explained that he supplied information he had obtained in the DeFeo case and that the Lutzes used it to fabricate their own account. As one example, he stated, the Lutzes' tale about a stench and flies in a bedroom actually came from the police who described a stench that arose from a bedroom where one of the murder victims had been discovered.[54]

Weber informed Kathy Lutz that the murders were reported to have taken place about 3:00 A.M. "So Kathy said, 'Well, that's good. I can say I'm awakened by noises at that hour . . . and I could say I had dreams at that hour of the day about the DeFeo family." As to why he had not come forward earlier, Weber answered: "They haven't violated the law. If the public is gullible enough to believe the story, so be it." Weber did file a $2 million suit against the couple, charging them with fraud and breach of contract for reneging on their book deal. The suit, during which George Lutz admitted making $100,000 each from the book and film, was settled out of court for an undisclosed amount, and the Lutzes' countersuit was dismissed.[55]

Later, Ronald DeFeo himself came forth to admit that his claims to having heard voices telling him to kill were false. He said his lawyer, Weber, had talked him into the insanity plea so he could peddle a bogus "haunted house" tale to Hollywood and share the expected revenues.[56]

The Cromartys also sued the Lutzes, Anson, and the publishers. They maintained that their fraudulent claim of haunting had resulted in sightseers destroying any privacy they might have had. According to the *Chicago Tribune*, the suits were settled in favor of the Cromartys, reportedly for a six-figure sum.[57] The *Encyclopedia of Hoaxes* concluded: "The campaign to sell this hoax to the public was masterfully handled. To this day, few people know that the whole episode was a hoax, yet a number of exposures of the hoax are offered. The exposures did not realize the broad publicity that the book or movie did."[58]

Helping to keep belief in the story alive are Ed and Lorraine Warren. Of course, they have egg on their faces from the whole embarrassing affair, since the allegedly "clairvoyant" Lorraine and her "psychic" colleagues failed to pick up any hint of the outrageous fakery. They continue to promote the case as evidence of the "demonic world." When I appeared with the demon-promoting couple on the "Sally Jessy Raphael" show, Ed Warren loudly denied the story was a hoax.[59] In their book *Ghost Hunters,* Ed will say only that "my sense is that some things got dramatized beyond reality," but he denies that that discredits the case. Lorraine adds: "*The Amityville Horror,* if nothing else, showed how a cursed house can affect very different families. And it showed how demonic infestation is a reality that can invade anyone's life."[60]

Despite the Warrens' claims, of course, the evidence is clear that the Lutz-Anson story was a hoax. A transcript of the September 1979 trial of George and Kathy Lutz *vs.* Paul Hoffman— Hoffman being perhaps the first writer to publish an account of the Amityville happenings—reveals the Lutzes' admission that virtually everything in *The Amityville Horror* was pure fiction.[61] Indeed, *Newsday* columnist Ed Lowe observes: "It had to have been a setup since Day 1. The day after the Lutzes fled, supposedly in terror, they returned to hold a garage sale—just lots of junk. It was obvious they hadn't moved in there [the $80,000 house] with anything worth anything." Lowe added, confirming the findings of other investigators, "And during the entire 28-day 'siege' that drove them from the house, they never once called the police." Lowe should know: His father was the Amityville police chief at the time of the alleged demonic events.[62]

Undaunted, the Warrens went on to help peddle the movie *Amityville II: The Possession,* for which they were the film's "demonology advisors." The *Chicago Tribune,* to its credit, reminded its readers of the Lutz hoax and added: "What's more, the Warrens' investigation, which lent support to the Lutzes' story, failed to unearth some telling evidence to the contrary." The *Tribune* wondered: "So which is it—are the Warrens hoaxing or have they themselves been hoaxed?"[63]

West Pittston Succubus

The Associated Press reported on August 18, 1986, that demons had invaded a house in West Pittston, Pennsylvania, a small mining town near Scranton. The house at 330–332 Chase Street was occupied by the Smurl family: Jack and Janet and their four children.

The Smurls claimed that "strange goings-on" began in the house eighteen months previously, but in later news stories they extended the period to five years and again to twelve.[64] Whatever actually transpired there, as early as January of that year and again in August, the Smurls had invited Ed and Lorraine Warren to investigate. The Warrens quickly determined there were *several* demons in the Smurl house. In fact, it appears to have been at the Warrens' urging that the press was informed of the story. Soon the Smurls had signed a book contract.[65]

The August 18 AP story gave the following account:

> The Smurls said they have smelled the stench of smoke and rotten meat, heard pig grunts, hoofbeats, and blood-curdling screams and groans. Doors have opened and shut, lights have gone on and off, formless ghostly glows have traveled before them, and the television set has shot across the room. Even the family dog, a 75-pound German shepherd, has been slammed against the wall while [Jack] Smurl said he stood nearby.[66]

Smurl also told the reporter: "Sometimes when I say my rosary it drags me from my knees and tries to beat me into submission."[67]

At the Warrens' instigation, two exorcisms were conducted by a Roman Catholic priest—apparently without the church's sanction, however. In any event, these proved unsuccessful, and the Smurls appealed to people to pray for them.[68] However, when two investigators were dispatched to the site by the Committee for the Scientific Investigation of Claims of the Paranormal (CSICOP), they were refused admittance by the Smurls and Ed Warren. According to CSICOP's journal, the *Skeptical Inquirer*, "Warren began a dispute about their credentials, and the Smurls eventually called the police. The house was thus closed to independent scientific investigators."[69]

A psychiatrist and a psychologist also offered their help, but the family declined, saying that none of them was in need of such assistance. The psychologist, Dr. Robert Gordon, suggested the family may have been suffering from mass hysteria, rather like that present during the Salem witch delusion of 1692. Dr. Gordon explained that a shared tension could cause such hysteria, with symptoms also being shared, and that it could possibly involve hallucinations or delusions. The Smurls' deep belief in demonology, he theorized, could intensify the delusional belief system.

Interestingly, one of the demonic events reported by Jack Smurl makes Dr. Gordon's ideas seem most appropriate: Smurl claimed he was raped by a succubus! As Ed Warren describes it: "He was asleep in bed one night and he was awakened by this haglike woman who paralyzed him. He wanted to scream out, of course— he was horrified by what he saw, the woman had scales on her skin and white, scraggly hair, and some of her teeth were missing— but she paralyzed him in some manner." Warren added, "Then she mounted him and rode him to her sexual climax."[70]

One immediately recognizes how perfectly this description tallies with a "waking dream" or "night terror," as we discussed earlier in this chapter, specifically in relationship to the succubus. Note that Smurl was asleep, that he felt "paralyzed," that his experience was extremely vivid, and that the content of the experience was bizarre—all features of the waking dream.[71] Given the description of Jack Smurl's "rape" it seems extremely likely that he experienced a waking dream.

Dr. Gordon's speculations about hysteria seem borne out by another incident. As Lorraine Warren describes it: "Dawn Smurl [age seventeen] . . . was taking a shower when she felt a presence seize her arms and then brush up against her in an unmistakable way. It took all her strength to get from the shower to the hallway where she started screaming for her parents."[72]

Interestingly, prior resident Steve Ellis, who had resided in the West Pittston house prior to the Smurls' acquisition of it (fourteen years before), said that nothing of a paranormal or supernatural nature had occurred during the seventeen years of his residency. He said he doubted the Smurls' claims.[73]

CSICOP investigators Barry Karr and Mary Beth Gehrman searched the neighborhood around the Smurl house and discovered plausible sources for the reported stench and smell of smoke: a faulty sewer pipe and a fire that had recently occurred at a lumberyard nearby.[74]

Some of the other disturbances may well have been "poltergeist" type pranks. According to an investigative report on the case by Paul Kurtz, chairman of CSICOP, "Some neighbors were quick to point out that, if the house is infested by demons, the Smurl children do not seem frightened but take it as great sport and are sometimes left alone in the house by their parents." "Moreover," Kurtz added, "there is no police record that the Smurls have ever filed a complaint or called the department for help, although Mrs. Smurl maintains that they did."[75]

Just four days before Halloween 1986, the Smurls claimed the events had ceased, and that the demons had vacated their home. They credited their newfound peace to "the intercession of the Most Blessed Virgin Mary, St. Michael, and the Sacred Heart of Jesus." Unfortunately, the demons soon returned and followed the Smurls to their new house.[76] On November 14, St. Martin's Press announced the Smurls had signed a book contract with them. Titled *The Haunted: The True Story of One Family's Nightmare*, the book was written by Robert Curran "with Jack & Janet Smurl and Ed & Lorraine Warren."[77]

Whatever may actually lie behind the Smurl claims—and I suggest it is contagious hysteria coupled with natural events and childish pranks—the book exaggerates the claims in typical Warren style. And once again proof is elusive. The Warrens claim that they have captured various paranormal events in the house on audio- and videotapes, but have consistently refused to make them available to scientific investigators. Ed Warren has said that he will eventually release the tapes, but only to the Catholic church.[78]

Paul Kurtz said of the publicity seekers' new book, "I doubt virtually everything in this book. I think most of it is fiction." Kurtz went on to call the case "an affront to common sense. I consider the publication of this book nothing short of scandalous. It's exaggeration, imagination, fantasy. And it's deplorable—a modern society going back to the Dark Ages."[79]

When asked if they "play on people's fears for profit," Ed Warren told a reporter, "Sure, we want all the publicity we can get." He added: "That's what we're all about. We want to tell people that if a psychiatrist can't help them, then there must be another explanation."[80]

Southington Demons

In 1986 the Snedeker family moved from northern New York to Southington, Connecticut, because their oldest son was receiving treatment for Hodgkin's disease at a nearby hospital. The family consisted of Allen, a stone-quarry foreman; his wife Carmen, a former bowling alley cocktail waitress and self-described "devout Catholic"; Carmen's two sons by a previous marriage, Philip (thirteen) and Brad (eleven); a daughter, Jennifer (six); another son, Allen, Jr. (three); and a pet ferret.[81] Later, two nieces would live in the house also.

The Snedekers' new residence was a white clapboard, two-and-a-half-story Colonial Revival house, built in 1916.[82] Known locally as the Hallahan House, it is located at 208 Meriden Avenue, a street listed in the National Register as a historic neighborhood. The house was used since 1936 as a funeral home, and zoning prevented its being converted to a real-estate office in the mid-1980s; instead it was transformed into upstairs and downstairs apartments. The "For Rent" sign caught Carmen's eye and she promptly rented the downstairs residence.[83] On June 30 the Snedekers moved in.[84]

Whether or not the Snedekers knew when they moved in that the place had been a funeral home has been disputed. They say they did not, but some neighbors insist otherwise. The owners state emphatically that the couple was informed before moving into the house as to its previous use. In any event, the Snedekers soon discovered in the basement a box of coffin handles, a blood drainage pit, and a chain-and-pulley casket lift—unmistakable leftovers from the previous business known as the Hallahan Funeral Home.

Certainly, the creepy setting may have had an overpowering

psychological effect. Indeed, the phenomena began with Philip, whose bedroom was in the basement, in a room partitioned from the remainder of the grisly area. Soon Philip reportedly began to see ghosts, including an old man in a gray, pinstriped suit and a young boy dressed in Superman pajamas. "We didn't believe him," said Carmen Snedeker, saying they thought Philip's behavior was due to the effects of his cobalt cancer treatments.[85]

Philip's personality underwent a drastic change. He started to wear leather, developed an interest in demonology, and, according to one news report, "broke into a neighbor's house and told his mother he wanted to get a gun and kill his stepfather." Philip (who survived his cancer) was diagnosed a schizophrenic and hospitalized in January 1988. The Snedekers told reporters they had believed that with Philip gone there would be an end to the ghost reports, but soon their seventeen-year-old niece (who had come to live with them in September 1987) reportedly "felt an unseen hand toying with her bra." There were other unwanted touchings.[86]

Two years after the phenomena reportedly began, the Snedekers contacted Ed and Lorraine Warren, who also live in Connecticut, and they, in turn, "alerted the media." The Snedekers' landlady, who had served them with an eviction notice for nonpayment of rent, was not amused. She said she and her husband had had no problems with the house.

> We've owned the property for two and a half years. We knew nothing of any so-called ghosts before we bought the house, nor did we hear anything until a couple of weeks ago. And we've had tenants upstairs and downstairs at all times.
>
> Personally, my husband and I do not believe in ghosts and to us, the whole issue seems ridiculous. I find it ironic that after more than two years as tenants, suddenly we are told about these alleged ghosts and then read in the paper that the Warrens will be conducting a seminar and will be charging the public for it.
>
> If the ghosts really are there, then why did the Snedekers stay there over two years and why are they staying there now? Are they looking for publicity or profit, or what?[87]

The Warrens, operating in the name of their nonprofit New England Society for Psychic Research, were promoting their "Supernatural Night," billing themselves as "America's top ghostbusters" and charging ten dollars per attendee. Having moved into the Snedekers' home for nine weeks, the Warrens also brought with them two men who were variously described as "psychic researchers" and "psychics." One of them, Chris McKinnell, happened to be the Warrens' grandson, while the other, John Zaffis, was their nephew.[88]

One newspaper seemed critical of McKinnell, stating: "Even though he seems to welcome interviews, he intends for the public to know only selected information about his organization and the case on Meriden Avenue." The news report added, "When told Monday night that he had to keep all of his comments on the record for publication, he almost ended the interview."[89] Soon McKinnell and his fellow "psychic" were reporting their own sightings of ghosts and other phenomena, and also denying that there was any book deal in progress regarding the case. In fact, Mrs. Snedeker had already told her upstairs neighbor about the deal, saying she and her husband were to get one-third of the profits (the customary amount the Warrens offer).[90] As we shall see, just such a book deal did materialize.

The media attention continued to focus on Meriden Avenue, and soon the Snedekers appeared on a national television program, "A Current Affair." In the meantime they had begun to claim that they and some of their family members and researchers had been attacked by the evil "presence." She and her husband, Carmen Snedeker maintained, had been raped and sodomized by demons. McKinnell, however, said he was "not quite sodomized."[91]

By this time neighbors and local residents had begun to come forward with negative comments. The Warrens were "con artists," according to the Snedekers' upstairs neighbor. "I haven't experienced anything," she said. "I definitely know that no one has been raped up here." She stated that the Warrens, whom she believed were exploiting the Snedekers for personal gain, "have caused a lot of problems here and they are not ghost problems."[92]

More negative comments awaited the Snedekers and Warrens when they appeared on the "Sally Jessy Raphael" show to promote their forthcoming book, *In a Dark Place: The Story of a True Haunting*. The show, taped on October 19, 1992, was carefully scheduled to air on October 30—just in time to provide spine-tingling thrills for Halloween. Indeed, a pre-publication copy of the book (which the "Sally" show producers gave me in preparation for appearing on the same program) listed the official publication date as "October 31, 1992." The professional author hired to turn the story into a sensational book was Ray Garton, shamelessly billed on the back cover as "author of five successful horror novels."[93] That seemed appropriate, since many people were branding the book fiction. Said the husband of the Snedekers' former landlady: "It's a fraud. It's a joke. It's a hoax. It's Halloween." He added: "It's a scheme to make money." Those comments appeared in the *Hartford Courant* in an article brilliantly titled "Couple Sees Ghost; Skeptics See Through It."[94]

Additional skeptics included several Meriden Avenue residents who appeared on "Sally Jessy Raphael"—some on the set with me, others who were asked to stand up from their seats in the studio audience. On the set for the Snedekers' interview was a brass bed for them to sit on while they told their story of demonic sexual attack.

Eventually Sally turned to the current resident of the apartment vacated by the Snedekers, asking, "Why don't you believe the Snedekers' story?" He replied, "Well, I think the most obvious reason for me was the inconsistencies in it." To Carmen he said, "As a matter of fact, a close relative of yours told me that there was nothing to it, that you were making it up just for the money." He added, "I have not heard anything that would suggest that that house is haunted whatsoever." Other participants accused the Snedekers of making up the haunting tale after being behind in their rent. Others mentioned that the older son took drugs, and Carmen Snedeker readily agreed, saying she was aware he took "illegal substances." That brought the specific statement that the teenager had used LSD, which "would allow him to see things" (i.e., have hallucinations). Still other audience members disputed whether there had actually been an exorcism at the house as the Warrens and Snedekers alleged, but which the local diocese refused to confirm.

At one point in telling their story, Carmen Snedeker actually made reference to the spirits "called incubus and succubus," suggesting that they had researched—or had been "prepped" on—demon lore. As one member of the audience said to the Snedekers, "You . . . sound like you're reading a script. I'm not saying spirits and ghosts don't exist, but you sound so rehearsed." That seemed to sum up the opinion of most, because at the end of the program Sally said: "We took a little poll in our audience. Our audience does not believe."[95]

One of the most effective critics of the Snedekers' claims was also on the "Sally" show: Mrs. Kathy Altemus, the across-the-street neighbor of the Snedekers during their entire tenancy in the Hallahan House. Beginning in mid-July 1988, she kept a journal of events relating to 208 Meriden Avenue. As a consequence, she told Sally, "I discovered that there were usually things going on in the neighborhood that explained the things they put in the newspaper."[96] The journal—a copy of which she generously shared with me in hopes it would help "expose the truth"[97]—is too lengthy to quote here, but it juxtaposes Mrs. Altemus's written records with newspaper clippings arranged chronologically among the entries.

For example, the program "A Current Affair" had mentioned the sound of clanking chains in the house, presumably from the coffin lift in the basement. But Mrs. Altemus's journal shows that the noise most likely was that from a truck that passed by, making a sound like it was "dragging a chain." Similarly, according to entries in the journal, "vibrations" felt in the house could easily be attributed to heavy trucks going by with noisy mufflers that rattled the house and also hitting a repair spot in the road. Other events could possibly be attributed to various passersby mentioned in the journal as "pulling pranks on the 'haunted house.' "[98]

The journal also sheds light on another event. As sensationalized in the *New Britain Herald*, either a "bizarre coincidence or ghost" was indicated by a power outage—caused by a tree limb that fell onto an electrical line at 208 Meriden Avenue and happening just after "A Current Affair" had broadcast "a segment on the Snedeker family of that address." According to the paper, a spokesman for the utility "was at a loss to explain just why the limb chose that particular time to knock out the power." In fact, however, the incident did not occur at the time of the TV program, but some two hours later. Moreover, as Kathy Altemus's journal makes clear, such outages have happened several times on the tree-lined Meriden, when limbs have fallen on the uninsulated line.[99] Such an event, in fact, occurred when I was in Southington at the Altemus home in June 1993; it seems unlikely that mysterious forces were heralding my humble arrival.

The journal also contained revealing information about the oldest Snedeker boy's drug use, vandalism, and other misbehavior. Revealingly, the Snedekers' own book (written with the Warrens and Ray Garton) acknowledges such behavior and even, unwittingly, seems to provide an explanation for the sexual touching that Carmen's niece had felt "from an unseen hand." The boy was actually caught fondling his nieces while they slept, behavior that caused Carmen Snedeker to call the police. "Steven" (as he is called in the book) "was taken away by the police that afternoon. He was questioned, at which time he confessed that he'd been fondling the girls while they slept at night, and that he'd attempted unsuccessfully to have sex with his twelve-year-old cousin."[100] He was later taken to the juvenile detention center, where a psychiatrist diagnosed him as schizophrenic.[101] As we see from the book, the reported ghostly touchings began while the older son was still in the house—not afterward, as implied in several newspaper articles quoting Carmen Snedeker.[102]

Taken together, the evidence in the Southington case does not warrant the conclusion that demons were at work in the Hallahan House. The combination of creepy surroundings and a mentally ill teenager on drugs, who was actually discovered to possess the "unseen hand" that fondled his cousin as she slept, could easily have triggered mass hysteria in the religiously superstitious family. Once fixated on demons, individuals could be expected to apply that explanation to mundane events such as those documented in Mrs. Altemus's journal. The admitted excess drinking of the boy's stepfather, Al, could also have contributed to the situation.[103]

Even so, the arrival of the Warrens on the scene, with their publicity-seeking actions in the case, appears to have grossly magnified and exaggerated whatever core of "real" events might have existed. Evidence that a book deal was discussed early but denied, together with the fact that a professional horror-tale writer was chosen to produce the text and that the book was timed for Halloween release and promotion, casts doubt on the motives of those involved. If the case did not begin as a hoax, perhaps people cannot be blamed for thinking it was turned into one.

Black Hope Terror

One more case study of a demonic attack will perhaps suffice— mercifully a brief one that does not involve Ed and Lorraine Warren. I was asked to look into the claims in preparation for my appearance on "The Maury Povich Show," where I was to meet the alleged victims, Ben and Jean Williams. (Also on the show for a brief appearance was Carmen Snedeker who seemed to amuse the audience with her tale about being sexually attacked by a demon.[104])

The Williams story properly begins at the home of a neighbor in 1983, three years after the Williamses moved into their new home in the Newport subdivision at Crosby, Texas, located on Lake Houston. Their neighbor, Sam Haney, was building a swimming pool in his yard when he received a visit. "An elderly man knocked on my door," Haney said, "and told me there was something I should know." The man pointed out an area about ten feet square that he said contained graves. Soon, elderly black folk in Crosby confirmed that Haney's house site had once been a cemetery for poor blacks—the abandoned Black Hope Graveyard—with some of the graves probably dating back to the 1880s.[105]

Haney hired a backhoe operator to begin excavation for the pool, but determined to stop at the first sign of a grave. It soon came, and Haney phoned the Harris County medical examiner's office, which in turn contacted the sheriff's department. The remains—a portion of an arm—were found to be human but lingered on the examiner's office shelf for several months. At length, Haney and his wife Judy received permission to rebury them, using a small casket they had fashioned. Later, they discovered there were a pair of graves, apparently belonging to a couple named Betty and Charlie Thomas, and the subdivision developers had them reburied in a cemetery.[106]

In the meantime, the Haneys began to suffer from stress and to experience some strange happenings. For example, a pair of shoes mysteriously vanished from their home, only to turn up in Charlie Thomas's open grave. Such incidents figured in the lawsuit the Haneys eventually brought against the developers, the Purcell Corporation. As the *Houston Chronicle* reported: "The Haneys contended that the developers had deceived them by not informing them about the location of the old burial ground and that disturbing the graves agitated the ghosts of those buried there."[107] The *Chronicle* added: "The story told in court sounded like the script for a low-budget remake of the movie *Poltergeist*, which concerned a family's struggle to cope with ghosts who revolted because the family's home had been built over their graves."[108]

Although the Haneys sued for $2 million, the jury awarded them only $142,600—including $115,000 for mental anguish due to their distressing discovery. The jury refused the Haneys' request for punitive damages, determining that the Purcell Corporation did not intentionally build the home over the cemetery. Based on that finding, however, State District Judge Ruby Kless Sondock entered a final judgment that negated the jury's award and ordered the Haneys to pay court costs.[109]

Although Judy Haney had testified about mysterious happenings, "She later said," reported the *Houston Chronicle*, "she believes there were logical explanations for those occurrences."[110] In the case of the displaced shoes, for instance, a possible explanation is found in Mrs. Haney's earlier statement to a reporter: "We searched the house and places the dog would have taken them."[111]

Now enter Ben and Jean Williams. They report much more extensive and persistent paranormal phenomena, and claim it goes back to the time they moved into their new home in 1980.[112] Interestingly, however, it appears it was not until the Haneys' trial was underway against the developers that the Williamses—

who were themselves attempting to negotiate a settlement with Purcell—first came forward with their story.[113] Eventually they produced a book, *The Black Hope Horror: The True Story of a Haunting.* The book is "ghost written" with John Bruce Shoemaker, a professional writer. Although the book does not mention Ed and Lorraine Warren, the Williamses appear to have taken a page or two from their works.

Specifically, every odd occurrence, no matter how unlikely it is to have an occult cause and no matter what rational explanations may be at hand, is interpreted as providing further evidence of a ghost or demon. Snakes in the backyard, an infestation of ants in the house—surely most rational people would not rush to equate these with sinister forces, yet Ben and Jean Williams do.[114] When their automatic garage door malfunctioned, it was considered an example of "paranormal experiences, both bizarre and malicious,"[115] even though Ben Williams conceded the possibility that the mechanism was faulty.[116]

And when their eight-year-old granddaughter came to live with them and frequently saw "ghosts" or other "shadowy presences," this was considered still more proof of haunting. Yet the girl loved to "daydream" and "pretend"—indeed, had several "imaginary playmates" that she conversed with—and often could not distinguish between what was real and what was imaginary.[117]

The most profound event the Williamses attributed to "the force"—which they equated with "the Devil"—was the death of their daughter, Tina. While tragic, the death need not be attributed to anything of a supernatural nature. Tina had Hodgkin's disease, which had been in remission, but then she acquired a virus that caused her own immune system to attack her heart muscle. She died, in fact, of "a massive heart attack."[118]

The Williamses are emotional people, very religious, and given to outbursts—Jean to crying and Ben to shouting at whomever would challenge him—as they demonstrated on "The Maury Povich Show." Jean Williams avidly read books on "supernatural and paranormal phenomena" and at times almost wished she were a Catholic so she could "attempt an exorcism." When it became awkward to carry a Bible through the house, she purchased a crucifix, and, "The time came when she was walking the halls of her own home, reciting prayers aloud, carrying the crucifix in one hand and a thirty-eight pistol in the other."[119] Ben, nicknamed "Shag," is an asthmatic with elevated blood pressure, and he sometimes attributed what he had experienced to "nerves."[120]

The Williamses' book emphasizes that other neighbors also experienced paranormal phenomena, but the salient fact is that according to the *Houston Chronicle*, "most of the residents think the neighborhood is haunted only by overactive imaginations." For example, the Haneys' next-door neighbor, Karen Regini, a twenty-eight-year-old homemaker and mother of two children, stated, "I've seen nothing spooky at all."[121]

Perhaps Ida Ruth McKinney, the then seventy-nine-year-old ranch owner whose father once owned the subdivision property, summed up the affair most succinctly. "I think it's a hoot. Just ridiculous," she said. Insisting she had never heard even a "boo" on the property, she added, "I think somebody's a little off in the head or wants a little money." Referring to the case's similarity to the movie *Poltergeist*, McKinney said, "Maybe we'll see a sequel from this."[122] Indeed, on March 3, 1992, CBS aired the made-for-TV movie based on the Williamses' story, *Grave Secrets: The Legacy of Hilltop Drive*. But as a reviewer observed, "The ghosts aren't as convincing as they should be, and the movie is not scary enough to quicken your pulse."[123]

Recommended Works

Beyerstein, Barry L. "Naturopathology and the Legacy of Spiritual Possession," *Skeptical Inquirer* 12, no. 3 (Spring 1988): 248–62. A demonstration that three brain syndromes—epilepsy, Tourette's, and migraine—probably fostered ancient notions of "possession."

Cavendish, Richard. *The Powers of Evil: In Western Religion, Magic and Folk Belief*. New York: Dorset Press, 1975. Comprehensive introduction to the subject of evil supernatural beings through the ages.

Guiley, Rosemary Ellen. *Harper's Encyclopedia of Mystical & Para-*

normal Experience. New York: HarperCollins, 1991. Uncritical guide
to mystical and magical claims.

Hicks, Robert D. "Police Pursuit of Satanic Crime," *Skeptical Inquirer*
14, no. 3 (Spring 1990): 276–86 and 14, no. 4 (Summer 1990): 378–
89. Penetrating critical analysis of topic.

Huston, Peter. "Night Terrors, Sleep Paralysis, and Devil-Stricken
Telephone Cords from Hell," *Skeptical Inquirer* 17, no. 1 (Fall 1992):
64–69. Vivid discussion of hypnopompic/hypnogogic hallucinations
("waking dreams").

Morris, Robert L. Review of Jay Anson's *The Amityville Horror,* in
Skeptical Inquirer 2, no. 2 (Spring/Summer 1978): 95–102. Review-
article exposing a major hoax.

Rachleff, Owen S. *The Occult Conceit: A New Look at Astrology, Witchcraft & Sorcery.* Chicago: Cowles Book Co., 1971. A highly readable,
skeptical look at witchcraft, Ouija boards, and other occult interests.

Scot, Reginald. *The Discoverie of Witchcraft.* 1584; reprint of 1930
edition, New York: Dover 1972. Surprisingly modern in its view,
a sixteenth-century discrediting of the black arts by a witness to
witch-hunting mania.

Notes

1. Gerald Larue, *The Supernatural, the Occult and the Bible*
(Amherst, N.Y.: Prometheus Books, 1990), p. 68; Rosemary Ellen Guiley,
Harper's Encyclopedia of Mystical & Paranormal Experience (New York:
Harper Collins, 1991), pp. 144–46, 647.

2. Larue, *The Supernatural, the Occult and the Bible,* p. 68.

3. Ibid.

4. Ibid.; A. E. Garvie, "Devil," *Encyclopedia Britannica,* 1960.

5. Owen S. Rachleff, *The Occult Conceit* (Chicago: Cowles, 1971),
p. 104.

6. Richard Cavendish, ed., *Encyclopedia of the Unexplained*
(London: Routledge & Kegan Paul, 1974), p. 219.

7. Ibid.

8. Garvie, "Devil."

9. Ibid.; Owen S. Rachleff, *The Occult Conceit,* p. 107; Richard
Cavendish, *The Powers of Evil* (New York: Dorset Press, 1975), pp.
170–71.

10. Simon Welfare and John Fairley, *Arthur C. Clarke's Mysterious World* (New York: A & W Visual Library, 1981), pp. 45–48.

11. I published the first part of this story in my column, "Rappings," in the *SCM Levitator* (the newsletter of the Society of Canadian Magicians) 1, no. 6 (May 1972): 6–7. Other information is from my case file.

12. See Daniel Farson, *Vampires, Zombies, and Monster Men* (New York: Doubleday, 1976), p. 32.

13. John Anderson with Rich Monk, *Psychic Phenomena Unveiled: Confessions of a New Age Warlock* (Lafayette, La.: Huntington House, n.d.), pp. 103–104, 108.

14. "Satanic Hoaxes," in *Encyclopedia of Hoaxes*, ed. Gordon Stein (Detroit: Gale Research, 1993), pp. 237–38. See also Robert D. Hicks, "Police Pursuit of Satanic Crime," *Skeptical Inquirer* 14, no. 3 (Spring 1990): 276–86 and 14, no. 4 (Summer 1990): 378–89; Robert D. Hicks, *In Pursuit of Satan: The Police and the Occult* (Amherst, N.Y.: Prometheus Books, 1991).

15. Hicks, "Police Pursuit of Satanic Crime," p. 279.

16. Ibid., pp. 279–80.

17. Guiley, *Harper's Encyclopedia*, pp. 145–46.

18. Maria Leach, ed., *Funk & Wagnall's Standard Dictionary of Folklore, Mythology, and Legend* (New York: Harper & Row, 1984), pp. 515–16; Cavendish, *The Powers of Evil*, pp. 102–103.

19. Cavendish, *The Powers of Evil*, p. 103.

20. Robert A. Baker and Joe Nickell, *Missing Pieces* (Amherst, N.Y.: Prometheus Books, 1992), pp. 130–31.

21. Guiley, *Harper's Encyclopedia*, p. 457.

22. Ibid.

23. Barry L. Beyerstein, "Naturopathology and the Legacy of Spiritual Possession," *Skeptical Inquirer* 12, no. 3 (Spring 1988): 248–62.

24. Robert A. Baker, *Hidden Memories: Voices and Visions from Within* (Amherst, N.Y.: Prometheus Books, 1992), p. 192.

25. Ibid., pp. 194–95.

26. "The Exorcism," ABC's "20/20" program, April 5, 1991. See also "ABC to Televise an Exorcism in Florida," *USA Today*, April 5, 1991, and "Real Life Exorcism Hits Prime-Time Television," *Newark Star-Ledger*, April 5, 1991.

27. Rev. Richard McBrien, interview on ABC's "Nightline," April 5, 1991.

28. Larue, *The Supernatural, the Occult and the Bible*, p. 95.

29. Guiley, *Harper's Encyclopedia*, p. 647.

30. Rachleff, *The Occult Conceit,* pp. 99–100.

31. Guiley, *Harper's Encyclopedia,* pp. 647–48.

32. Ibid; *Encyclopedia Britannica,* 1960, s.v. "Salem."

33. Rachleff, *The Occult Conceit,* p. 121.

34. Ibid.

35. Jay Anson, *The Amityville Horror: A True Story* (New York: Bantam Books, 1977), pp. 7–8. Robert L. Morris, book review of *The Amityville Horror,* in *Skeptical Inquirer* 2, no. 2 (Spring/Summer 1978): 95.

36. Anson, *The Amityville Horror,* passim; Morris, review, pp. 95–96.

37. Anson, *The Amityville Horror,* pp. 23–24, 37, 126, 157, 215, 226.

38. Ibid., pp. 3–5; Morris, review, pp. 95–96.

39. Anson, *The Amityville Horror,* pp. 287–88.

40. Ibid., pp. 288–90.

41. See the Bantam edition (n. 32), including the front cover and preliminary pages.

42. Anson, *The Amityville Horror,* pp. 293–94.

43. Ibid., pp. 294–95.

44. Ibid., pp. 226–27.

45. Ibid., pp. 299–300.

46. Frank Burch, *New York Daily News,* quoted in Kendrick Frazier, "Amityville Hokum: The Hoax and the Hype," *Skeptical Inquirer* 4, no. 2 (Winter 1979–80): 3.

47. Author's case file; see also Frazier, "Amityville Hokum," p. 3.

48. Rick Moran and Peter Jordan, "The Amityville Horror Hoax," *Fate,* May 1978: 44–45.

49. Ibid., p. 46; Morris, review, p. 97.

50. Morris, review, pp. 99–100; cf. Anson, *The Amityville Horror,* pp. 263–65.

51. Barbara Cromarty, interview with author, May 1, 1979 (author's case file).

52. Moran and Jordan, "The Amityville Horror Hoax," p. 45.

53. Frazier, "Amityville Hokum," p. 2.

54. William Weber, interview with Associated Press, distributed July 26, 1979, quoted in Frazier, "Amityville Hokum," pp. 2–3.

55. Ibid.

56. *New York Times* story, quoted in *North Texas Skeptic* (August 1992): 8.

57. Clarence Peterson, "Demonologists Hellbent on Selling 'Amityville II,' " *Chicago Tribune,* September 23, 1982.

58. Gordon Stein, ed., *Encyclopedia of Hoaxes* (Detroit: Gale Research, 1993), p. 63.

59. "Sally Jessy Raphael" show, taped October 19, aired October 30, 1992.

60. Ed and Lorraine Warren, with Robert David Chase, *Ghost Hunters* (New York: St. Martin's Paperbacks, 1989), pp. 166, 171.

61. Stein, *Encyclopedia of Hoaxes*, p. 63.

62. Quoted in Peterson, "Demonologists Hellbent."

63. Peterson, ibid.

64. Paul Kurtz, "A Case Study of the West Pittson 'Haunted' House," *Skeptical Inquirer* 11, no. 2 (Winter 1986–87): 137–38; Michele Leslie, "Nightmare on Chase Street," *Cleveland Plain Dealer*, April 9, 1988.

65. Kurtz, "A Case Study," pp. 137–38, 146.

66. Ibid., p. 138.

67. Associated Press story, August 18, 1986, quoted in ibid., p. 138.

68. Kurtz, "A Case Study," p. 138, and clippings shown in illustration on p. 139.

69. Ibid., p. 138.

70. Warren and Warren with Chase, *Ghost Hunters*, pp. 105–106.

71. Baker and Nickell, *Missing Pieces*, p. 226.

72. Warren and Warren with Chase, *Ghost Hunters*, p. 105.

73. Kurtz, "A Case Study," p. 145.

74. Ibid.

75. Ibid.

76. Ibid.; Leslie, "Nightmare on Chase Street."

77. Robert Curran with Jack and Janet Smurl and Ed and Lorraine Warren, *The Haunted* (New York: St. Martin's, 1988).

78. Kurtz, "A Case Study," p. 142.

79. Ibid.

80. Quoted in Leslie, "Nightmare on Chase Street."

81. Kathy Rivard, "Southington Family Spooked by House," *Bristol Press* (Bristol, Conn.), August 11, 1988; Susan Corica and Glenn Smith, "Haunted House Claim Clouded by Tenant, Landlord Dispute," *Herald* (New Britain, Conn.), August 29, 1988, and "An Unworldly Being," *Herald Extra*, August 15, 1988; Ed and Lorraine Warren and Al and Carmen Snedeker, with Ray Garton, *In a Dark Place: The Story of a True Haunting* (New York: Villard Books, 1992), pp. 3, 6. The book fictionalizes all of the children's names.

82. Historic Resources Inventory, No. 175, Connecticut Historical Commission, 1985. This source lists the house as having two stories, the book (n. 77) as three; the two-and-a-half figure is my own.

83. Kathy Altemus (across-the-street neighbor of the Snedekers), letter to author, January 16, 1993.

84. Warren and Warren et al., *In a Dark Place*, p. 17.

85. Rivard, "Southington Family Spooked"; Bryant Carpenter, "Southington Haunting Is Daunting," *Record-Journal* (Meriden, Conn.), August 13, 1988.

86. Corica and Smith, "An Unworldly Being"; Rivard, "Southington Family Spooked"; Carpenter, "Southington Haunting."

87. Ken DiMauro and Jeanne Starmack, "Demonic Presence Said to Plague Family," *Observer*, August 18, 1989; Corica and Smith, "Haunted House Claim."

88. Ibid.; Carpenter, "Southington Haunting"; Corica and Smith, "Haunted House Claim"; Rivard, "Southington Family Spooked."

89. DiMauro and Starmack, "Demonic Presence."

90. Bryant Carpenter, "Researcher Says Home Haunted by Evil Presence," *Record-Journal*, August 18, 1988; Corica and Smith, "An Unworldly Being" and "Haunted House Claim."

91. DiMauro and Starmack, "Demonic Presence"; Glenn Smith, "Bizarre Coincidence or Ghost? Limb Falls at 'Haunted House' Seen on TV; 1,830 Left in Dark," *Herald*, September 13, 1988.

92. Corica and Smith, "Haunted House Claim."

93. See n. 76.

94. Karen Schmidt, "Couple Sees Ghost; Skeptics See Through It," *Hartford Courant*, October 30, 1992.

95. Quotations are from the official transcript, no. 1084, of the "Sally Jessy Raphael" show, "I Was Raped by a Ghost," air date October 30, 1992, Multimedia Entertainment, Inc.

96. Ibid.

97. Cover letter by Kathy Altemus, January 16, 1993, sending photocopy of her journal to author.

98. Mrs. Altemus's journal entries of July 13, August 19 and 21, and September 12, 1988; cf. Warren and Warren et al., *In a Dark Place*, p. 93. Al Snedeker attributed some of the vibrations to an upstairs refrigerator (pp. 97–98). See also the "Sally Jessy Raphael" show transcript, p. 6.

99. Smith, "Bizarre Coincidence"; Mrs. Altemus's journal, entries of September 12–13, 1988, and November 13, 1992.

100. Warren and Warren et al., *In a Dark Place*, pp. 145–47.

101. Ibid.

102. Corica and Smith, "An Unworldly Being"; Carpenter, "Southington Haunting."

103. Warren and Warren et al., *In a Dark Place*, pp. 97, 185.

104. "The Maury Povich Show" was taped on March 2, 1992.

105. Steve Friedman, "Man Sues After Finding Grave in His Yard," *Houston Chronicle*, July 4, 1987.

106. Bob Tutt, "Ghost Trial Opens Grave Discussion of Fears That Won't Die," *Houston Chronicle*, July 4, 1987; Steve Friedman and Cindy Horswell, "Testimony Details Eerie Occurrences," *Houston Chronicle*, June 27, 1987.

107. Tutt, "Ghost Trial."

108. Ibid.

109. Steve Friedman, "Award to Couple in Cemetery Case Overruled," *Houston Chronicle*, July 29, 1987.

110. Ibid.

111. Friedman and Horswell, "Testimony Details Eerie Occurrences."

112. Ben Williams, Jean Williams, and John Bruce Shoemaker, *The Black Hope Horror: The True Story of a Haunting* (New York: William Morrow, 1991), pp. 21–30.

113. Of three clippings reproduced in the Williamses' book, the earliest is an article by Cindy Horswell and Steve Friedman, " 'Nothing But Hell There,' Says Man Who Fled 'Haunted' House," *Houston Chronicle*, June 26, 1987.

114. Williams, Williams, and Shoemaker, *The Black Hope Horror*, p. 33.

115. Jean Williams, quoted in Greg Lakes, "Flight of Fright: Texas Couple Flee Ghostly Goings-on," *Missoulian* (Missoula, Mon.), 1987 clipping reproduced in the Williamses' book, p. 124.

116. Lakes, "Flight of Fright."

117. Williams, Williams, and Shoemaker, *The Black Hope Horror*, pp. 60–61.

118. Ibid., pp. 172–73, 223, 227–29.

119. Ibid., pp. 179, 203, 204.

120. Ibid., pp. 32, 43, 71.

121. Horswell and Friedman, " 'Nothing But Hell There.' "

122. Friedman and Horswell, "Testimony Details Eerie Occurrences."

123. "Grave Doubts," *Courier-Journal* (Louisville, Ky.), March 3, 1992.

5

Divine Visitations

Ancient Concepts

Turning from sinister and malevolent supernatural beings, since
ancient times shamans, mystics, and prophets have also given
accounts of deities, angels, and other beneficent beings. Many
of the most ancient gods were connected to natural phenomena.
For example, the Babylonian Shamash and the Egyptian Ra were
sun-gods and the Greek Zeus a sky-god. Deities were sometimes
thought of as human in form, or as wholly or partly animal
(theriomorphic), or as trees (dendromorphic), or simply as powers,
taking on no specific shape.[1]

Some of the ancient Hebraic concepts were quite imaginative. In the vision of Ezekiel, for instance, the Lord's throne was
guarded by four "cherubim" having "the likeness of four living
creatures" and

> they had the likeness of a man. And every one had four faces,
> and every one had four wings. And their feet were straight
> feet; and the sole of their feet was like the sole of a calf's foot:
> and they sparkled like the color of burnished brass. And they
> had the hands of a man under their wings. . . . Their wings
> were joined one to another; they turned not when they went;
> they went every one straight forward. As for the likeness of
> their faces, they four had the face of a man, and the face of
> a lion on the right side: and they four had the face of an ox
> on the left side; they four also had the face of an eagle. Thus

149

were their faces: and their wings were stretched upward; two
wings of every one were joined one to another, and two covered
their bodies. (Ezek. 1:5-11KJV)

Also above Yahweh's throne, according to Isaiah, were "seraphim"
each having six wings: "with twain he covered his face, and with
twain he covered his feet, and with twain he did fly" (Isa. 6:2).

Angels were represented in various ways. Often they looked
like ordinary men (Gen. 18, 19), whereas the "angel of the Lord"
who spoke to Moses on Mount Horeb appeared in the form of
a burning bush (Exod. 3:2).

Often man interacted or had encounters with the deities or
their representatives. In the Old Testament, for example, Lot
conversed with angels (Gen. 19:1-3), and angels saved Elijah from
starvation in the wilderness (1 Kings 19:5-8). Similarly, Abraham
spoke with God in a dream (Gen. 20:6), and Moses talked with
him upon Mount Sinai where he received the stone tablets of
the law (Exod. 24:112, 31:18). In the New Testament, divine
visitations are central to the story of Jesus. The angel Gabriel
announced his conception (Luke 1:26-31), the "Spirit of God"
heralded him at his baptism (Matt: 3:16), and an angel confronted
Mary Magdalene at his tomb (Matt. 28).[2]

Responses to heavenly visitors ranged from fear to adoration.
For example, the guardians at Christ's sepulcher were terrified
of the angel: "And for fear of him the keepers did shake" (Matt.
28:4). On the other hand, John, author of the book of Revelation,
fell at the feet of an angel in worship. However, the angel
admonished him, saying, "See thou do it not: for I am thy fellow
servant, and of thy brethren the prophets, and of them which
keep the saying of this book: worship God" (Rev. 22:9). Despite
this admonition, the Roman Catholic church has encouraged the
veneration of angels since the late fifth century. Several angels
such as Gabriel and Raphael have been promoted to sainthood
and churches are sometimes named after those so designated.
Although defenders of the practice observe that the veneration
of angels is of a lesser form than the veneration of God, Bible
scholar Gerald Larue states simply, "But worship is worship and
angels are worshipped within Catholicism."[3]

The same can be said of the veneration of the Virgin Mary. Mary's status has been increasingly elevated by the Catholic church. The ecclesiastical term *hyperdulia* is used to describe the special veneration she is accorded—a status in which, as Marcello Craveri pointedly observes in *The Life of Jesus*, the Virgin eventually "assumed the functions of divinity."[4] Early on, Mary became not merely the mother of Christ, but, much more importantly, the "Mother of God." Indeed, so much emphasis has been placed on Mary and so many divine attributes conferred on her (such as the ability to produce miracles of her own accord) that some have labeled Marian devotion, especially when expressed before statues and other images, as "Mariolatry."[5] Be that as it may, dramatic illustrations of Mary's special status and supposedly miraculous powers are provided by the Marian apparitions that have come to proliferate throughout the Catholic world.

Divine visitations—particularly those of guardian angels and the Virgin Mary—are more fully discussed in the sections that follow, as are so-called "near-death experiences": the visions and other phenomena reported by people on the verge of death. The focus will be primarily on the modern evidence for divine encounters.

Guardian Angels

The earliest depiction of an angel—or a precursor of angels— may be a winged figure on an ancient Sumerian stele who is pouring the water of life into the king's cup from a jar. Other precursors may be the giant, winged, supernatural beings, part animal and part human, that guarded the temples in ancient Assyria and thus may have served as models for the concept of angels as protectors.[6]

The Judeo-Christian word *angel* derives from the Greek *angelos*, meaning "messenger." Certainly some fulfilled this role, such as the angel who appeared to Joseph in a dream, telling him, "fear not to take unto thee Mary thy wife: for that which is conceived in her is of the Holy Ghost" (Matt. 1:20). Angels could also be avengers (2 Sam. 24:16), protectors (Ps. 91:11), rescuers (Dan. 6:22), and so on.[7]

Interest in angels has waxed and waned. In 1975 Billy Graham began his book *Angels: God's Secret Agents* with this paragraph:

> When I decided to preach a sermon on angels, I found practically nothing in my library. Upon investigation I soon discovered that little had been written on the subject in this century. This seemed a strange and ominous omission. Bookstores and libraries have shelves of books on demons, the occult and the devil. Why was the devil getting so much more attention from writers than angels? Some people seem to put the devil on a par with God. Actually, Satan is a fallen angel.[8]

Some 2.6 million copies of Graham's book later, things have changed. Now angels are everywhere—if not in reality at least in nearly every other way. According to *Newsweek*: "Driven by book sales approaching a heavenly 5 million copies, the angel subculture is off on more than a wing and a prayer."[9] Almost overnight angel books began to proliferate and to head the religious best-seller lists. In addition to reissuing Graham's book, publishers have rushed into print additional copies of Eileen Elias Freeman's *Touched by Angels*; Alma Daniel, Timothy Wyllie, and Andrew Rahmer's *Ask Your Angels*; and Joan Wester Anderson's *Where Angels Walk*—not to mention Sophy Burnham's *A Book of Angels*, which sold over half a million copies in thirty printings between 1990 and 1993.[10]

In addition to angel books, there have appeared angel focus groups and workshops, an AngelWatch Network with a bimonthly journal, and an Angel Collectors Club of America together with mechandizers eager to supply things to collect: angel statues, dolls, rings, pins, watches, calendars, T-shirts, napkin rings, posters, thank-you notes, greeting cards, plates, and so on and on—even a new "Angel" perfume sold at Saks Fifth Avenue.[11]

Not surprisingly, perhaps, belief in angels went up from 50 percent in 1988 to 69 percent at the end of 1993, with 66 percent believing they are actually watched over by their "own personal guardian angel."[12]

According to *Newsweek*: "It may be kitsch, but there's more to the current angel obsession than the Hallmarking of America.

Like the search for extraterrestrials, the belief in angels implies that we are not alone in the universe—that someone up there likes me."[13] Theologian Ted Peters of Pacific Lutheran Theological Seminary in Berkeley says: "It's a New Age answer to the homelessness of secularity."[14] *Newsweek* adds:

> Much of the new angelology is lifted from Roman Catholic sources—though without much regard for church tradition. "Angels represent God's personal care for each one of us," says Father Andrew Greeley, the sociologist-novelist. But all too often these days, it is the angels—not the Lord—who get all the credit. To some extent the church itself is to blame. Although the invocation of angels continues in some churches—especially in the vibrant Orthodox liturgies, where the faithful join the heavenly host in singing the Lord's praises—their existence is rarely remarked. Children's prayers to their guardian angels, like other popular Catholic devotions, have declined since Vatican Council II. Among many otherwise upright believers, angels have become optional accessories, articles of hope but not quite faith.[15]

The books on angels are filled with inspirational stories about people's personal encounters with angels. One such account appears in Joan Wester Anderson's *Where Angels Walk: True Stories of Heavenly Visitors.* This "true" story—in a chapter titled "Callers in the Night"—is about a little girl who seeks a doctor's help for her ailing mother. As it happens, the all-too-brief, too-good-to-be-true tale appeared in Billy Graham's book in a slightly expanded version, which we here look at in its entirety (complete with Graham's source):

> Dr. S. W. Mitchell, a celebrated Philadelphia neurologist, had gone to bed after an exceptionally tiring day. Suddenly he was awakened by someone knocking on his door. Opening it he found a little girl, poorly dressed and deeply upset. She told him her mother was very sick and asked him if he would please come with her. It was a bitterly cold, snowy night, but though he was bone tired, Dr. Mitchell dressed and followed the girl. . . .
> As *Reader's Digest* reports the story, he found the mother

desperately ill with pneumonia. After arranging for medical care, he complimented the sick woman on the intelligence and persistence of her little daughter. The woman looked at him strangely and then said, "My daughter died a month ago." She added, "Her shoes and coat are in the clothes closet there." Dr. Mitchell, amazed and perplexed, went to the closet and opened the door. There hung the very coat worn by the little girl who had brought him to tend to her mother. It was warm and dry and could not possibly have been out in the wintry night. . . .

Could the doctor have been called in the hour of desperate need by an angel who appeared as this woman's young daughter? Was this the work of God's angels on behalf of the sick woman?[16]

Graham provides no documentation beyond the vague "*Reader's Digest*," which in any event is hardly a scholarly source. The story does sound familiar—in part because of a striking similarity to the "Phantom Hitchhiker" legend we studied in chapter 2 (in the section "Case Motifs"). Note, for example, the supposedly confirming coat-in-the-closet detail, which functions just like the jacket-atop-the-tombstone motif in the Phantom Hitchhiker yarn.

In fact, I have discovered that the tale is an old one, circulated in various forms with conflicting details. For example, as "The Girl in the Snow," it appears in Margaret Ronan's anthology of *Strange Unsolved Mysteries*. Whereas Graham's version is of implied recent vintage, the Ronan one is set on a "December day in 1880." Graham states that the doctor was "awakened by someone knocking on his door," yet Ronan tells us "the doorbell downstairs was ringing violently." Missing from the Graham version are the suggestions that the little girl was a *ghost*, not an angel; for example, Ronan says the child looked "almost wraithlike in the whirling snow," and that "at times she seemed to vanish into the storm. . . ." Again, in Graham's account, the doctor is credited with simply "arranging for medical care," while Ronan insists Dr. Mitchell "set about at once to do what he could for her" and "by morning he felt that at last she was out of danger." Although both versions preserve the essential element that the woman's little girl had died a month before, Graham's version quotes the mother as saying, "Her shoes and coat are in the clothes closet there," while Ronan's has her stating: "All I have left to remember her by are those clothes hanging on that peg over there." Indeed the latter account describes not a coat and shoes but states: "Hanging from the peg was the thin dress he had seen the child wearing, and the ragged shawl."[17]

In short, Rev. Graham has passed on a version of an old narrative about a ghost, presenting it as a supposedly true account suggestive of angelic visitation. No doubt he has done so in good faith (no pun intended), but the fact is that many of the angel narratives lack verification and thus cannot constitute proof of transcendent realms.

In contrast to the foregoing, many of the currently popular angel stories are personal narratives. Among these are tales of "mysterious stranger angels," ordinary-looking people who appear suddenly when they are needed, and disappear just as suddenly when their job is done."[18]

One subtype of this genre is the "roadside rescue" story which, one source admits, "happens so often that it is almost a cliché in angel lore." Essentially, "In the roadside rescue, the mysterious stranger arrives to help the motorist stranded on a lonely road at night, or who is injured in an accident in an isolated spot. Or, human beings arrive just in the nick of time."[19] One such testimonial has come from Jane M. Howard (who is described as an "angel channeler and author"):

> One night, the gas pedal in Janie's car became stuck, and she ran off the freeway near Baltimore. She stopped the car by throwing the transmission into park. It would not restart, and she began to panic. It was ten P.M. and she was miles from the nearest exit. She prayed to the angels for help, and within minutes, a van pulled up, carrying a man and a woman.[20]

As the story continues:

> The woman rolled down her window and told Janie not to be frightened, for they were Christians. Even so, many people would have been wary of strangers at night. But the angels

gave Janie assurances, and she accepted a ride to a gas station. She discovered that the couple lived in a town near hers, and knew her family. They pulled off to help Janie, they said, because they had a daughter, and they hoped that if their daughter ever was in distress, she, too, would be aided.[21]

The question immediately comes to mind, of course: Why assume that *angels*, or anything of a supernatural order, had something to do with such a mundane event?

Often, however, the disappearance is described so as to leave little doubt that it was a preternatural occurrence. One such story involved a visit to an electronics store and a young man who helped the woman's son with a bit of technical knowledge. The woman stated:

> I was just dumbfounded. The young man wished us a nice day and left the store. A couple of seconds later, I rushed out the door to thank him, but he was gone. He literally disappeared. The store is in the middle of the block, so you would still be able to see someone walking down the sidewalk. Obviously, this was not an ordinary human. I still get chills when I think about it.[22]

Rationally, however, we must ask: Was it really only "a couple of seconds later" or might it really have been *several* seconds— long enough for the man to have entered a waiting car or stepped into an adjacent store?

Then there are the angelic encounters of the bedside variety. Such is a story told by a Louisville woman in Burnham's *A Book of Angels*. One of the woman's good friends had died but seemed to linger as a "presence." Moreover, she says,

> Twice I have awakened from sleep to see something mystical. I sat up in bed to convince myself I was not dreaming.
>
> To the right of me, hovering about five feet from the floor, was a bright mass of energy, a yellow and orange ball about six inches in diameter. I closed my eyes and reopened them. I even pinched myself to make sure I was really seeing what was before my eyes, and there it remained until I fell asleep again.

Left: Countless "spirit" pictures like this one were produced in the nineteenth and early twentieth centuries as an outgrowth of the spiritualism craze and the advent of photography. Photo courtesy of Dr. Gordon Stein, *Encyclopedia of Hoaxes.*

Below: One of the author's earliest occult investigations focused on this strange creature with budding horns, hooves, and a tail—an apparent devil baby mummy—that reportedly came from an Irish museum. Photo made for the author by Chris Tammaro.

The "House of Blood" mystery—in which the walls and floor of an elderly Atlanta couple's home inexplicably began to bleed in 1987—has been attributed to a "poltergeist." Official police photograph, Atlanta Police Department.

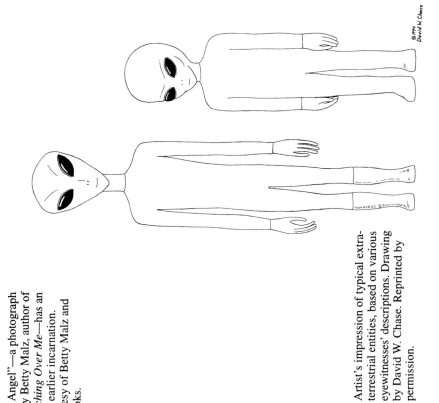

© 1994
David W. Chase

Artist's impression of typical extra-terrestrial entities, based on various eyewitnesses' descriptions. Drawing by David W. Chase. Reprinted by permission.

The "Cloud Angel"—a photograph circulated by Betty Malz, author of *Angels Watching Over Me*—has an unfortunate earlier incarnation. Photo courtesy of Betty Malz and Chosen Books.

Right: At Marian apparition site at Conyers, Georgia, author Joe Nickell examines a statue of the Virgin Mary that some pilgrims claim exhibits a heartbeat. Photo made for the author by William Evans.

Left: According to legend, the ghost of a resentful spinster causes this old wedding dress to sway mysteriously before onlookers at central Pennsylvania's Baker Mansion. Photo by the author.

I was frightened. About a year later, the same thing happened under the same circumstances. However, this time I asked
questions subconsciously and they were answered. They were
all in reference to my friend who had left this world. And the
overall summation was, I was not to fear or worry, because
I was being watched over. His protection, caring, and love were
continuing, though his physical being was gone.[23]

The astute reader, of course, immediately recognizes in this account the unmistakable characteristics of a hypnopompic
hallucination—i.e., a "waking dream" like those we have
encountered in our discussions of ghosts and succubi.

In still other cases the percipient may be a fantasy-prone
personality. Children may easily fall into this category. Consider,
for instance, this anecdote related by Sophie Burnham:

Once my mother saw an angel. She was five years old at the
time, just a little girl in her nightie, getting ready for bed, when
she looked up and saw an angel standing in the bedroom door.
"Auntie!" She pointed at the figure. "Look!" But her beloved
auntie could not see.
"Go to sleep, child," she said. "There's nothing there." I don't
know what her angel looked like. When I asked her, my mother's
face took on a dreamy and exalted look, simultaneously nostalgic
and alight. She used words like *brilliance* or *radiance,* and I
have the impression of many colors. But I have no idea what
she saw.[24]

No one does, of course. As indicated by the aunt's inability to
see it, it was clearly only a product of a child's imagining, no
more credible than an eyewitness account of Santa Claus or an
elf or leprechaun.

Stress can even produce angels in crisis situations. As psychologist Robert A. Baker observes, there is a "well-known psychological fact that human beings, when subjected to extreme
fear and stress, frequently hallucinate. These hallucinations, in
many instances, take the form of phantom helpers, aides, guides,
assistants, et al., playing the role of Savior." Adds Dr. Baker,
"If the hallucinator also has religious leanings it is easy to

understand how such a 'helper' is converted into one of the heavenly host, i.e., a guardian angel."[25]

If personal accounts represent only what serious researchers disparage as "anecdotal evidence," then what about *photographic* evidence—photos offered to support accounts of angelic encounters? Alas, as we saw with spirit photographs in chapter 1, such evidence is easily faked. Consider, for example, the "Cloud Angel" circulated by Betty Malz, author of *Angels Watching Over Me* and other books. The picture Ms. Malz was kind enough to send me was accompanied by the following brief narrative:

> A couple flying for their first airplane ride, on their honeymoon, took a whole roll of photos out the window of the plane. They were fascinated by the topside of clouds, so much like Cool Whip or Dairy Queen ice cream! The pilot announced on the intercom that they were flying into turbulence that would last about twenty minutes. Bill and his wife prayed aloud, "Oh Lord, protect us, send the Angels of the Lord to hold this plane upright and keep us safe." Almost immediately the choppy wind subsided. The second officer got on the intercom and announced, "It is amazing. The monitor showed turbulence for twenty minutes and it was over in two minutes." Returning home they found this photo when they picked up their prints at Anderson Pharmacy.[26]

Unfortunately, my attempts to track down the airborne, honeymooning couple who allegedly took the photograph proved futile. Ms. Malz stated that she had "not kept background material" on her earlier publications.[27] Even more unfortunate is the fact that the picture appears to be (except for minor areas of tonal dissimilarity attributable to multiple-generation copying) the same as one in a book by Hans Holzer. It illustrates chapter 19, "A Ghostly Apparition in the Sky," in his *America's Restless Ghosts: Photographic Evidence of Life After Death*. Holzer says his photograph was "taken in 1971 during a terrible storm in rural Pennsylvania" by a friend of an "ordained spiritual minister."[28]

As these cases illustrate, the evidence for angels seems as ethereal and elusive as the winged creatures themselves. Nevertheless, belief in them continues. To many, they offer comfort in trying times; to others they are confirmation of their deeply held religious views; and to still others they are intriguing elements of New Age mysticism. Unfortunately, to many others, they are merely the seraphic heralds of that great deity known as the Almighty Dollar.

Marian Apparitions

Devotion to Mary increased in western Christianity in the eleventh and twelfth centuries, and apparitions of the Virgin began to outnumber those of Jesus, saints, and angels. The early sixteenth century, however, brought a diminution in Marian sightings, apparently as the result of the Protestant Reformation (which rejected, among many other things, the veneration of the Virgin) and the Inquisition (whose witchhunting proclivities could dampen a seer's desire to claim any sort of experience that might be equated with the occult).[29]

The first Marian apparition deemed authentic by the Roman Catholic church was that at Guadalupe, Mexico, in 1531. Desiring a shrine to be built in her honor, the Virgin supposedly appeared to a peasant named Juan Diego, giving him—as a "sign" to a skeptical bishop—her full-length self-portrait, miraculously imprinted on Diego's cactus-fiber cloak. Devotees of the Image of Guadalupe claim its coloration is "inexplicable" and cite other evidence of its reputedly divine origin. So popular is the image of the Virgin that

> [y]ou will find every imaginable representation of her in the churches. . . . You may find her outlined in neon as part of a downtown spectacular, chalked into a hillside, on a throwaway advertising a mouthwash, pricked out in flowers in public parks; clowns and hucksters will distribute booklets about her as a preliminary to hawking patent medicines. . . . Bullfighters have her image woven into their parade capes; she is a popular tattoo subject; almost everyone wears her medal.[30]

Jody Brant Smith, author of *The Image of Guadalupe*, tells us that "yearly, an estimated ten million bow down before the mysterious Virgin, making the Mexico City church the most popular shrine in the Roman Catholic world next to the Vatican."[31]

Although direct examination of the image is not permitted, forensic analyst John F. Fischer and I conducted an investigation of the legend and historical record of the cloth and the iconography (the study of the artistic elements) of the image, together with an examination of close-up and infrared photographs showing various details of the Guadalupan image.[32]

In addition to suspicious elements of religious dogma found in the earliest account of the Virgin's appearance, and the incorporation into the legend of hyperdulia (Mary's special veneration), the Guadalupan legend itself appears to have been borrowed. The very name Guadalupe (which had been given to the site by 1556, the date of a formal investigation of the cloth) arouses further suspicion. As one historian has observed, the Mexican tale is quite similar to an earlier Spanish legend in which the Virgin appeared to a shepherd and led him to discover a statue of her. The Spanish site was even on a river known as Guadalupe (that is, "hidden channel"), strongly suggesting that the Mexican tale was derived from the Spanish tale.[33]

Another element smacks of deliberate legend manufacture. As Smith states: "The Shrine which held the Image of Guadalupe had been erected on a hill directly in front of the spot where there had been an important temple dedicated to the Aztec virgin goddess Tonantzin, 'Little Mother' of the Earth and Corn."[34] Thus the Christian tradition became grafted onto the Indian one, a process folklorists call *syncretism*.

Turning to iconography, we again find considerable borrowing. The image of Mary is the traditional *artistic* one (no one knows what she actually looked like), and it contains a number of specific artistic motifs, like the crescent moon in the picture (taken from Rev. 12:1), gold fleur-de-lis designs (symbolic of the Virgin Mother), and an angel at the lady's feet. In fact, a Spanish painting is said to be "of the exact form as the Virgin of Guadalupe," even with "a similar brooch at the throat," according to Philip Serna Callahan, who terms it "strikingly imitative of the Virgin of Guadalupe"—although it preceded the latter picture by nearly a century![35]

Although there are copious amounts of paint on the image, pro-authenticity writers such as Callahan suggest these are later additions and that the "original" portions are therefore "inexplicable" and even "miraculous," as Callahan terms the "original figure, including the rose robe, blue mantle, hands and face."[36] Yet while those areas are less thickly painted, evidence that they *are* painted is abundant and comes from infrared photos which reveal reworking of the hands; also close-up photographs show that the texture of the cloth has been obscured by the coloration. Professional artist and art scholar Glenn Taylor has pointed out that the part in the Virgin's hair is off-center; that the eyes, including the irises, have outlines, as they often do in paintings, but not in nature, and that the outlines appear to have been done with a brush; and that "the detailing of the features exhibits the characteristic fluidity of painting." Taylor describes the work as obviously "mannered" (in the artistic sense) and suggests it was probably copied by an inexpert copyist from an expertly done original.[37]

In fact, evidence that the image is indeed only a painting dates from as early as 1556, when a formal investigation of the cloth was held. Father Alonzo de Santiago testified that the image was "painted yesteryear by an Indian," and another Franciscan priest, Juan de Maseques, supplied more specific information, testifying that the image "was a painting that the Indian painter Marcos had done." Indeed, there was an Aztec painter known as Marcos Cipac active in Mexico at the time the Image of Guadalupe appeared.[38]

Certainly, the artist was familiar with one or more Spanish paintings of the Virgin Mary, a fact that suggests he may have been commissioned to produce the pious fraud. It is certainly well known that "the propogation of Christianity was one of the main purposes of Spanish imperialism, and church and state were closely connected."[39] No doubt as expected, the "miracle" played a "major role" in hastening the conversion of the conquered Indians. Countless thousands came to view the image and, "In just seven years, from 1532 to 1538, eight million Indians were converted to Christianity."[40]

After Guadalupe, no further authenticated Marian apparitions occurred for three centuries.[41] Then in the nineteenth century—when there flourished such occultish interests as popular
mesmerism, spiritualism, Theosophy, and clairvoyance[42]—came
a revival in reports of Marian apparitions which drew great
crowds to certain sites in Catholic Europe.[43] These interests
evidently served as models for such reports and their attendant
responses in that century. In her scholarly book *Encountering
Mary*, Sandra L. Zimdars-Swartz comments on the phenomenon:

> The peculiar importance that has become attached to some of
> the Marian apparitions of the past two centuries can be ex-
> plained, in part, by the fact that many of these have been both
> "serial" and "public." A serial apparition is one in which the
> seers have been led in an initial experience to expect that this
> experience will be repeated, and when they speak about it to
> relatives and friends and suggest that it will happen again, word
> spreads and people gather around the seers at the announced
> or expected time. The subsequent experiences of the seers, then,
> occur in the presence of anywhere from a few to several thousand
> people, giving rise to public events of sometimes immense pro-
> portions. A public apparition is simply one in which people
> surround the seers during their experiences. While those gath-
> ered may witness a sign, such as a sun miracle, generally speak-
> ing they do not see (or expect to see) the Virgin themselves.[44]

Four major Marian apparitions during the nineteenth century
were those at Paris (1830), La Salette (1846), and Lourdes (1858),
all in France, and at Knock, Ireland (1879).[45] The first of these
was reportedly seen by a peasant-born Sister of Charity,
Catherine Laboure, but she also claimed to have a personal "angel"
and exhibited every sign of having been a classic, fantasy-prone
personality.

The second apparition, the first modern Marian one to occur
outside a cloistered setting, occurred when two shepherd children
at La Salette claimed a single encounter with a figure described
in Marian terms. A spring near the site of the apparition became
a "miraculous spring" that supposedly had healing powers. But
as Zimdars-Swartz says in *Encountering Mary*, "Many of La

Salette's healings, particularly those that were said to have occurred at the site itself, were associated with mass pilgrimages involving very large numbers of people, and this suggests that psychological factors could have played a considerable part in these healings."[46]

Among other supposedly miraculous aspects of the affair were certain prophecies the children claimed to have been given by the apparition. Although these have been cited as having come true and thus providing proof of the apparition's supernatural powers, the fact is that the "prophecies" about a famine become less than impressive when we consider additional facts: The 1840s had brought a famine to Europe; by the time of the Virgin's alleged visitation, it had already reached the southeastern portion of France (i.e., the LaSalette/Grenoble area), resulting in shortages of food and consequently bringing higher prices. Certain other prophecies—about war and floods, for example—were not in fact contained in any of the early accounts of the children's messages. And as to certain secret messages that the children received, these were obtained by local officials and sent to Pope Pius IX at his specific request. Unfortunately, as even the credulous writer Scott Rogo admitted, they are "so cryptic that it would be difficult to offer an objective or concise evaluation of them."[47]

The most significant nineteenth-century Marian apparition was that claimed to have been witnessed at Lourdes, a town in the foothills of the Pyrenees, by the illiterate daughter of a local miller. On February 11, 1858, Bernadette Soubirous, age fourteen, was gathering firewood along the river bank with her sister and a friend. Suddenly, hearing a rustling above a nearby grotto, she looked up to see "something white" in the form of a young girl. Subsequently, she returned to the site with a group of schoolgirls. On a third visit to the grotto on February 18, Bernadette claimed the apparition requested her to visit the grotto for each of fifteen days. Now, with up to a thousand people watching, Bernadette would stand stiffly, occasionally smiling or moving her lips as if she were actually in communication with an invisible being. Those who came to witness the spectacle or who sought Bernadette elsewhere "already saw and treated her as if she were a saint."[48]

On February 25, Bernadette crawled on her knees to the back of the grotto where she dug some muddy water, later explaining that she had been directed by the Virgin to drink and wash there. Soon miraculous cures were being credited to the spring and people began to carry away bottles of the water. Eventually millions of pilgrims would annually visit the massive basilica built at the site, with the sick and the dying all waiting in line to enter the sacred grotto either to be bathed in its cold mountain water or to take water home from the holy spring. And despite "multitudinous failures" over the years, the crowds continue to prove the truth of the statement that "one apparent cure will efface the memory of a hundred failures."[49]

Early on, however, the curé of the parish, Dominique Peyramale, had accused Bernadette of perpetrating an outrageous hoax. He called for her to ask the entity for a sign: to cause a rosebush in the grotto to bloom. The sign failed to appear, and Peyramale noted other suspicious factors. For example, the figure identified herself by stating, "I am the Immaculate Conception." But this was a logical/grammatical inaccuracy—one which the skeptical priest was quick to note as more likely to be uttered by an untutored schoolgirl than by "the Mother of God." Thereupon Bernadette quickly amended the statement to "I am the Virgin of the Immaculate Conception."

Ironically, all her life Bernadette endured ill health. As a child she had had asthma, and she later suffered from tuberculosis of the bone in the right knee as well as from attendant complications, being bedridden for the last years of her life. At her death in 1879, she was only thirty-five years old; the "healing" water of Lourdes had never been for her. Nevertheless, she was canonized a saint in 1933.[50]

Bernadette inspired imitators. Long before her death, as the site became an established shrine, other alleged visionaries came forth, including (as they were described by the police commissioner) a "bad woman devoted to drink," a prostitute with "disgusting morals," and some fifty others, among them many schoolchildren.[51]

The last significant nineteenth-century Marian apparition took place at the little village of Knock, County Mayo, Ireland, on August 21, 1879. However, the "apparition" was quite different from the others we have discussed, consisting of a glow that seemed to emanate from the church's southern gable, within which a "tableau" of immobile figures was seen: Mary, Joseph, and a bishop, standing beside an altar. Now it is impossible to recreate the exact conditions that prevailed at that time and place, although we know the day had been a dismally rainy one. However, considering that the tableau figures were unmoving and unspeaking, the possibility of the ethereal scene being merely some kind of optical illusion seems likely. Given any potential source for the illumination, such as the moon or a reflection of light from some other source, together with its diffusion by the misty atmosphere, a play of light and shadow could result which would be eminently capable of stimulating pious imaginations. The climate of social stress at the time was probably conducive to wishful thinking, given the fact that the country was undergoing especially hard times: a bad harvest and a typhus epidemic. Although the "apparition" was investigated and deemed authentic by a commission of three priests, they obviously had little to go on other than the testimony of the credulous villagers.[52]

The twentieth century has brought a proliferation of alleged apparitions of the Virgin, the most important of which are those at Fatima and Medjugorje—one deemed authentic, the other not.

The story of Fatima begins near the town of that name in Portugal. On May 13, 1917, three shepherd children were tending their flock in a pasture two miles to the west of the town. The children were ten-year-old Lucia de Jesus dos Santos and her two cousins, Francisco Marto, age nine, and his sister Jacinta, seven. A sudden flash of lightning sent the children fleeing down a slope, whereupon the two girls beheld a dazzling apparition: a beautiful woman, radiant in white light, standing among the leaves of a small holm oak. Only Lucia talked with the figure, who she said instructed them to return on the thirteenth of each month; at the end of six months, she would identify herself.

News soon spread throughout Fatima and, when the children revisited the site on June 13 they were accompanied by approximately fifty devout villagers. Kneeling in prayer at the tree, the children presently saw the woman gliding down from heaven and again taking up a position amid the oak's foliage. This was repeated each month. At the end of the six-month period, on a stormy and rainy October 13, an estimated seventy thousand people were in attendance at the site, anticipating the Virgin's final visit and with many fully expecting that she would work a great miracle.[53]

After supposedly discoursing with the lady, Lucia suddenly exclaimed, "The sun!" As everyone gazed upward, and saw that a silvery disc had emerged from behind clouds, they experienced what is known in the terminology of Marian apparitions as a "sun miracle." This was variously described: some claimed the sun spun in pinwheel fashion with colored streamers, others that it "danced," still others that it seemed to fall toward the spectators. Exactly what did happen at Fatima has been the subject of much controversy. Church authorities made inquiries, collected eyewitness testimony, and declared the events worthy of belief as a miracle.[54]

Since several eyewitnesses specifically stated they were looking "fixedly at the sun" or "tried to look straight at it,"[55] then the phenomena were most likely due to optical effects resulting from such factors as temporary retinal distortion caused by staring at the intense light, or by the effect of darting the eyes to and fro so as to avoid fixed gazing (but thus combining image, afterimage, and movement), or other illusory effects, such as the eyes' inability to focus on such a bright light source and thus resulting in a pulsating effect.

Mass hysteria may also have been engendered by the dramatic way Lucia directed people to look skyward, and people may have influenced each other as they excitedly discussed and compared their perceptions.[56]

Believers in a Fatima miracle also cite certain predictions that the lady allegedly made to Lucia, and that have since come true. However, the "predictions" and "secrets" were described in Lucia's memoirs written many years after the fact![57]

To fully comprehend what took place at Fatima in 1917, one must look more closely at its central figure—not the Virgin Mary but Lucia de Jesus dos Santos. A petted and spoiled child, she had a gift for telling stories—fairy tales, biblical narratives, and saints' legends—that made her popular with the village children. At festivals, Lucia would be placed on a crate where she would entertain an admiring crowd.

She was also overtly religious, and two years before the famous series of apparitions occurred at Fatima, eight-year-old Lucia was leading three girlfriends in praying the rosary when the children saw an apparition: a figure like "a statue made of snow" that was "rendered almost transparent by the rays of the sun." When news of this spread, Lucia's mother contemptuously exclaimed, "Childish nonsense!" Nevertheless, the children "saw" the apparition on two further occasions. The following year, Lucia supposedly began to experience supernatural encounters while in the company of her impressionable little cousins, Francisco and Jacinta. They were visited three times by an "angel"—an apparition of a boy of about fifteen. He materialized suddenly, exhorting the children to pray, and on another occasion he gave them Communion.[58]

Lucia's background is revealing. Clearly she was a fantasy-prone personality with childhood experiences that led to her later visionary experiences. Her own mother was convinced that her precocious daughter was, in her words, "nothing but a fake who is leading half the world astray."[59]

The apparitions at Fatima were put into perspective in the 1960s with a complex series of alleged Marian apparitions that took place in the village of San Sebastian de Garabandal from 1961 to 1965. Four young girls were involved, ages ten to twelve. Eventually, however, the girls made a rather equivocal confession, but three of them retracted it. The fourth child did not withdraw her confession. Whereas her three companions moved to the United States and "to differing degrees . . . remained accessible to Garabandal devotees," Mari Cruz Gonzalez stayed in Spain and continued to deny that the apparition was authentic. She stated that she and her companions had used the fake trances and apparition claims as a means to get away from the village and play! Ecclesiastical authorities eventually ended their investigation by concluding that there had been no apparition and that nothing had occurred there that did not have a natural explanation.[60]

Young children were also central to the events at Medjugorje in the former Yugoslavia that provoked a raging controversy with claims of great miracles and accusations of outright trickery.

On June 24, 1981, on a rocky hill overlooking the village, six children (four girls, ages fifteen to seventeen, and two boys, ten and sixteen) claimed that at dusk they were suddenly startled by an extremely bright light, at the center of which was a beautiful woman wearing a gray dress with white mantle and veil. Events continued but were moved from the hill (by police), then from other locations (on the bishop's orders), and eventually to St. James Catholic Church. There the children would stand in a line facing one wall and begin reciting the Lord's Prayer. Suddenly they would kneel in unison and enter their visionary state wherein—their lips moving inaudibly—they allegedly communicated with the Virgin. In 1984 the Virgin began giving weekly messages to the parish and, in 1987, to the world.[61]

Until war greatly reduced pilgrimages to the site by 1991, Medjugorje attracted crowds of up to fifty thousand on holy days, and an estimated nineteen million over the ten-year period. Villagers built additions onto their homes, and "apparition watch" gazebos and a pavilion of confessional booths sprang up. Incredible claims were attributed to the site. In addition to the daily visitations and messages, there were sun miracles (like those at Fatima), images of Jesus and Mary that sometimes appeared in the clouds, numerous healings, and other supposedly miraculous occurrences such as rosary beads turning from silver to gold![62]

Medjugorje mania was not going unchallenged, however. Although the local bishop, Pavao Zanic, at first accepted the claims as genuine, he soon changed his view. One revelation occurred when a message allegedly from the Virgin took the side of the Franciscan friars against the bishop in a rather petty matter. Once his suspicions were aroused, Bishop Zanic found additional evidence that things were not as they seemed. For example, the children had changed their story about why they had gone to the hill on the day they first saw the apparition. In addition, some of the alleged messages from the Virgin became progressively elaborated—another indication that they may have been spurious. The bishop also found points of incompatibility with

Catholic theology, and other problems. Eventually, Bishop Zanic stated publicly:

> The majority of the pious public has naively fallen victim to the great propaganda, the talk of the apparitions and the feelings. These people themselves have become the greatest propaganda for the event. They do not even stop to think that the truth has been hidden by deliberate falsehood. They do not know that not one miraculous healing has occurred that could have been verified by competent experts.[63]

In 1986 the Vatican became involved in the Medjugorje affair, taking the matter out of Bishop Zanic's hands and entrusting the question of authenticity to Yugoslavia's national bishops conference. That group's work is apparently still in progress and could take years to complete. In the meantime, the bishops conference issued a warning against any public worship that is directly linked to the alleged apparitions. However, until civil war came to the region, Medjugorje seemed unaffected by any such warnings.[64]

In the meantime, however, apparition sites had begun to spring up across the United States as pilgrims brought the "Medjugorje pox" home. The *Hartford Courant* noted that: "A 'copycat' effect may be at work similar to what happened all over France in 1858 after Bernadette of Lourdes said Mary was appearing to her in visions."[65] The sites include the following (with dates they became public): Conyers, Georgia (1990); Mother Cabrini Shrine near Denver, Colorado (1991); Marlboro Township, New Jersey (1992); Cold Spring, Kentucky (1992); and Falmouth, Kentucky (1993).

Three of these have not fared well. The diocesan bishop said at the time of the initial Cold Spring event, at which the Virgin Mary was to appear at midnight, that "nothing of a miraculous nature" had occurred there.[66] At Marlboro Township, where Joseph Januszkiewicz began to see visions six months after visiting Medjugorje, a church commission dismissed the reported visions.[67] And at the Mother Cabrini Shrine, where a laywoman, Theresa Antonia Lopez, said she had visions which began at Medjugorje, a commission's investigation prompted the archbishop to say that the visions were "devoid of any supernatural origin."[68]

I have had the opportunity to visit and investigate three of the sites at the time the apparitions are said to appear (typically at a specified monthly date). These were Cold Spring (which I reported on for *Skeptical Inquirer* magazine), Conyers (which an Atlanta television station commissioned me to visit and which I did accompanied by members of Georgia Skeptics), and Falmouth (which I investigated at the request of "Forces Beyond," a Learning Channel television program).[69] In each case my main interest was in examining allegedly miraculous occurrences. My results are given below, in claim-by-claim fashion.

Rosary transmutation. The claim that rosaries change from silver to gold apparently began at Medjugorje, but is now common at sites across the United States. Rosaries that I have been able to examine on site (using a Bausch & Lomb illuminated 10X magnifying loupe) have typically been those with a thin silver plating over a brassy metal base; as the plating is rubbed off the yellowish metal shows through, giving the illusion that the metal is undergoing transmutation. Others report similar findings, while in some instances (including rosaries from Conyers) the effect is simply due to oxidation.[70] Apparently aware that the rosaries are not yielding real gold, in several recent instances claimants have been careful to use the term "gold color."

Sun Miracles. Standard fare at all apparition sites are so-called sun miracles—effects of the sun pulsating, dancing, etc., like those reported at Fatima in 1917 and similarly explained as optical illusions resulting from the eyes' inability to focus on such a bright light source. Retinal damage may explain some effects, and reports of eye damage have come from several sites, including the Mother Cabrini Shrine and Falmouth.[71] At Conyers, the Georgia Skeptics set up a telescope outfitted with a mylar solar filter. Becky Long, president of the organization, stated: "I estimate that well over two hundred people viewed the sun through one of our solar filters, and without exception they saw nothing unusual when looking through the mylar."[72]

Golden Door Photos. A type of sun miracle is purportedly captured on film. As pilgrims take Polaroid snapshots of the sun, even seasoned reporters have been astonished to see what often develops: not a picture of the sun but instead what resembles an arched doorway flooded with golden light. As I can also attest, these can appear quite striking. However, as Dale Heatherington (a member of Georgia Skeptics) discovered, the effect is one that is produced by the Polaroid One-Step camera whose aperture (lens opening) is in the very shape of the "Golden Door." Commenting on claims that the photos depict the doorway to heaven (mentioned in Rev. 4:1), Heatherington noted that instead it was "actually the doorway into the camera." Heatherington has demonstrated that a photo of a halogen spot lamp can also yield a Golden Door picture.[73]

Other miracle photographs. Many other unusual photos can usually be seen at an apparition site, and Conyers has albums of them on display. Some are double exposures and similar obvious fakes, while others result from optical effects. At Cold Spring, for example, I saw many such photos that were caused by simple lens flares, although earnest miraculists were turning their prints this way and that, attempting to discern a face or figure in the anomalous glare shapes. (For a more extensive discussion of "miracle" photos, see my *Camera Clues: A Handbook for Photographic Investigation.*[74])

Weeping statues. The statues, icons, and other images that are often said to "weep,"—when found inside churches or other indoor locations—invariably prove to be hoaxes, as I discuss in my book *Looking for a Miracle.*[75]

Outdoor statues could easily become damp from rain, fog, and the like. While the moisture would not selectively collect in the region of the eyes, that might be the only area that a pilgrim who was checking for just such a miracle would think to touch.

It is one thing to venerate someone by means of a statue, but quite another to suggest that a statue or other image has attributes of a living entity: the latter crosses the line into idolatry.[76]

Effigies with heartbeats. Another miracle claim that smacks of outright idolatry is one that attributes a heartbeat to a picture, such as a photograph of the Image of Guadalupe, or a statue, such as those at Conyers, Georgia. The photo of the Guadalupan image has toured the United States since 1991, frequently tied to anti-abortion activities. Reports of its miraculous powers yield clues to what is really going on: an Associated Press article refers to "the feel of a heartbeat on the image."[77] Similarly at Conyers the percipients explained that they reached up and *felt* the heartbeat.[78] Under those conditions, the most likely explanation for the "heartbeat" would be the pulse in the person's own thumb.

This list is not exhaustive. Claims of healings are more difficult to assess (for a discussion see sources in the Recommended Works at the end of this chapter); however, many of the "cures" that supposedly occur at apparition sites prove to be something less than a miracle. In the excitement of the moment, there may well be a reduction of pain (due to the body's release of endorphins) that leads people to believe and act as if they have been miraculously healed, whereas later investigation reveals their situation is as bad—or even worse—than before.[79]

As the claims of divine visions and miracles continue, the lack of convincing evidence remains. One wonders why the Virgin Mary's appearances must always be so equivocal, so dubious, so controversial and divisive. If she indeed has messages for us, why does she not appear in person instead of through some intermediate person, often one of dubious credibility or even questionable reputation? Until the situation changes, the mystery will not be why some doubt, but why so many are willing to believe so much on so little evidence.

Near-Death Experiences

If evidence for earthly visitations of angels, the Virgin Mary, and other celestial beings is weak, what about that for travel in the opposite direction: humans making the journey to heaven and living to tell about it? The evidence is provided in the form of personal testimonials by those who claim they have "come back" from death (or a state verging on death), that is, who have undergone "a near-death experience" (NDE).

As scientific knowledge has progressed, many people have come to feel that the concept of the soul (or individual spirit popularly believed to survive death) was being pushed aside.

Spiritualism, which purports to contact the spirits of the dead, offers one type of proof for survival. The NDE offers another.

In earlier times, people who were dying sometimes described otherworldly visions they were having, some even reporting that they were conversing with dead loved ones. More familiar are today's close encounters with death that result from heart failure, with revived persons occasionally providing testimonials of NDEs. Some describe out-of-body experiences, others a sense of passing through a tunnel; still others see their life flash before them, or they visit otherworldly realms. British parapsychologist Susan Blackmore has looked at each of these with illuminating results.[80]

The out-of-body experience. This is quite common. Typically, the patient has a vivid sense (as one woman cardiac patient describes it) of "looking down from the ceiling at them working on my body."[81] In fact, however, such experiences—while seeming quite real—are actually hallucinations that can also occur under anesthesia *when one is nowhere near death,* as well as when one is falling asleep, or even just relaxing or meditating, or that can be experienced in migraine and epilepsy.[82] Blackmore attributes the vividness of the scene allegedly viewed during the experience to a "memory model." As she explains the out-of-body experience: "A memory model in bird's-eye view has taken over from the sensory model. It seems perfectly real because it is the best model the system has got at the time."[83]

Tunnel travel. Another commonly reported aspect of the near-death experience is the sense of traveling through a tunnel. As one person described it: "I found myself in a tunnel of concentric circles. Shortly after that I saw a TV programme called 'The Time Tunnel,' where people go back in time through this spiralling tunnel. That's the closest to it I can think of."[84] Another said:

> I do remember thinking to myself that I was dying. I felt I was floating through a tunnel. . . . When I say tunnel the only thing I can think of is—you know, those sewer pipes, those big pipes they put in? It was round like that, but it was enormous. I couldn't really see the edges of it; I got the feeling that it was round. ["What kind of feeling did you have as you were floating through this tunnel?"] Very peaceful, almost as if I were a raft in the ocean, you know?[85]

As with the out-of-body experience, the tunnel experience can occur under many other conditions besides the NDE: when meditating or relaxing, in migraine and epilepsy, with certain drugs (such as LSD and psilocybin), and even with simple pressure on both eyeballs. Lack of oxygen (which can occur near death) can also produce the tunnel experience.

Again, however, the effect is a hallucination, in this case one attributed to the particular structure of the visual cortex (the visual-information-processing portion of the brain).

The impression that one is moving is part of the physiology behind the hallucination. Because the brain "infers our own movement to a great extent from what we see," explains Blackmore, "[t]herefore, presented with an apparently growing patch of flickering white light your brain will easily interpret it as yourself moving forward into a tunnel."[86]

The life review. In some reports of near-death experiences the percipient sees his or her life flash by, as if in a final predeath review. But as Susan Blackmore observes, "The experience of seeing excerpts from your life flash before you is not really as mysterious as it first seems." As she explains:

> It has long been known that stimulation of cells in the temporal lobe of the brain can produce instant experiences that seem like the reliving of memories. Also, temporal-lobe epilepsy can produce similar experiences, and such seizures can involve other limbic structure in the brain, such as the amygdala and hippo-campus, which are also associated with memory.
>
> Imagine that the noise in the dying brain stimulates cells like this. The memories will be aroused and, according to my hypothesis, if they are the most stable model the system has at that time they will seem real. For the dying person they may well be more stable than the confused and noisy sensory model.[87]

However, Blackmore is quick to acknowledge:

> Of course there is more to the life review than just memories. The person feels as though she or he is judging these life events, being shown their significance and meaning. But this too, I suggest, is not so very strange. When the normal world of the

senses is gone and memories seem real, our perspective on our life changes. We can no longer be so attached to our plans, hopes, ambitions, and fears, which fade away and become unimportant, while the past comes to life again. We can only accept it as it is, and there is no one to judge it but ourselves. This is, I think, why so many NDEers say they faced their past life with acceptance and equanimity.[88]

Visiting other worlds. Blackmore acknowledges that these visits might seem to be the most remarkable part of the near-death experience. "But I think you can now see that they are not so extraordinary at all." As she explains:

> In this state the outside world is no longer real, and inner worlds are. Whatever we can imagine clearly enough will seem real. And what will we imagine when we know we are dying? I am sure for many people it is the world they expect or hope to see. Their minds may turn to people they have known who have died before them or to the world they hope to enter next. Like the other images we have been considering, these will seem perfectly real.[89]

Blackmore goes on to acknowledge: "Finally there are those aspects of the NDE that are ineffable—they cannot be put into words." She continues:

> I think we can now see why an essentially physiological event can change people's lives so profoundly. The experience has jolted their usual (and erroneous) view of the relationship between themselves and the world. We all too easily assume that we are some kind of persistent entity inhabiting a perishable body. But, as the Buddha taught, we have to see through that illusion. The world is only a construction of an information-processing system, and the self is too. I believe that the NDE gives people a glimpse into the nature of their own minds that is hard to get any other way. Drugs can produce it temporarily, mystical experiences can do it for rare people, and long years of practice in meditation or mindfulness can do it. But the NDE can out of the blue strike anyone and show them what they never knew before, that their body is only that—a lump of flesh—

that they are not so very important after all. And that is a
very freeing and enlightening experience.[90]

In a 1992 television appearance on the "Jerry Springer Show,"
I shared the stage with a woman whose five-year-old son had
reportedly had a near-death experience in which he went through
a tunnel to heaven. (The child no longer remembers the experience,
but his mother says she wrote it down at the time.) Also on
the program were Joan Wester Anderson, author of *Where Angels
Walk*, mentioned earlier in this chapter; Eileen Freeman, the
founder of Angel Watch Network (also mentioned earlier), who
has seen angels since childhood; and Jane Howard, who claims
she can see an individual's very own guardian angel.

At one point, an audience member accused me of making
fun of the other guests, to which I clarified that I regarded them
with degrees of seriousness. I said I found the little boy's near-
death encounter very moving, but simply did not consider his
reported experience to be a real supernatural occurrence; skipping
over Ms. Anderson, I noted that Eileen Freeman had the characteristics of a fantasy-prone personality (at which point there
were some boos from the audience); but, I said, indicating Jane
Howard who was sitting beside me, when someone claims to
see angels on demand, "That beeping sound you hear is my
baloney detector going off." This produced some laughter and
applause and—I think—helped put the various claims into proper
perspective.[91]

Recommended Works

Blackmore, Susan. "Near-Death Experiences: In or Out of the Body?"
Skeptical Inquirer 16, no. 1 (Fall 1991): 34–45. Excellent scientific
explanation of the NDE, yet one which is sympathetic with the
profundity of the experience to the person undergoing it.

Burnham, Sophy. *A Book of Angels: Reflections on Angels Past and
Present and True Stories of How They Touch Our Lives.* New York:
Ballantine Books, 1990. Unabashedly credulous treatment of angels
aimed at a popular audience.

Larue, Gerald A. *The Supernatural, the Occult and the Bible.* Amherst, N.Y.: Prometheus Books, 1990. A distinguished bible scholar's examination of occult and supernatural beliefs together with their biblical underpinnings.

Moody, Raymond. *Life After Life.* Covington, Ga.: Mockingbird Books, 1975. A true believer's pioneering work in the field of near-death experiences, providing accounts by those who have "died" and returned to tell tales of going into light, being out of body, etc.

Nickell, Joe. *Looking for a Miracle: Weeping Icons, Relics, Stigmata, Visions & Healing Cures.* Amherst, N.Y.: Prometheus Books, 1993. A wide-ranging investigative study of allegedly miraculous phenomena.

Rogo, Scott. *Miracles: A Parascientific Inquiry into Wondrous Phenomena.* New York: Dial Press, 1982. An overly credulous view of alleged supernatural phenomena by a partisan researcher in the field of parapsychology.

Wilson, Ian. *The After Death Experience: The Physics of the Non-Physical.* New York: William Morrow, 1987. An accumulation of supposed evidence for the soul's survival of death.

Zimdars-Swartz, Sandra L. *Encountering Mary: From La Salette to Medjugorje.* Princeton, N.J.: Princeton University Press, 1991. A scholarly, phenomenological approach to the study of Marian apparitions; attempting to be unbiased, it is necessarily skeptical given the weight of the evidence.

Notes

1. Maria Leach, ed., *Standard Dictionary of Folklore, Mythology, and Legend* (New York: Harper & Row, 1984), p. 457; *Encyclopedia Britannica,* 1960, s.v. "Religion."

2. For a further discussion of these, see Isaac Asimov, *Asimov's Guide to the Bible,* vols. 1 and 2 (New York: Avon, 1968).

3. Gerald A. Larue, *The Supernatural, the Occult and the Bible* (Amherst, N.Y.: Prometheus Books, 1990), p. 63.

4. Marcello Craveri, *The Life of Jesus,* trans. Charles Lam Markmann (New York: Grove, 1967), pp. 27–28.

5. Joan Ashton, *The People's Madonna: An Account of the Visions of Mary at Medjugorje* (London: Fount, 1991), p. 29.

6. Sophy Burnham, *A Book of Angels* (New York: Ballantine Books, 1990), pp. 81–82.

7. Ibid., p. 82; Larue, *The Supernatural, the Occult and the Bible,* pp. 57-61; Rosemary Ellen Guiley, *Harper's Encyclopedia of Mystical & Paranormal Experience* (New York: HarperCollins, 1991), p. 20.

8. Billy Graham, *Angels: God's Secret Agents* (Garden City, N.Y.: Doubleday, 1975), p. ix.

9. Kenneth L. Woodward, et al., "Angels," *Newsweek,* December 27, 1993, p. 54.

10. Ibid.

11. Ibid., pp. 53-54; Sarah Rilling, "Born-Again Angels," *Express-News* (San Antonio, Tex.), September 19, 1993.

12. Woodward, "Angels," p. 54; CNN/*Time*/*Newsweek* poll, CNN "Headline News," December 18, 1993.

13. Woodward, "Angels," p. 54.

14. Quoted in ibid, p. 54.

15. Ibid.

16. Graham, *Angels,* pp. 2-3.

17. Ibid.; *cf.* Margaret Ronan, *Strange Unsolved Mysteries* (New York: Scholastic Book Services, 1974), pp. 99-101.

18. Rosemary Ellen Guilley, "A Radiance of Angels," *Fate* (December 1993): 65.

19. Ibid., p. 66.

20. Ibid.

21. Ibid.

22. Ibid., p. 65.

23. Quoted in Burnham, *A Book of Angels,* pp. 275-76.

24. Burnham, *A Book of Angels,* p. 3.

25. Robert A. Baker, typescript article/review, "Angels," March 1, 1993.

26. Photograph and letter of permission to publish from Betty Malz, March 17, 1993.

27. Ibid.

28. Hans Holzer, *America's Restless Ghosts* (Stamford, Conn.: Longmeadow Press, 1993), pp. 112-13. The Malz picture represents only a detail of the larger Holzer photo.

29. Sandra L. Zimdars-Swartz, *Encountering Mary: From La Salette to Medjugorje* (Princeton, N.J.: Princeton University Press, 1991), p. 4. (Note: This section on Marian apparitions is largely abridged from my *Looking for a Miracle* [Amherst, N.Y.: Prometheus Books, 1993].)

30. Donald Demarest and Coley Taylor, eds., *The Dark Virgin* (N.p.: Academy Guild Press, 1956), p. 2.

31. Jody Brant Smith, *The Image of Guadalupe* (Garden City, N.Y.: Doubleday, 1983), p. 4.

32. See Joe Nickell and John F. Fischer, "The Image of Guadalupe: A Folkloristic and Iconographic Investigation," *Skeptical Inquirer* 8, no. 4 (Spring 1985): 243–55; reprinted in Joe Nickell with John F. Fischer, *Secrets of the Supernatural* (Amherst, N.Y.: Prometheus Books, 1988), pp. 103–17.

33. Jacques LaFaye, *Quetzalcoatl and Guadalupe: The Formation of Mexican National Consciousness 1531–1813* (Chicago: University of Chicago Press, 1976), pp. 231–53.

34. Smith, *The Image of Guadalupe*, p. 20.

35. Philip Serna Callahan, *The Tilma under Infra-red Radiation* (Washington, D.C.: Center for Applied Research in the Apostolate, 1981), p. 10.

36. Callahan, *The Tilma*, pp. 18, 20.

37. Glenn Taylor, personal communication, October 4, 1983.

38. Smith, *The Image of Guadalupe*, pp. 20–21.

39. *Encyclopedia Britannica*, 1973, s.v.: "Mexico."

40. Smith, *The Image of Guadalupe*, pp. 10–11.

41. Guiley, *Harper's Encyclopedia*, p. 343.

42. Richard Cavendish, ed., *Encylopedia of the Unexplained* (London: Routledge & Kegan Paul, 1974), pp. 114–21, 181, 205, 230–25, 248–54.

43. Zimdars-Swartz, *Encountering Mary*, pp. 4–5; Guiley, *Harper's Encyclopedia*, p. 343.

44. Zimdars-Swartz, *Encountering Mary*, p. 5.

45. Guiley, *Harper's Encyclopedia*, p. 343.

46. Zimdars-Swartz, *Encountering Mary*, p. 17.

47. Ibid., pp. 40–41; D. Scott Rogo, *Miracles* (New York: Dial Press, 1982), p. 210n.

48. Zimdars-Swartz, *Encountering Mary*, p. 50.

49. Keith Thomas, *Religion and the Decline of Magic*, quoted in Larue, *The Supernatural, the Occult and the Bible*, p. 157.

50. For a more complete discussion of Bernadette, see Zimdars-Swartz, *Encountering Mary*, pp. 43–67; John Coulson, ed., *The Saints: A Concise Biographical Dictionary* (New York: Hawthorn Books, 1958), pp. 85–86; Joan Carroll Cruz, *The Incorruptibles* (Rockford, Ill.: Tan Books and Publishers, 1977), pp. 288–89.

51. Zimdars-Swartz, *Encountering Mary*, pp. 57–67.

52. Rogo, *Miracles*, pp. 218–19.

53. Michael Arvey, *Miracles: Opposing Viewpoints*, Great Mysteries Series (San Diego, Calif.: Greenhaven Press, 1990), pp. 66–69; Rogo, *Miracles*, pp. 221–23.

54. Arvey, *Miracles*, pp. 230–231.

55. Quoted in Rogo, *Miracles*, pp. 230–31.

56. Larue, *The Supernatural, the Occult and the Bible*, pp. 195–96; Rogo, *Miracles*, pp. 229–30; Nickell, *Looking for a Miracle*, pp. 177–78, 197.

57. Zimdars-Swartz, *Encountering Mary*, pp. 68–72, 194, 197–99, 218.

58. Ibid., pp. 68, 73–74, 90–91; Rogo, *Miracles*, p. 222.

59. Quoted in Zimdars-Swartz, *Encountering Mary*, p. 86.

60. Rogo, *Miracles*, pp. 238–50; Zimdars-Swartz, *Encountering Mary*, pp. 124–56.

61. Joan Ashton, *The People's Madonna: An Account of the Visions of Mary at Medjugorje* (London: Fount, 1991), *passim*; John Thavis, "Girls Who Say They See Visions Interviewed," *The Tidings* (Los Angeles), March 25, 1988.

62. Chuck Sudetic, "In Shrine to Virgin, Threat of War Darkens Streets," *New York Times*, September 27, 1991; Jeffrey L. Sheler et al., "What's in a Vision?" *U.S. News & World Report*, March 12, 1990; Kenneth L. Woodward with Andrew Nagorski, "Visitations of the Virgin," *Newsweek*, July 20, 1987; "Reported Apparitions by the Virgin Mary Put a Yugoslav Village on Map," *Sunday Star-Ledger* (Newark, N.J.), December 13, 1987; Dusko Doder, "Religious Boomtown Rakes in Cash," *Rocky Mountain News*, June 20, 1991.

63. Ashton, *The People's Madonna*, pp. 34–72; Rev. Father Gerard Dunn, "Medjugorje: Reasons for the Bishop's Condemnation," a recorded audio program distributed by Keep the Faith, North Haledon, N.J. Chuck Sudetic, "Do 4 Behold the Virgin? Bishop Is Not a Believer," *New York Times International*, September 28, 1990.

64. Sheler et al., "What's in a Vision?"; Sudetic, "In Shrine to Virgin."

65. Gerald Renner, "Reports of Divine Visions Increase," *Hartford Courant* (Hartford, Conn.), May 18, 1994.

66. Paul Prather, "Cold Spring Wasn't Visited by Virgin Mary, Bishop Says," *Lexington Herald-Leader* (Lexington, Ky.), September 2, 1992.

67. Renner, "Reports of Divine Visions Increase."

68. Ibid.

69. I was at Cold Spring, Kentucky, on August 31 and September 1, 1992; at Conyers, Georgia, on February 12–13, 1994; and at Falmouth, Kentucky, on August 8, 1994. My article, "Miraculous Signs in Cold Spring?" appeared in *Skeptical Inquirer* 17, no. 2 (Winter 1993): 120–22.

70. Richard Bush (Chair, Paranormal Investigating Committee of Pittsburgh), typescript report, "The Non-Miracle of Medjugorje," May

1988; Torri Minton, " 'Miracle' Changes in Rosary Beads," *San Francisco Chronicle*, May 13, 1988; Becky Long, personal communication.

71. Al Galipeau, "A Holy Vision Reported in Rocky Mountains," Part II, *Rocky Mountain Skeptic* 9, no. 5 (January/February 1992): 4; Laura Goldberg, "Thousands to Hail Mary," *Cincinnati Enquirer*, May 8, 1994 (sidebar, "Sun Can Permanently Damage Eyes").

72. Becky Long, "The Conyers Apparitions," *Georgia Skeptic* 5, no. 2 (March/April 1992) :3.

73. Dale Heatherington, "The Mystery of the Golden Door," *Georgia Skeptic* 5, no. 3 (May/June 1992): 1.

74. Joe Nickell, *Camera Clues: A Handbook for Photographic Investigation* (Lexington: University Press of Kentucky, 1994), p. 190.

75. Nickell, *Looking for a Miracle*, pp. 48–57.

76. Ibid., pp. 46–48.

77. "Photo Draws Believers in Power of Cloak" (Associated Press), *Lexington Herald-Leader* (Lexington, Ky.), December 26, 1992.

78. Interviews at Conyers, February 12, 1994.

79. William A. Nolen, M.D., *Healing: A Doctor in Search of a Miracle* (1974), cited in Terence Hines, *Pseudoscience and the Paranormal* (Amherst, N.Y.: Prometheus Books, 1988), p. 236.

80. Susan Blackmore, "Near-Death Experiences: In or Out of the Body?" *Skeptical Inquirer* 16, no. 1 (Fall 1991): 34–45.

81. Quoted (from another source) by Ian Wilson, *The After Death Experience* (New York: William Morrow, 1987), p. 132.

82. Blackmore, "Near-Death Experiences," p. 41.

83. Ibid., p. 42.

84. Quoted in Wilson, *The After Death Experience*, p. 139.

85. Quoted in ibid.

86. Blackmore, "Near-Death Experiences," pp. 39–41.

87. Ibid., p. 43.

88. Ibid., pp. 43–44.

89. Ibid., p. 44.

90. Ibid., pp. 44–45.

91. "Jerry Springer Show," aired December 16, 1992.

Part Three
Alien Creatures

6

Extraterrestrial Invasions

Man has always interacted with the heavens. As the source of lifegiving sun and rain, of calamities, of signs and portents, the sky—the abode of the gods—has seemed to hold the promise of human destiny. The ancient Babylonians even theorized that there was a direct accord between the stars and occurrences in people's lives. The biblical prophets engaged in visionary celestial travel (Rev. 4:1), communicated with holy messengers (Exod. 3:2; Luke 1:11-20), and were even taken up bodily into heaven (2 Kings 2:11).

Therefore, as Gerald Larue observes, "One might argue that if angels, as creatures from another dimension who have visited earth, are to be accepted as real, there is no reason to doubt recent claims of encounters with aliens from outer space. In other words, the Bible serves to authenticate the reality of space creatures."[1] Indeed, the connection between the two has frequently been made, recently at book length by Keith Thompson's *Angels and Aliens: UFOs and the Mythic Imagination* (which, despite its subtitle, takes neither a debunking nor a credulous stance). Speaking of the "common ground between the modern imagination of aliens and the traditional imagination of angels and daemons" (recalling that the latter term did not originally have its current, exclusively evil connotation), Thompson states:

> Beings from these realms appear to be intermediate between mind and matter, able to change their forms at will in the sight of select witnesses in select locations.

185

Over forty years of UFO sightings have led to the creation of an alien hierarchy (tall, Nordic-looking "blonds" and short, repulsive "grays" being only two types) no less daunting than the multileveled choir of angels, a richness bound to be documented in vivid detail someday by some enterprising folklorist.

Just as most information about angels comes from outside "approved" theological channels, and is based to a considerable extent on eyewitness testimony, likewise there is no room in the orthodox texts of Big Science for a class of phenomena that dares to originate outside the halls of orthodox institutes and academies, among "mere folk." In their own ways, angels and aliens are both heretical. . . .

Angels and aliens alike can easily be seen as messengers, as both are more visible in their functions—their effects—than as any known essence. But of course questions about what aliens and their amazing vehicles *are made of and where they are from* continue to haunt much ufological discourse, no less so than Thomas Aquinas's speculations about precisely how many angels could dance on the head of a pin.

For example, if angels can be said to have "subtle bodies," what should we say about aliens who pass through walls, float inches above the ground, and withstand (inside their vehicles) extraordinary accelerations in velocity and shifts in trajectory?[2]

In the following sections we will examine the persistent claims that celestial beings—angels or extraterrestrials—have visited our planet since ancient times and continue to do so at this very moment. Our discussion will focus on ancient astronauts, UFO sightings, crashed saucers, and alien abductions.

Ancient Astronauts

Since its publication in 1967, Swiss writer Erich von Däniken's book *Chariots of the Gods?* has become immensely popular and at one time was an international bestseller. It advanced the notion "that in the earth's remote past the planet was visited by beings from space who perhaps fathered humanity as we know it."[3] Not only did the aliens mate with early humans to produce *Homo sapiens*, suggests von Däniken, but they are also responsible for many of antiquity's great works, such as the Egyptian pyramids, the stone statues on Easter Island, and the giant Nazca drawings in Peru. Let's examine each of these in turn.

The Pyramids. To convince his readers that ancient "primitive" man could not have produced great structures like the pyramids of Egypt, von Däniken mentions that their stones weigh up to twelve tons each, that the Egyptians lacked the means to quarry them and had neither rope nor sufficient wood for rollers or sledges with which to transport the stones, and that there was no means of raising them in place.[4]

In fact, however, as Egyptologists well know, the great majority of the pyramid stones weigh an average of only two and a half tons.[5] They are of soft limestone rather than the formidable granite von Däniken leads readers to believe, and the Cairo Museum has a copper saw and chisels that were used to cut the blocks; the quarries are still extant, one of them being the hollow area in which the Sphinx stands.[6]

As well, the "non-existent" rope that von Däniken refers to is actually displayed in quantities in several Egyptian museums, and specimens are reported from numerous excavations. In fact, the Egyptians themselves left depictions of rope making on certain Fifth Dynasty tomb walls. It is also known that the Egyptians imported wood in great quantities from no fewer than nine countries. Moreover, there is not only an Egyptian hieroglyph for "sledge" but the Egyptians also left a drawing showing how they transported a colossal statue weighing an estimated sixty tons: 172 men are using four ropes to pull the statue on a wooden sledge, while one workman pours lubricant from a pitcher to lessen the friction. The Egyptians also used boats to transport stones through channels that were built close to the Great Pyramid and that were filled by flood waters of the Nile.[7]

As to raising the stones, the Egyptians not only had ropes and levers, but they also employed great earthen ramps, traces of which still exist. Presumably the ramps were progressively lengthened as the pyramid grew taller in order to lessen the steepness of the incline. One should keep in mind that pyramid building evolved over many dynasties from relatively small structures with stepped sides to the Great Pyramid of Cheops that is thought to have been built over a period of some thirty years with many tens of thousands of laborers being involved.[8]

Easter Island statues. Von Däniken's "theory" (which in any event is not original[9]) represents only one of many fanciful notions about the mysterious great stone heads that flank the coastal area of Easter Island, a tiny isolated isle in the Pacific Ocean. Some think they are the remains of lost Atlantis, others that the native islanders possessed magical, antigravitational powers, merely *willing* the statues into place.[10]

Archaeological investigation, however, together with scholarly interrogation of the present-day islanders, plus some practical experimentation, has solved many of the fundamental questions about the strange effigies. According to tradition, the island was populated by a chief and his followers who were forced to flee their homeland, reportedly one of the Marquesas Islands where the language and types of artifacts are similar. The curious statues were erected at various religious sites (called *ahu*) to honor respected ancestors.[11]

An open quarry, where statues are found in various states of completion along with discarded tools, provides detailed evidence of how the statues were created. Despite the assertions of writers like von Däniken,[12] experimenters have demonstrated that the natives could indeed move the statues. They have used a simple bipod (an inverted V made of logs) with ropes to "walk" a statue a few inches at a time, and they have shown that men using a lever could raise a statue a few inches, with rocks then being tossed underneath and the process repeated.[13] The latter feat—as described by explorer Thor Hyerdahl in his book *Aku-Aku*—took only two poles, ten men, and eighteen days.[14]

Nazca drawings. Called "riddles in the sand,"[15] they are the famous Nazca lines and giant ground drawings etched across thirty miles of gravel-covered desert near Peru's southern coast. Von Däniken argues that the huge sketchpad's lines and figures could have been "built according to instructions from an aircraft." He envisions flying saucers hovering above and beaming down instructions for the markings to awed primitives in their native tongue. To von Däniken, the large drawings are "signals" and the longer and wider lines are "landing strips."[16] But would extraterrestrials create signals for themselves in the shape of spiders and monkeys? And would such "signals" be less than eighty feet long (like some of the smaller Nazca figures)? As to the "landing strip" idea, Maria Reiche, the German-born mathematician who for years has mapped and attempted to study the markings, has a ready rejoinder. Noting that the imagined runways are clear of stones and that the exposed earth is quite soft, she says, "I'm afraid the spacemen would have gotten stuck."[17]

That the giant markings were produced by the Nazca Indians is demonstrated in several ways. The striking similarity of the stylized figures to those of known Nazca art has been clearly demonstrated.[18] There is also the evidence from carbon-14 analysis: Wooden stakes mark the termination of some of the long lines, and one of these was dated to A.D. 525 (plus or minus 80), consistent with the presence of the Nazcas in the area from 200 B.C. to about A.D. 600. Their graves and the ruins of their settlements lie near the drawings.[19]

To demonstrate that the Nazcas could indeed produce the giant figures, I launched a project in 1982 called "Project Nazca." Privately, we termed it "Project Big Bird": we determined to recreate one of the largest of the Nazca figures, the giant "condor," which measures 440 feet from beak to tail feathers. Studying photos of the Peruvian plain, and also visiting similar (if more simplistic) giant figures in the Mojave Desert (accompanied by an Indian guide), I was able to discount some previous theories and to come up with a method the Nazcas might have employed.[20]

Using only sticks and knotted cord, six of us (including my late father, J. Wendell Nickell; nephew, Con Nickell; and three cousins: John May, Sid Haney, and Jim Mathis) reproduced the giant bird actual size in less than two days (marking it with white lime like one would use for a playing field). *Scientific American* magazine termed our drawing "remarkable in its exactness" to the original.[21]

Regardless of the purpose for which such giant effigies were made (perhaps as offerings to the gods in the sky), it is clear that they—like the pyramids, Easter Island statues, and other works von Däniken cites as evidence for ancient spacemen—were actually made by those noble entities called humans.

UFO Sightings

First as an occasional incident beginning about 1880, then progressing to a full-fledged "flap" by the mid-1890s, strange "airships" were reportedly observed by thousands of Americans. Called the "Great Airship Wave," it existed primarily between November 1896 and May 1897.[22]

As typically described, the vessel was cigar-shaped, with wings or propellers or both, as well as an undercarriage; yet, historically, that era lacked the technology to fly such heavier-than-air craft. The Wright Brothers were not to make their pioneering flight until the end of 1903, and "attempts at earlier heavier-than-air flight were crude and erratic at best."[23]

In the early evening of November 17, 1896, something resembling an "electric arc lamp propelled by some mysterious force" passed over Sacramento, California, traveling at low altitude. As witnessed by hundreds of people, the craft carefully avoided tall buildings and hills; some persons reported hearing human voices. According to UFO historian Jerome Clark:

> The incident sparked enormous excitement and much press comment. Rumors spread that an airship had been secretly developed in Oak Park or that one had flown in from the East Coast. There was also, however, great skepticism. The *San Francisco Chronicle* called the Sacramento airship "probably one of the greatest hoaxes . . . ever sprung on any community" but, in practically the next breath, acknowledged "it is hard to account for the evident sincerity of those who claim they saw the machine and heard the voices" (November 19). The next day, however, it approvingly quoted Prof. George Davidson's remark that the affair was the "outcome of a sort of freemasonry of liars. Half a dozen fellows have got together, sent up a balloon with some sort of an electric light attachment, and imagination has done the rest. It is a pure fake." The *Oakland Tribune* likened the airship to the sea serpent, which "never appeared . . . when there was any dearth of whiskey. The air ship . . . cannot be verified properly without a liberal use of stimulant." To the *Woodland Mail* the airship was "about the thinnest fake yet set afloat."[24]

Be that as it may, the airship—or "mysterious lights moving through the air a great distance from the earth"—returned to Sacramento on November 20. On succeeding days others saw a strange contrivance with a headlamp. On the twenty-third, the *Call* published a letter from a man who claimed that while hunting in the mountains he had chanced upon a secluded machine shop. Swearing the hunter to secrecy, the mechanics confided that they were at work on an airship which was nearing completion. Clark says that the man, William Jordon, "may be the first person to claim an encounter with the aeronauts," adding, "He certainly would not be the last."[25]

The great airship scare was off and flying. Eventually reports came in from across the United States but mostly from the Midwest and, of course, the Pacific coast. According to UFO authority Philip J. Klass, author of *UFOs Explained*:

> Because of some similarities between the numerous reports of "mysterious airships" in the 1890s and the UFO flaps that began half a century later, there are those who suggest that the "mysterious airships" were really spaceships from other worlds that were erroneously described in terms of the emerging technology familiar to observers of that earlier era. But the fatal flaw in this hypothesis is that in the 1890s many persons reported having seen, and talked with, the very earthy members of the crews that allegedly operated the "mysterious airships." There were numerous reports of landings to enable the crew to replenish food and water. Not infrequently, it was said that the pilot sought directions to his destination. Some accounts said the pilot had confided to the "observer" that a revolutionary new airship design or "anti-gravity technique" was being tested that would be made public as soon as it had been patented. One of my favorite accounts involved an observer who claimed to have heard the crew of a "mysterious airship" singing "Nearer My God to Thee."[26]

Needless to say, there were no propelled airships in the American skies during the 1890s. Behind the reports was no doubt an increasing interest in air machines, with many people believing heavier-than-air flight was imminent and a few inventors securing patents for proposed aircraft.[27] These expectations led to hoaxes and to the misperception of natural phenomena such as meteors or ball lightning.[28] The "yellow journalism" of the day further augmented the hysteria (contagion) which occurred in two major waves correlating with newspaper accounts of where the "airship" was supposed to be. In other words, the expectation of seeing airships prompted people to see them.[29]

After World War I, "the world's first ufologist," Charles Fort, stirred interest in mysterious phenomena, including unidentified objects in the sky that Fort believed indicated visits from space aliens.[30] Fort (1874-1932) did not actually investigate the alleged occurrences but simply relied on reports in old newspapers and magazines.[31] In the 1920s, 1930s, and 1940s, science-fiction pulp magazines became popular, especially *Amazing Stories*, which made its debut in 1929. However, when its circulation began to lag, a new editor named Ray Palmer boosted sales with wild stories of extraterrestrial visitations, and decorated the covers with occasional illustrations of strange, circular spaceships.[32]

The term "flying saucers" came following a sighting in 1947. On June 24, businessman Kenneth Arnold was flying his private airplane over the Cascade Mountains in Washington State when he saw what he described as a chain of nine disc-like objects, each flying with a motion like "a saucer skipped across water."[33] According to one writer: "Possibly no one was more surprised by Kenneth Arnold's 1947 story, regarded as the UFO sighting that triggered off the 'modern era' and certainly gave the phenomenon its first popular name—flying saucers—than Ray Palmer. Palmer's fiction had become a reality! Viewed with hindsight, Arnold's sighting came in the middle of a UFO-flap in the United States that lasted into July."[34]

Theories about exactly what Arnold saw abound, ranging from "a group of aircraft"[35] to "mirages due to temperature inversion."[36] In any case, additional sightings of "flying saucers" (later termed by Air Force investigators "unidentified flying objects" or "UFOs") soon proliferated across the United States. On July 4, 1947, in Seattle, Washington, one of the "saucers" was photographed. After considerable publicity, however, it was identified as a weather balloon.[37]

Two major types of UFOs are commonly reported, the first being dubbed "daylight discs": metallic, phototypically saucer-shaped objects.[38] When properly investigated, these often turn out to be lens flares; weather, research, and other balloons; aircraft (for example, an airplane seen from the front or rear can look like a shiny domed saucer); meteors; lenticular (lens-shaped) clouds; kites, blimps, and hang gliders; windborne objects of various kinds; and many others, including, of course, outright hoaxes.[39] (Many faked UFO photos have been produced by sailing a model spaceship in the air Frisbee style, or suspending it on a thread, or using one or another methods of trick photography.[40])

A second type of UFO sighting consists of nighttime UFOs—so-called "nocturnal lights"—which represent the most frequently reported UFO events and also the "least strange events" according to the late Dr. J. Allen Hynek, astronomer and former consultant to the U.S. Air Force Project Blue Book (a UFO research program, 1952-1969). Although Blue Book determined there was no evidence that saucers were extraterrestrial craft, Hynek later actively promoted interest in UFOs. Still, he conceded: "It should be clearly understood that *initial* light-in-the-sky reports have a very low survival rate." He continued:

> An experienced investigator readily recognizes most of these for what they are: bright meteors, aircraft landing lights, balloons, planets, violently twinkling stars, searchlights, advertising lights on planes, refueling missions, etc. When one realizes the unfamiliarity of the general public with lights in the night sky of this variety, it is obvious why so many such UFO reports arise.[41]

Most UFO researchers—proponents and skeptics alike—agree that the majority of UFO reports can be explained. The controversy is over a small residue—say 2 percent—of unsolved cases. Proponents often act as if these cases offer proof of extraterrestrial visitation, but to suggest so is to be guilty of the logical fallacy *argumentum ad ignorantiam* (i.e., "arguing from ignorance"). Skeptics observe that what is unexplained is not necessarily *unexplainable*, and they suspect that if the truth were known such cases would fall not into the category of alien craft but into the realm of mundane explanations.

Philip J. Klass's *UFOs Explained* discusses many cases that, unsolved at first, were later shown to have a prosaic explanation. One such case was that of Capt. Thomas Mantell, who was leading a flight of P-51 fighter planes into Godman Air Force Base, near Fort Knox, Kentucky, when he was asked to investigate reports of a mysterious UFO in the area. Soon the pilots had it in view. Observers described the UFO as resembling a parachute or "an ice cream cone topped with red," as appearing "round like a tear drop . . . at times almost fluid," and as looking "metallic and of tremendous size." Mantell closed in on the object, but eventually decided to "abandon chase" at twenty thousand feet since his plane was not oxygen-equipped. Then there was silence from Capt. Mantell, and he failed to acknowledge a message from one of the other planes. Soon it was learned that Mantell's plane had crashed. Speculation and rumors grew that he had been shot down by a spacecraft from another world.

Mantell's UFO remained unidentified for several years, but eventually it was learned that a "Skyhook" balloon (used for secret cosmic-ray research) had been launched from southern Ohio "on or about 7 January 1948," the date of the Mantell encounter. Such balloons fit the description of the cone-shaped object seen over Godman Air Force Base. Depending on how sunlight strikes the plastic covering, the balloon can appear to be white, metallic, red, glowing, and so on. Mantell had not been shot down, of course, but had blacked out from lack of oxygen and crashed.[42]

Another initially unsolved case was one I investigated in 1993 with psychologist Robert A. Baker. The case even made the cover of the May 4 *Weekly World News*, which headlined: "UFO Fires on Louisville, Ky. Police Chopper." As the tabloid reported, the police first saw what looked like "a fire" off to the patrol craft's left; the "pear-shaped" UFO was seen in the police spotlight "drifting back and forth like a balloon on a string"; after circling the helicopter several times, the object darted away before zooming back to shoot the "fireballs" (which fortunately "fizzled out before they hit"); and then—as the helicopter pilot pushed his speed to over 100 mph—the UFO "shot past the chopper, instantly climbing hundreds of feet," only to momentarily descend again before flying into the distance and disappearing.[43]

As it turned out, just before the police encounter, a young man named Scott Heacock had launched a homemade hot-air balloon made from a plastic dry-cleaning bag, strips of balsa wood, and a dozen birthday candles. No sooner had the balloon cleared the trees, Heacock told us, than the county police helicopter encountered it and began circling, shining its spotlight on the glowing toy. The encounter was a comedy of errors and misperceptions. Like a dog chasing its tail, the helicopter was actually pushing the lightweight device around with its prop wash. As to the "fireballs," they may have been melting, flaming globs of plastic, or candles that dislodged and fell, or some other effect. (Heacock used the novelty "relighting" type of birthday candles as a safeguard against the wind snuffing them out. Such candles may sputter, then abruptly reflame.[44])

The very number of reported UFOs actually argues against the extraterrestrial hypothesis. As Ian Ridpath observes:

> Imagine, for a moment, that there are one million other civilizations in the galaxy, all sending out starships. Since there must be something like 10 billion interesting places to visit (one-tenth of all stars in the galaxy), then each civilization must launch 10,000 spaceships annually for only one to reach here every year. If each civilization launches the more reasonable number of one starship annually, then we would expect to be visited once every 10,000 years. Alternatively, the higher number of reported UFOs might be taken as indicating that we are something special. If so, then life cannot be a very common phenomenon in the galaxy—and thus there would be fewer civilizations to send out starships, and we would expect a smaller number of UFOs.[45]

Nevertheless, ufologists are undeterred and have even postulated that if the UFOs are not coming from *outer* space then they must be coming from *hyper* space—i.e., from the future or some other dimension. "Yet the fact remains," observes Dr. Baker, "that as of this date the UFOlogists have yet to produce one concrete bit of material evidence of an alien visitation from anywhere. What evidence we have been able to amass over the past forty years of searching all points to the fact that the aliens are coming from *inner* space, i.e., the space between the two ears of the human head. What aliens there are are the imaginary creations of the human mind."[46]

Crashed Saucers

It is a bizarre story, surfacing in 1950, of how flying saucers crashed in the American Southwest, were retrieved by the United States Air Force, and their preserved little humanoid occupants secretly stored at Wright-Patterson Air Force Base in Dayton, Ohio. It has been the subject of several magazine articles and books, as well as the recent motion picture, *Hangar 18*, named after the (nonexistent) building supposed to house the pickled aliens.[47]

Over several years, Leonard Stringfield, a public relations man—both for a chemical company and for a UFO organization—collected a number of such "crash/retrieval syndrome" stories (as he called them). In a booklet published in 1980, Stringfield relates nine "firsthand" cases and fourteen "new leads, or other pertinent material." An example of one of his "firsthand" sources (all of his informants, Stringfield says, have insisted on anonymity) is an unnamed "member of a group of twenty-five pilots" who he claims approached him after he gave a talk on UFOs at a September 1977 meeting of the Cincinnati chapter of World Wings. The man led Stringfield to a back room with a large map, and, as Stringfield relates:

> Staring at the map he said bluntly, "I have seen the bodies." Still looking at the map and noting my protracted silence, he pointed vaguely to an area inside the state of Arizona. "There's approximately where the saucer crashed," he said. "It was in a desert area, but I don't know the exact location. I'm almost positive it happened in 1953."
>
> The pilot was my first encounter with a firsthand witness. As he stood at the map with a straight-on glance, he impressed

me as a person who is sincere and forthright, possessing a no-nonsense character. "I saw the bodies at Wright-Patterson," he said. "I was in the right place at the right time when the crates arrived by night by DC-7."[48]

Stringfield continues:

As we lingered at the map he recalled that he had stood inside a hangar at a distance of about 12 feet, peering at five crates on a forklift. In his judgment, the crates appeared to be hastily constructed and were made of wood. In three of these, little humanoids appearing to be 4 feet tall were lying unshrouded on a fabric, which he explained prevented freeze burn from the dry ice packed beneath. As a number of Air Police stood silent guard nearby the crates, he managed to get a reasonably good but brief glimpse of the humanoid features. He recalls that their heads were hairless and narrow, and by human standards were disproportionately large, with skin that looked brown under the hangar lights above. The eyes seemed to be open, the mouth small, and nose, if any, was indistinct. The arms were positioned down alongside their bodies, but the hands and feet, he said, were indistinct. When asked about their attire, he said they appeared to be wearing tight-fitting dark suits, and, because of the tight-fitting suit, there was one revealing feature—a surprising feature. One of the humanoids appeared to him to be female. He said, "Either one of the aliens had an exceedingly muscular chest or the bumps were a female's breasts." Later, he learned from one of the crew members, with whom he bunked at the barracks, that the body of one of the aliens was believed to be that of a female.[49]

As we shall see, such tales not only exist in great number and in an astonishing variety, but they have a long history as well. From a folkloristic point of view, the crash/retrieval stories seem to function as "belief tales."[50] It has even been plausibly argued that the broader category of UFO phenomena "constitutes a modern-day myth couched in space-technology symbols."[51]

To put the crashed saucer accounts into perspective, let us look at their antecedents. A profitable place to start is 1884, when a June issue of the *Nebraska Nugget* ran a story about four cowboys who allegedly witnessed the crash of a cylindrical object and found "fragments of cog wheels and other pieces of machinery" glowing with intense heat. States UFO historian Jerome Clark:

> It is almost certainly a hoax, concocted like so many others which appeared in nineteenth-century newspapers, at a time when America's tall tale tradition was very much alive. . . . The *Nugget's* evident uncertainty about the chief "witness' " name— it refers to him variously as Ellis, Wilks, Willis, and Williamson—tips us off that the story is not all it appears to be.[52]

The next crashed saucer tale comes from the airship wave hysteria of 1896–1897 (discussed in the previous section of this chapter). On April 17, 1897, an "airship" crashed at Aurora, Texas, striking Judge J. S. Proctor's windmill, and exploded. According to the *Dallas Morning News*, the Aurora townsfolk reportedly found papers amid the wreckage (with an indecipherable writing) along with the horribly disfigured body of the "Martian" pilot, who, after the debris had been cleaned up, was given a Christian burial at noon in the local Masonic cemetery. (In recent years the story was branded a hoax and supposedly traced to an Iowa telegrapher.[53])

A 1937 science-fiction story by R. De Witt Miller described much earlier visitations. His "Within the Pyramid" involved the discovery of subterranean chambers in South America containing the "living dead" bodies of four ancient astronauts, each encased in a translucent sarcophagus. (An astonishingly similar story was related as true by Erich von Däniken of *Chariots of the Gods?* fame, who told the *National Enquirer* in 1979 that he knew the location of the underground chambers and would, that summer, lead an expedition to bring back the ultimate proof.[54])

On October 30, 1938, the Martians crash-landed in rural New Jersey, the octopus-like monsters spewing forth destruction from their heat rays. Panic set in:

> Thousands wept, prayed, closed their windows to shut out poison gas, or fled from their homes expecting the world to

end. Phone lines were tied up for hours. The panic was from coast to coast, but the greatest hysteria was in the southern states among the poorly educated.[55]

This Halloween invasion was, of course, only the famous stunt broadcast, Orson Welles's radio version of H. G. Wells's *The War of the Worlds*. But in less than a decade, strange new visitations would allegedly be made.

After his famous "flying saucer" encounter of June 24, 1947, Kenneth Arnold wrote a pamphlet and a number of articles discussing his experience along with what he considered evidence of extraterrestrial visitations. As one example, Arnold cited a fourteen-inch-tall mummified man discovered in the Rocky Mountains in 1932.[56]

Jacques Vallee, in "A Century of UFO Landings,"[57] lists no fewer than nine saucer landings for 1947, from June 10 to August 14. All but two of these were American and one was the infamous Maury Island hoax in which two Puget Sound harbor patrolmen took photos of six UFOs. They also allegedly retrieved chunks of metal spewed out by one of the craft which had seemed temporarily disabled. Soon they claimed to have had encounters with mysterious persons who warned them to forget what they had seen. This "first, possibly second-best, and the dirtiest hoax in the UFO history" was soon acknowledged by the pair.[58]

A book by Charles Berlitz and William L. Moore, *The Roswell Incident*, which tells "the never before published, fully documented story of a manned UFO landing in New Mexico," relates fourteen sightings reported in or near that state between June 25 and July 2, 1947. Then on July 8 came a bizarre and unauthorized press release from a young but eager public information officer at the Roswell Army Air Base who reported that a "flying disc" had been retrieved from an area ranch.[59]

The young officer was reprimanded and soon new information was released: The saucer had been an airborne weather device. The *Fort Worth Star-Telegram* published a photograph of two amused officers posing with the "wreckage"—some flexible, silvery-looking material.[60] The Air Force first identified the device as a "Rawin sonde" (a polyethylene balloon with a two-pound instrument package) and then corrected that to a "Rawin target" (a radar target formed of foiled paper stapled to a balsa frame and carried aloft by a cluster of balloons). The two authors of *The Roswell Incident* consider this a "cover story" that was "hastily contrived." They argue that the original wreckage (from a crashed saucer) had been flown to Carswell Air Force Base and then on to Wright-Patterson Field, while wreckage of a Rawin device was "hastily substituted," apparently so that the news photographers could be fooled and the public kept from learning the fearful truth.[61]

The July 9 *Roswell Daily Record*, which carried the news that the "saucer" was a balloon, also featured an interview with the rancher, William Brazel, who had reported the odd debris to the Roswell sheriff's office. Brazel stated, "I am sure what I found was not any weather observation balloon. [It wasn't.] . . . But if I find anything else besides a bomb, they are going to have a hard time getting me to say anything about it."[62]

Moore and Berlitz interviewed the aging former Roswell staff officer, Major (now Lieutenant Colonel, retired) Jesse A. Marcel, who was in charge of intelligence at Roswell at the time of the incident. Marcel insisted the debris, which he described as in copious quantity, "certainly wasn't anything built by us and it most certainly wasn't any weather balloon." He described

> small beams about three-eighths or a half-inch square with some sort of hieroglyphics on them that nobody could decipher. These looked something like balsa wood, and were of about the same weight, except that they were not wood at all. They were very hard, although flexible, and would not burn. There was a great deal of an unusual parchment-like substance which was brown in color and extremely strong, and a great number of small pieces of a metal like tinfoil, except that it wasn't tinfoil.[63]

He stated that the pieces of metal were "so thin, just like the tinfoil in a pack of cigarettes," and added: "It was possible to flex this stuff back and forth, even to wrinkle it, but you could not put a crease in it that would stay nor could you dent it at all. I would almost have to describe it as a metal with plastic properties."[64]

Again Marcel stated:

> One of the other fellows, Cavitt, I think, found a black, metallic-looking box several inches square. As there was no apparent way to open this, and since it didn't appear to be an instrument package of any sort (it too was very lightweight), we threw it in with the rest of the stuff.[65]

Rancher Brazel's son described materials similar to those seen by Major Marcel, referring to "wooden-like particles . . . like balsa wood in weight, but a bit darker in color and much harder." As to the foil, "You could wrinkle it and lay it back down and it immediately returned to its original shape." And there had been "some thread-like material . . . not large enough to call it string." He adds, "None of this stuff had an exactly natural appearance about it, it was more like something synthetic now that I think about it." He said that the pieces of "material" he had seen did not have any markings on it but that his father had referred to "figures." (His sister used the word "designs.") The son of a man who had interviewed rancher Brazel described similar debris.[66]

It certainly seems remarkable that 1947-model saucers would be constructed of materials so closely resembling those of a weather target (again, not a balloon)—materials resembling balsa, foil, and string. If so, they seem to have been surprisingly flimsy!—by our pathetically terrestrial standards, of course. In any case, citing vague rumors of a saucer alleged to have crashed approximately 125 miles west of Brazel's ranch, Berlitz and Moore postulate an "explosion on board the stricken saucer." Presumably, this caused debris to fall at the first location while the craft itself crashed at the second site.[67]

To continue our chronology, in 1950 Frank Scully published his *Behind the Flying Saucers*, which told of three "spacecraft" that had crashed—one near Phoenix, Arizona, and the other two in the vicinity of Aztec, New Mexico. A total of thirty-four little humanoids were recovered, ranging in size from 36 to 42 inches tall, and dressed in blue uniforms. The little men, Scully said, were being studied at undisclosed locations along with several items found on board the craft, including an "unknown" metal and booklets written in a pictorial script that government experts were attempting to decipher.[68] Alas, in September 1952, *True* magazine exposed the story as a hoax. Scully's chief source was a friend named Silas M. Newton who in turn had obtained the story from a mysterious "Dr. Gee." Although Scully described the latter as "the top magnetic research specialist in the United States," he turned out to be one Leo A. GeBauer, proprietor of a Phoenix radio- and TV-parts business.[69]

According to UFO researcher Kevin D. Randle:

> Between 1950 and 1974, further rumors of the "little bodies" surfaced periodically, only to be swatted by careful research. In almost every case, the rumors were traced to Scully's book and Newton's claims.[70]

In 1974, Robert Carr claimed he had talked with several people who had seen the little creatures secretly stored at Wright-Patterson. Carr, who once wrote space stories and worked for Walt Disney Studios as a film research director, was at the time generating publicity for "Operation Lure," a scheme to attract UFOs to land by building a saucer greeting station atop an Arizona mountain. Carr, apparently basing his information on the discredited Scully book, claimed one of the saucers had crashed at Aztec, New Mexico.[71] (The year before Carr made his claims, there had been a brief revival of the 1897 Aurora crashed "airship" story, reportedly attracting some 3000 persons to the site, many with metal detectors. Three elderly residents—aged 78, 91, and 98—claimed parents or friends had visited the site of the "explosion" and told them about it. However, further investigation tended to reconfirm the tale as a hoax.[72])

In 1977 Leonard Stringfield began to apply his public relations talents to the crash/retrieval rumors. His book *Situation Red* cried cover-up, while he observed that a UFO "occupant—humanoid or bestial, found dead or captured alive—would constitute the *final proof* of the UFO's extraterrestrial origin."[73]

Stringfield presented a signed statement by a pseudonymous engineer, "Fritz Werner," who claimed that "during a special assignment with the U.S. Air Force on May 21, 1953, I assisted in the investigation of a crashed unknown object in the vicinity of Kingman, Arizona."[74] But Jerome Clark points out suspicious "coincidences" between the "Werner" and Scully stories.[75]

From Leonard Stringfield (mentioned earlier), we learn that the crash/retrieval cases continued to proliferate. Anonymous informants supposedly claim to have witnessed (or have seen a film of) crashed saucers and/or little bodies, on various occasions between 1952 and 1973. One saw nine bodies, about four feet tall, "preserved in deep freeze conditions" at Wright-Patterson. Another saw only four bodies there, and they were about a foot taller and were "badly burned" (like Scully's creatures). Yet another "source" was taken blindfolded (in 1973) through an underground corridor to a room where he saw "specialists" viewing 3-foot-tall alien corpses "stretched out on a table." And so on.

One "noted doctor" (alas also anonymous) claimed to have autopsied "an alien being in the early 1950s, but was not only disconcertingly vague about the date but also about the internal organs, if any. However he did supply several details of the creature's appearance: It had an oversized head—oversized in relation to its four-foot, three-eighths-inch height. The skin was "not green" (as Stringfield emphasizes) but grayish. The eyes were "mongoloid in appearance" and there was only a "wrinkle-like fold" for the mouth. The arms were overly long; there was no thumb; the legs were short and thin. The sexual organs (this was a male specimen) were said to be "atrophied."[76]

In 1980 there surfaced several photographs purported to show the little bodies. Investigators concluded one set of these was almost certainly of "a rhesus monkey killed in a V-2 rocket test" thirty years earlier. The other set was traced to a publication that, says Jerome Clark, "routinely prints absurd fiction as 'documented fact' " and to a 1977 issue of a sister publication that had featured one of the photos on its cover next to the heading, "*Exclusive Proof Positive: Space Alien Discovered Beneath the Empire State Building!*" During the controversy over the photos, two rival UFO groups were up in arms, and the conspiracy-minded Stringfield (who had been taken in by one set of photographs) could not "help but wonder if somebody in a powerful position pressed the 'silence' button." "In intelligence circles," he said, "they call it 'disinformation.' "

Clark, on the other hand, thought it merely the act of "a hoaxer with a cruel sense of humor." He added, "It's time to close the book on this embarrassing episode before all ufology succumbs to a case of terminal silliness."[77]

Alleged documentary proof that a saucer had indeed crashed at Roswell, and that its humanoid occupants were recovered and hidden away, came in 1987. Two documents were supposedly sent by an unidentified source to Jaime Shandera, an associate of *Roswell* author William L. Moore, and later a third document surfaced, discovered at the National Archives by Moore and Shandera. The documents purported to show that there was a secret "Operation Majestic Twelve" (MJ-12), authorized by President Truman to handle clandestinely the crash/retrieval at Roswell.

Investigation, however, soon showed that the MJ-12 documents were obvious forgeries, and that the one at the National Archives was a "plant" (i.e., a paper brought *into* the archives and placed among others). Proof that the documents were fake came from Philip J. Klass, as well as from an independent investigation I conducted with forensic analyst John F. Fischer (with encouragement from Jerome Clark, editor of the center for UFO Studies' journal, the *International UFO Reporter*).[78]

As it happens, what *really* crashed on rancher Brazel's property on June 14, 1947, was learned in 1994 when investigations by both the U.S. Air Force and UFO researchers, notably Robert G. Todd, uncovered the truth in once-classified documents. The device was a balloon-carried "radar corner reflector" that at the time was part of a top secret *Project Mogul*—an effort to use high-altitude balloons to detect nuclear explosions in the former Soviet Union.[79]

In summary, we have a long tradition of flying-saucer crash/retrieval tales—an obvious amalgam of misreported incident, science-fiction story, rumor, urban legend, and hoax. The concept seems to be flitting across the country—not unlike a "saucer" itself. One wonders if it will ever crash.

Alien Abductions

Not all of the purported evidence of extraterrestrial visitations comes from distant sightings of UFOs or legends and hoaxes about crashed saucers and embalmed humanoids. To study what he termed "close encounters" with alien beings, Dr. J. Allen Hynek devised the following classification system:

> *Close Encounters of the First Kind* (CE-I): A UFO is seen at close range without interaction between the UFO and the environment (apart from the evoked psychological reaction of the observer).
>
> *Close Encounters of the Second Kind* (CE-II): A UFO is observed at close range and physical effects on the environment (disabled vehicles, frightened animals, ground indentations, broken or crushed plants, burned or scorched ground) are reported.
>
> *Close Encounters of the Third Kind* (CE-III): "Intelligent beings" are reported in or around the UFO, sometimes apparently collecting rock samples or "repairing" their craft. Interactions between human "contactees" and UFO occupants fall into this category.[80]

Later, investigators added a fourth type:

> *Close Encounters of the Fourth Kind* (CE-IV): The contactee is abducted by the UFO occupants, taken aboard the landed craft, and subjected to a variety of "tests" and "experiments." Some investigators claim to have recovered physical evidence of these interactions in the form of scars from alien surgical incisions. Some abductees report memories of devices being implanted within their bodies, typically through the nose.[81]

If true (an important caveat as we shall see), the first UFO abduction occurred on a farm on the outskirts of South Bend, Indiana, on Christmas Eve, 1889. While a snowfall accumulated outside, the Larch family, their minister, and some friends were in the parlor singing to Mrs. Larch's organ music. Shortly before eleven o'clock, Mr. Larch sent his eleven-year-old son, Oliver, to the well for water. But no sooner had the lad slipped on his overshoes and started on his errand than the adults heard his frantic screams: "Help! Help! Help!"

The adults rushed outside, with Oliver's father carrying a kerosene lamp. The boy's cries—which were already growing faint—seemed to come from the blackness overhead! And lamplight revealed that Oliver's tracks led about halfway to the well—and ended abruptly! According to the account in Frank Edwards's *Strangest of All*, "There were no other marks of any kind in the soft snow. Just Oliver's footprints . . . and the bucket . . . and silence." Edwards adds that subsequent investigation proved the truth of the story.[82] Some modern clippings from the local newspaper mentioned speculations that the disappearance was a flying saucer kidnapping, with one reporter claiming that next to Oliver's footprints had been the tracks of "little men."[83]

Is there evidence to confirm the disappearance? Actually, despite Edwards's insistence on the truth of the tale, it is not only fictitious—my investigation revealed that no such family and no such case ever occurred in the area—but it exists in various other versions, attributing similar events to an Oliver Lerch, 1890; Oliver Thomas, 1909; and so on. In fact, the story is a plagiarized version of Ambrose Bierce's short story, "Charles Ashmore's Trail," one of a trilogy of "Mysterious Disappearances" related in his *Can Such Things Be?*[84]

Jerome Clark, in his comprehensive reference work *The UFO Encyclopedia*, relates "what has to be the first would-be abduction in history." It occurred during the "Great Airship Wave" when one Col. H. G. Shaw told the Stockton, California, *Evening Mail* that on November 25, 1896, while out jogging, he and a companion encountered "three strange beings." Tall, naked, and rather human-like, the creatures attempted, but failed, to carry him to their airship, which hovered nearby. However, Shaw's account is clearly tongue-in-cheek, made clear at the end when he inveighs against other airship storytellers. They are "clumsy fakes," he says, and "should not be given credence by anyone."[85]

The first noteworthy modern abduction case was that of an interracial couple named Betty and Barney Hill which reportedly occurred in September 1961. As Jerome Clark states:

When first reported to investigators shortly after its occurrence, the Hills' story of a UFO sighting on a lonely New Hampshire road seemed to be a more-or-less-typical close encounter of the third kind (a UFO sighting in which occupants are reported); Barney claimed to have seen a being inside the object as it hovered over their car. What made the incident unique was the Hills' conviction that two hours had passed unaccountably following the sighting. Two and a half years later, when the couple, suffering from stress which they linked to the sighting, underwent hypnosis in the office of Boston psychiatrist Benjamin Simon, they related that gray-skinned humanoids with large heads and small mouths had taken them aboard the UFO and given them a medical examination.[86]

Dr. Simon's conclusion was that the Hills had experienced a "shared dream" and, indeed, specific inconsistencies in Mrs. Hill's story are characteristic of dreaming. Dr. Simon observed: "At one point when Betty tried to explain why Barney had 'removable teeth,' she referred to people getting older. When the 'spacemen' didn't understand, Betty explained 'with the passage of time . . . ,' but the spaceman said he didn't understand what 'time' was because there was no such thing on their planet." Yet, moments afterward, as the Hills were ready to leave, the *same* alien said, "Wait a minute," asking them to delay their departure and demonstrating a full awareness of time.[87]

When Philip Klass interviewed Dr. Simon in 1966, the psychiatrist commented on the difference between their respective accounts "relived" under hypnosis. Whereas Mrs. Hill recalled numerous, particular details, her husband recalled very little. This indicated, Dr. Simon said, that the "abduction" was not a shared experience; rather, it indicated Mr. Hill had obtained his knowledge of the incident after he repeatedly heard his wife tell her nightmares to neighbors and friends.[88]

On October 20, 1975, NBC-TV first aired its movie on the Hill case. Titled *The UFO Incident*, the movie starred James Earl Jones and Estelle Parsons in the lead roles. The airing sparked additional "abduction" reports including one told by six Arizona woodcutters just two weeks afterward (on November 5). The men claimed that while at work in the Sitgreaves National Forest, they saw a fellow woodcutter, Travis Walton, get "zapped" by a flying saucer. Indeed, Walton failed to appear for five days, then returned to tell how he had been taken aboard an alien spacecraft and given an examination.

Although one UFO organization termed the case "one of the most important and intriguing in the history of the UFO phenomena,"[89] investigation by skeptical UFO expert Philip Klass revealed many indications that the case was a hoax. These included the fact that Walton and his brother had discussed what to do if they ever had a close encounter with a UFO; that shortly before the incident Walton told his mother not to worry if a UFO abducted him; that his brother seemed unconcerned with his safety during the five days he was "missing"; and that an experienced polygraph examiner reported Walton had exhibited "gross deception" and even tried to "beat the machine" by holding his breath.[90]

Further investigation showed that in 1971 Walton and the brother of his logging crew chief had pleaded guilty to committing a burglary and forging stolen checks. (However, after making restitution and living up to the terms of their probation, they were allowed to "cleanse the record," pleading "not guilty" to the crimes they originally pled guilty to.[91])

In his *UFO Abductions: A Dangerous Game*, Klass explained the alleged abduction as a hoax concocted by Walton and the crew leader, Michael Rogers. The motive, Klass argues was twofold: first, to create an excuse for Rogers having missed a contract deadline, and, second, to win a UFO-sighting contest sponsored by the tabloid newspaper, *National Enquirer*. Walton did win, collecting a $5,000 prize.[92]

Just two months after the Walton case had provided additional national publicity to UFO abductions, three Kentucky women were snatched by aliens. However, they did not reveal this publicly until a year later.

In 1994 psychologist Robert A. Baker and I took a fresh look at the eighteen-year-old case. Dr. Baker was to be interviewed about the incident for a British TV program, and I volunteered to drive the two of us on an investigative trip to the southern Kentucky area. After talking to neighbors and relatives of the women, and conducting research at the local library, we had a good start on our review.[93] The television producer did not want us to actually approach either of the two surviving women until they themselves made contact, but Dr. Baker was finally able to talk with one of the abductees and to formulate an opinion about the "abduction."

Their story began on January 6, 1976, when they drove to a restaurant in Lancaster, thirty miles from their homes in Liberty, to celebrate one of the women's thirty-sixth birthday. If what happened on their way home seems quite similar to the account by Betty and Barney Hill, there is a good reason.

What actually happened was that while traveling on the deserted road after their very late meal, about 11:30 P.M., one of them saw a light in the sky and mentioned it to the others. (At dinner they had been discussing recent reports of UFOs in the area.) The driver eventually became sleepy and, the other two having already fallen asleep, pulled off the road. Having struggled to stay awake, she now experienced a "waking dream" about a UFO and later—according to Dr. Baker, who describes her as the "dominant personality"—"talked the other two into agreeing that something strange had happened."

Explains Dr. Baker:

Over the subsequent months, she was visited by another alien that looked like an angel. Again, she managed to convince the other two that very strange things had happened to them and to convince them to go along with her story. The dreamer herself was not exactly sure about what had occurred until she managed to talk to Betty Hill, the famous (and original) UFO abductee from the 1960s.

As it turned out, most of the content of their abduction story came directly from the lips of Betty Hill, after a little alteration and elaboration from the persuasive one of the three.[94]

As Dr. Baker concludes:

All in all, it was a typical abduction report blown up and elaborated to make an intriguing and incredible story. Sadly enough, the three actually believe they were picked by the Lord for this very holy mission of peace and revelation. They were very saddened that so many people didn't believe them.[95]

Dr. Baker says the three women were also victimized by overzealous ufologists who subjected the women to regressive hypnosis and thus inserted various concepts of UFO mythology into their memories.[96]

One of my own meetings with an abductee occurred on a Canadian television program, "The Shirley Show," when I appeared with Dorothy Wallis. She claims she has been abducted more than fifteen times since she was a child, her first abduction occurring in 1947 when she was eight. In a pre-show interview (a copy of which I obtained prior to my appearance so I could examine her claims) she says she awoke with a compulsion to go out into a field. She did not want to go, she insists, but could not resist. In the field was a bright light emanating from the door of some kind of craft. A humanoid creature having a small, spindly body but with very large head and large eyes communicated telepathically with her and told her to enter the craft. After examining her on a table and inserting a spiked ball up her nose, the aliens took her to an "observation area" in a "giant hangar" where she was shown revelations of the earth's future—visions so horrific that she tried to turn away but could not move. Afterward she was returned to the field and released; when she arrived at her house she discovered three hours had elapsed.

Mrs. Wallis says she was abducted again at age fifteen, at which time the aliens used a probe inserted through her navel to collect ova. Other abductions were spaced a few years apart; she does not have total recall of each but has recovered more memory through hypnotic regression. She kept her experiences secret, she said, until recent years, only telling her husband in 1986. She adds that he supports her and that her friends say she is the most honest person they know so the events must be true. Since "going public" she has given dozens of interviews, appearing on such shows as "Oprah" and "Sally Jessy Raphael." "The Shirley Show" preappearance interview gave her a "storyteller" rating of ten on a ten-point scale and noted that she is a "great talker" who "paints incredible word pictures."[97]

Mrs. Wallis's case is typical of abductees and seems clearly to be part of an evolving mythology. For example, the spiked-ball-up-the-nose motif seems to have been "lifted" from a popular abductee case publicized in a 1979 book titled *The Andreasson Affair*. When I mentioned this on "The Shirley Show," Mrs. Wallis retorted that her implant occurred before that of Betty Andreasson, to which I responded that, in terms of what could be proven, Mrs. Andreasson's earlier publication gave her the stronger claim.

As another example, consider Mrs. Wallis's description of the alien spacemen: as little, big-headed humanoids familiar to moviegoers as "E.T." in Steven Spielberg's 1982 motion picture. (The mythological implication of this description seems to be that the "aliens" are "time travellers"—in effect, they are us as it is assumed we *will be* in our distant evolutionary future; however, the evidence for equating brain size with intelligence is at best dubious.[98])

I also provoked Mrs. Wallis by suggesting she had the characteristics of a fantasy-prone personality. But consider her repeated experiences since childhood; the otherworldly content of her experience, including her strong sensory awareness; her role as a type of visionary; her early secrecy; her telepathic ability; her receptivity to hypnosis; and other characteristics, together with the fact that she seems basically a normal, healthy individual.[99]

Apart from the abductees themselves, the abduction phenomenon has been largely fostered by several individuals, notably Budd Hopkins, a New York artist whose book *Intruders* renewed interest in the subject in the 1980s; David Jacobs, a long-time UFO proponent who says he is now "frightened" of the UFO phenomenon that has assumed "realistic dimensions"; Whitley Strieber, who wrote the fantastically bestselling *Communion: a True Story* about his own repeated abductions; Thomas Bullard, a folklorist who conducted a survey of the phenomenon but could only conclude that "at least something goes on"; and John Mack, a Harvard psychiatrist.[100]

Dr. Mack, says *Time* magazine, "is more than a Harvard

Professor; he is a respected author"—one whose biography of
T. E. Lawrence won the 1977 Pulitzer Prize. In 1994, however,
Mack lent his considerable reputation to UFO kidnapping claims
with his book *Abduction: Human Encounters with Aliens.* This
led *Time* to report:

> Psychologists and ethicists do not question Mack's sanity so
> much as his motives and methodology. They charge that he
> is misusing the techniques of hypnosis, trying to shape the
> "memories" of his subjects to suit his vision of an intergalactic
> future, and very possibly endangering the emotional health of
> his patients in the process. "If this were just an example of
> some zany new outer limit of how foolish psychology and
> psychiatry can be in the wrong hands, we'd look at it, roll our
> eyes and walk away," says University of California, Berkeley,
> psychologist Richard Ofshe. "But the use of his techniques in
> counseling is substantially harming lots of people."
>
> The scientific skepticism is bolstered by some unusual first-
> hand evidence. One of Mack's "experiencers" has revealed to
> *Time* that she was actually an undercover debunker who worked
> her way into Mack's confidence and rose high in the ranks of
> his subjects. She found that Mack's work was riddled with
> scientific irregularities; it lacked a formal research protocol as
> well as legally required consent forms that advise research sub-
> jects of potential risks. She also discovered that Mack billed
> the insurance companies of at least some patient-subjects for
> what he described as therapy sessions.[101]

Although Mack has questioned the motives and reliability of the
interloper—Donna Bassett—I have met her and heard her account
of her undercover work and believe that it is an excellent example
of investigatory procedures.[102]

I have also met Dr. Mack and think he is a sincere, if
beleaguered, man. His major shortcoming, I think, has been well
pointed out by the *Time* article:

> Mack's view of the UFO phenomenon reflects a larger philo-
> sophical stance that rejects "rational" scientific explanations and
> embraces a hazier New Age reality. "I don't know why there's

such a zeal to find a conventional physical explanation," he says. "I don't know why people have such trouble simply accepting the fact that something unusual is going on here. . . . We have lost the faculties to know other realities that other cultures still can know. The world no longer has spirit, has soul, is sacred. We've lost all that ability to know a world beyond the physical. . . . I am a bridge between those two worlds."[103]

The New Age perspective has given the abductee promotors a mindset that has kept them from recognizing simpler explanations for the phenomenon. For example, like Bullard and others, Dr. Mack argues that evidence in favor of its genuineness includes a rather notable *consistency* of the accounts. However, Harvard Medical School professor and psychiatrist-in-chief at Beth Israel Hospital in Boston, Dr. Fred Frankel, observes: "Dr. Mack is ignoring the high level of suggestion and imagery that surrounds the way in which he deals with these people." He adds: "Hypnosis helps you regain memories that you would not have otherwise recalled. . . . But some will be true, and some will be false. The expectation of the hypnotist and the expectation of the person who is going to be hypnotized can influence the result."[104]

Mack and others also overlook—or dismiss out of hand— the evidence that many abductees are fantasy-prone personalities. Dr. Baker observes: "The reason we do not run into these types more often is that they have learned long ago to be highly secretive and private about their fantasy lives." However, when such persons are subjected to hypnosis by abduction proponents, "it provides them with a social situation in which they are encouraged to do, and are rewarded for doing, what they usually do only in secrecy and private."[105] Dr. Baker conducted an experiment on several hundred "very, very normal, sane, run-of-the-mill" volunteers, regressing them hypnotically to a "previous life"; he also projected about a hundred into the future. The volunteers were asked to describe their lives. "Some of these past and future lives were quite dramatic," reported Baker, "while others were dull and prosaic, depending upon the personality of the subject, his/her interest in science-fiction, and whether or not he/she was a fantasy-prone personality type."[106]

Dr. Baker also calls attention to the phenomenon of "waking dreams," the characteristics of which one frequently discovers in abductee accounts. He observes:

In Strieber's *Communion* is a classic, textbook description of a hypnopompic hallucination, complete with the awakening from a sound sleep, the strong sense of reality and of being awake, the paralysis (due to the fact that the body's neural circuits keep our muscles relaxed and help preserve our sleep), and the encounter with strange beings. Following the encounter, instead of jumping out of bed and going in search of the strangers he has seen, Strieber typically goes back to sleep. He even reports that the burglar alarm was still working—proof again that the intruders were mental rather than physical. Strieber also reports an occasion when he awakes and believes that the roof of his house is on fire and that the aliens are threatening his family. Yet his only response to this was to go peacefully back to sleep. Again, clear evidence of a hypnopompic dream. Strieber, of course, is convinced of the reality of these experiences. This too is expected. If he was not convinced of their reality, then the experience would not be hypnopompic or hallucinatory.[107]

Frequently, in abduction accounts there is also the motif of "missing time"—a period which the percipient cannot account for. But this is common to ordinary people in ordinary circumstances, such as daydreaming, driving down the highway (so-called highway hypnosis), and so on. As one authority explains, "What the time-gapper is reporting is not that a slice of time has vanished, but that he has failed to register a series of events which would normally have functioned as his time-markers."[108]

When abduction cases are carefully analyzed, we see that—apart from outright hoaxes—fantasy typically is responsible for the phenomenon, either as a personality characteristic, as a "waking dream" or other hallucination, as hypnotic confabulation, or in some other form. Apparently the only thing being abducted is some people's judgment.

Recommended Works

Baker, Robert A. "The Aliens Among Us: Hypnotic Regression Revisited," *Skeptical Inquirer* 12, no. 2 (Winter 1987–88): 147–62. Explains alien-abduction claims in light of anomalistic psychology.

Clark, Jerome. *The UFO Encyclopedia*, vol. 1, Detroit: Apogee Books, 1990; vol. 2, Chicago: Omnigraphics, 1992. Comprehensive survey of all aspects of saucer study by a respected UFO historian.

Klass, Philip J. *UFOs Explained.* New York: Vintage Books, 1974. Authoritative conversion of UFOs into IFOs using the scientific approach.

Klass, Philip J. *UFO Abductions: A Dangerous Game.* Amherst, N.Y.: Prometheus Books, 1989. Definitive book-length treatment of the subject.

Nickell, Joe. "The Hangar 18 Tales," *Common Ground* 9 (Britain), June 9, 1984: 2–10. Study of UFO crash/retrieval accounts as proliferating, evolving folktales.

Spencer, John, and Hilary Evans. *Phenomenon: Forty Years of Flying Saucers.* New York: Avon Books, 1988. Comprehensive overview of UFO phenomenon by both believers and skeptics.

Thiering, Barry, and Edgar Castle. *Some Trust in Chariots.* Toronto: Popular Library, 1972. Scholarly and scientific response to Erich von Däniken's *Chariots of the Gods?* with its "ancient astronauts" claims.

Notes

1. Gerald Larue, *The Supernatural, the Occult and the Bible* (Amherst, N.Y.: Prometheus Books, 1990), p. 64.

2. Keith Thompson, *Angels and Aliens: UFOs and the Mythic Imagination* (New York: Faucett Columbine, 1991), pp. 150–51.

3. Promotional blurb, Erich von Däniken, *Chariots of the Gods?* quoted in Barry Thiering amd Edgar Castle, *Some Trust in Chariots* (Toronto: Popular Library, 1972), p. 3.

4. Erich von Däniken, *Chariots of the Gods?* (London: Corgi, 1971), pp. 79–102.

5. Thiering and Castle, *Some Trust in Chariots*, p. 5; Basil Hennessy, "Archaeology of the Ancient Near East," in ibid., p. 10.

6. Hennessy in Thiering and Castle, *Some Trust in Chariots*, pp.

10–11; Christopher Baker, "Ancient Egypt without Astronauts," in ibid., p. 68.

7. Hennessy in ibid., pp. 10–11; Baker in ibid., pp. 68–72.

8. Baker in ibid., pp. 66–72.

9. Jerome Clark, The UFO Encyclopedia, vol. 2 (Detroit: Omnigraphics, 1992), p. 406.

10. Ron Fisher, "Easter Island: Brooding Sentinels of Stone," in Mysteries of the Ancient World (Washington, D.C.: National Geographic Society, 1979), p. 203.

11. Ibid., pp. 198, 201.

12. Von Däniken, Chariots of the Gods?, chapter 8.

13. Fisher, "Easter Island," pp. 211, 213.

14. Thor Heyerdahl, Aku-Aku: The Secret of Easter Island (London: George Allen and Unwin Ltd., 1958), pp. 132–51.

15. "Riddles in the Sand," Discover, June 1982: 50–57. This discussion is abridged from my article, "The Nazca Drawings Revisited," reprinted from Skeptical Inquirer in Science Confronts the Paranormal, ed. Kendrick Frazier (Amherst, N.Y.: Prometheus Books, 1986), pp. 285–92.

16. Von Däniken, Chariots of the Gods?, p. 17; Erich von Däniken, Gods from Outer Space (New York: Bantam, 1972), p. 105.

17. Quoted in Loren McIntyre, "Mystery of the Ancient Nazca Lines," National Geographic, May 1975, p. 718.

18. William H. Isbell, "The Prehistoric Ground Drawings of Peru," Scientific American, October 1978: 140–53; "Solving the Mystery of Nazca," Fate, October 1980: 36–48.

19. Isbell, "The Prehistoric Ground Drawings," p. 142; "Solving the Mystery of Nazca," p. 45.

20. For details of the various theories of Nazca figure construction, see Nickell, "Nazca Drawings."

21. "The Big Picture," Scientific American, June 1983: 84.

22. Clark, The UFO Encyclopedia, vol. 2, pp. 17–39; Robert E. Bartholomew, "The Airship Hysteria of 1896–97," Skeptical Inquirer 24, no. 2 (Winter 1990): 171–81; Philip J. Klass, UFOs Explained (New York: Vintage Books, 1974), pp. 302–15.

23. Bartholomew, "Airship Hysteria," p. 171.

24. Clark, The UFO Encyclopedia, vol. 2, pp. 19–20.

25. Bartholomew, "Airship Hysteria," p. 174.

26. Klass, UFOs Explained, p. 303.

27. Bartholomew, "Airship Hysteria," p. 174.

28. Klass, UFOs Explained, p. 312.

29. Bartholomew, "Airship Hysteria," p. 177.

30. Jerome Clark, *UFO Encounters: Sightings, Visitations, and Investigations* (Lincolnwood, Ill.: Publications International, 1992), pp. 21–23.

31. Robert A. Baker and Joe Nickell, *Missing Pieces: How to Investigate Ghosts, UFOs, Psychics, and Other Mysteries* (Amherst, N.Y.: Prometheus Books, 1992), pp. 261–66.

32. Ibid., pp. 186–87; Clark, *UFO Encounters*, p. 78.

33. Quoted in Edward T. Ruppelt, *The Report on Unidentified Flying Saucers* (New York: Ace Books, 1956), p. 23.

34. Lionel Beer, "The Coming of the Saucers," in John Spencer and Hilary Evans, *Phenomenon: Forty Years of Flying Saucers* (New York: Avon Books, 1988), p. 23.

35. William K. Hartmann, "Historical Perspectives: Photos of UFOs," in *UFOs: A Scientific Debate,* eds. Carl Sagan and Thornton Page (New York: W. W. Norton, 1974), pp. 248, 253–54.

36. Baker and Nickell, *Missing Pieces*, p. 187.

37. Ruppelt, *The Report on Unidentified Flying Saucers*, p. 32.

38. J. Allen Hynek, *The UFO Experience* (New York: Ballantine Books, 1972), p. 59.

39. Allen Hendry, *The UFO Handbook* (Garden City, N.Y.: Doubleday, 1979), pp. 57–69.

40. Joe Nickell, *Camera Clues: A Handbook for Photographic Investigation* (Lexington: University Press of Kentucky, 1994), pp. 159–69.

41. Hynek, *The UFO Experience*, pp. 41–42.

42. Klass, *UFOs Explained*, pp. 42–44; Joe Nickell, *The Magic Detectives* (Amherst, N.Y.: Prometheus Books, 1989), pp. 19–21.

43. "UFO Fires on Louisville, Ky. Police Chopper," *Weekly World News*, May 4, 1993.

44. Joe Nickell, "UFO 'Dogfight': A Ballooning Tale," *Skeptical Inquirer* 18, no. 1 (Fall 1993): 3–4.

45. Ian Ridpath, "Flying Saucers Thirty Years On," *New Scientist* (July 14, 1977): 77–79.

46. Robert A. Baker in Baker and Nickell, *Missing Pieces*, p. 208.

47. This section appeared in a slightly earlier form as "The 'Hangar 18' Tales: A Folkloristic Approach," *Common Ground* (England) (June 1984): 2–10.

48. In Leonard Stringfield, *The UFO Crash/Retrieval Syndrome, Status Report II: New Sources, New Data* (Seguin, Tex.: Mutual UFO Network, 1980), p. 2.

49. Ibid.

50. See Jan Harold Brunvand, *The Study of American Folklore: An Introduction* (New York: W. W. Norton, 1978), pp. 5, 108.

51. Stuart Campbell, "Myth Theory of UFOs," in *The Encyclopedia of UFOs*, ed. Ronald D. Story (Garden City, N.Y.: Doubleday, 1980), pp. 240–41.

52. Jerome Clark, "Crashed Saucers: Another View," *UFO Report* 8, no. 1 (February 1980): 29.

53. Story, *Encyclopedia of UFOs*, p. 32. See also J. Allen Hynek and Jacques Vallee, *The Edge of Reality* (Chicago: Henry Regnery Co., 1975), pp. 181–83.

54. See *Skeptical Inquirer* 3, no. 4 (Summer 1979): 14, and 4, no. 2 (Winter 1979–80): 110.

55. Martin Gardner, *Fads & Fallacies in the Name of Science* (New York: Dover, 1957), p. 67.

56. Ibid., p. 62.

57. Jacques Vallee, *Passport to Magonia: From Folklore to Flying Saucers* (Chicago: Henry Regnery Co., 1969), pp. 60–61.

58. Ruppelt, *The Report on Unidentified Flying Saucers*, pp. 37–41.

59. Charles Berlitz and William L. Moore, *The Roswell Incident* (New York: Grosset & Dunlap, 1980), pp. 22–23.

60. Ibid., p. 33.

61. Ibid., pp. 28–36.

62. Ibid., p. 40.

63. Ibid., p. 65.

64. Ibid., p. 66

65. Ibid., pp. 65.

66. Ibid., pp. 74–89.

67. Ibid., pp. 16, 84.

68. Story, *Encyclopedia of UFOs*, p. 326.

69. Ibid.

70. Randle in Story, *Encyclopedia of UFOs*, p. 171.

71. Ibid. See also David Quintner, "Ex-Disney Man Would Build Flying Saucer Pod," *Toronto Star*, November 2, 1974, A4.

72. See, for example, Sheila Wolfe, "UFO Pilot Buried in Texas?" *Chicago Tribune*, June 3, 1973.

73. Leonard H. Stringfield, *Situation Red: The UFO Siege* (Garden City, N.Y.: Doubleday, 1977), p. 177.

74. Ibid., p. 179.

75. Clark, "Crashed Saucers," p. 52.

76. Stringfield, *The UFO Crash/Retrieval Syndrome*, pp. 10–12.

77. Jerome Clark, "Into the Wild Blue Yonder," *Fate*, June 1981: 103-109.

78. Joe Nickell and John F. Fischer, "The Crashed-saucer Forgeries," *International UFO Reporter* (March/April 1990).

79. Philip J. Klass, "UFO Researchers, USAF Discover What Really Crashed on Brazel Ranch," *Skeptics UFO Newsletter* (July 1994): 7.

80. Thompson, *Angels and Aliens*, p. 144.

81. Ibid.

82. Frank Edwards, *Strangest of All* (New York: Signet, 1962), pp. 102-103.

83. *South Bend Tribune* clippings, May 14, 1967; December 9, 1974; August 21, 1979.

84. Joe Nickell with John F. Fischer, *Secrets of the Supernatural* (Amherst, N.Y.: Prometheus Books, 1988), pp. 61-73.

85. From Clark, *The UFO Encyclopedia*, vol. 2, p. 23.

86. Ibid., vol. 1, p. 1.

87. Quoted in Robert A. Baker, *Hidden Memories: Voices and Visions from Within* (Amherst, N.Y.: Prometheus Books, 1992), p. 318.

88. Klass, *UFOs Explained*, p. 299.

89. Philip J. Klass, *UFO Abductions: A Dangerous Game* (Amherst, N.Y.: Prometheus Books, 1989), p. 26. Klass is citing James and Coral Lorenzen, leaders of Aerial Phenomena Research Organization.

90. Ibid., pp. 25-31; press release by Committee for the Scientific Investigation of Claims of the Paranormal (in response to a Paramount movie on the Walton case, *Fire in the Sky*), March 3, 1993.

91. Klass, *UFO Abductions*, pp. 31-32.

92. Ibid., pp. 32-37.

93. For accounts of the case see Stringfield, *Situation Red*, pp. 198-212; see also Otto Billig, *Flying Saucers—Magic in the Skies: A Psychohistory* (Cambridge, Mass.: Schenkman, 1982), pp. 24-30, 103-106, 146-49, 160.

94. Robert A. Baker, "Was Abduction a Dream?" *KASES File* (newsletter of Kentucky Association of Science Educators & Skeptics) (March 1994): 7. Dr. Baker notes that his findings essentially agree with those of Dr. Billig (n.93).

95. Ibid.

96. Robert A. Baker, personal communication, July 29, 1994.

97. "The Shirley Show," preliminary interview notes for April 1, 1993, taping, n.d.; copy faxed to Joe Nickell by Shannon Wray, March 31, 1993.

98. "The Shirley Show," aired April 15, 1993; Vallee, in Hynek and Vallee, *The Edge of Reality,* p. 250.

99. For more on the fantasy-prone personality, see Baker and Nickell, *Missing Pieces,* pp. 221–27.

100. Clark, *The UFO Encyclopedia,* vol. 1, pp. 1–14.

101. James Willwerth, "The Man from Outer Space," *Time,* April 25, 1994, p. 74.

102. Donna Bassett spoke at a symposium on the abduction phenomenon at the conference of the Committee for the Scientific Investigation of Claims of the Paranormal held in Seattle, June 23, 1994.

103. Willwerth, "The Man from Outer Space," p. 75.

104. Quoted in ibid.

105. Robert A. Baker, "The Aliens Among Us: Hypnotic Regression Revisited," *Skeptical Inquirer* 12, no. 2 (Winter 1987–88): 153.

106. Robert A. Baker, speaking at the CSICOP conference in Chicago, November 5, 1988, quoted in Klass, *UFO Abductions,* pp. 201–202.

107. Baker, "The Aliens Among Us," p. 157. Dr. Baker cites Whitley Strieber, *Communion: A True Story* (New York: William Morrow, 1987), pp. 172–75.

108. Graham Reed, *The Psychology of Anomalous Experience* (Boston: Houghton Mifflin, 1972), cited in Baker, "Aliens Among Us," pp. 158–59.

7

Monster Sightings

Since the most ancient times people have been fascinated—and perhaps repulsed or terrified—by "strange" creatures. Some of these were great denizens of land and sea, like mastodons and the blue whale. Others were the stuff legends were made of, like the griffin and centaur of Greek mythology or the fabled medieval creature called the unicorn. Still others were animal or human oddities, like five-legged cows or "siamese" (conjoined) twins.

Many of the latter "monsters" were reported in ancient times (and may have prompted notions of still more fanciful creatures). In Babylonia a deformed infant could portend calamities (one lacking a nose meant "affliction will seize upon the country . . .") or good tidings (one with three feet signaling "great prosperity in the land"). In Rome, Cicero (106–43 B.C.) reported the birth of a two-headed girl. And in the twelfth century a pair of "joined twins" lived to the age of thirty-four; when one died doctors proposed to separate them, since they were only joined at shoulders and hips, but her sister refused, saying: "As we came together, we will also go together," and she followed suit after approximately six hours.[1]

When I worked in a carnival in 1969,[2] I met "El Hoppo, the living Frog Boy"—as Robert Ripley reportedly dubbed him, latterly an aging, sickly man in a wheelchair, eking out a living in what was popularly styled a "freak show." Billed as "the human most resembling a frog," and depicted on a giant banner as a

221

grotesque, hybrid creature, inside the tent "Hoppy" was discovered merely to possess spindly arms and a distended stomach, the rest of his supposedly remarkable appearance being due to a pair of green leotards.

Mercifully, ideas about people who are merely different are changing, and so are ideas about "monsters" in general. In the following pages we will discuss "Man-Beasts" (real or potentially real creatures that may be our evolutionary kin), "Night Creatures" (who inhabit horror movies and haunt people's dreams), "Denizens of the Deep" (both the legendary and the real creatures of lakes and seas), and other monsters.

Man-Beasts

Reports of various manlike creatures—the legendary "wild man of the woods," as well as the Yeti of the Himalayas, Bigfoot of North America, and a creature known as "Loy's Ape" in South America—continue to raise questions and controversy about man's evolution. This section examines claims for each in turn.

"*Wild Men.*" As early as the sixteenth century, in the writings of Aldrovandus (1522–1605),[3] are found tales of several "wild men of the woods"—actually men and women covered with hair and reportedly discovered inhabiting forests and mountains. Among such creatures Aldrovandus describes a man and his children from the Canary Islands, with hair all over their bodies. Exhibited as curiosities in Bologna, the family would seem merely to suffer from a genetic disorder.

Other "wild men" tales may have been hoaxes. For example, the July 4, 1884, *Daily British Colonist* told how a hairy "half man, half beast," four-feet-seven-inches tall and weighing 127 pounds was captured in British Columbia, Canada, by railway men. They supposedly caught the creature beside the railroad tracks some twenty miles from Yale and fed it milk and berries. It was claimed that "Jacko," as they named it, was being kept in the Yale jail, but was to be taken to London to be exhibited. "But," according to Janet and Colin Bord, "no more was heard, and it was supposed that Jacko had died on the journey."

Acknowledging that "some researchers tend to feel that the whole affair was a hoax of some kind," the Bords assert: "This has not been proved, though."[4]

Actually, according to the *Encyclopedia of Hoaxes,* a later newspaper article—in the July 9, 1884, *Mainland Guardian*— exposed the story as a hoax, including the claim that the creature could be seen at the town jail. "The jailer there was particularly annoyed at having to fend off all the people who came to see the nonexistent Jacko," says the *Encyclopedia.* "Apparently the originator of the hoax was a reporter for the newspaper that ran the original story."[5]

Some of the wild men stories, if not hoaxes also, may describe real men—unkempt, long-haired hermits, or deranged people of one type or another. The Bords provide the following 1885 newspaper account which offers various interpretations.

WILD MAN IN THE MOUNTAINS

Much excitement has been created in the neighborhood of Lebanon, Oregon, recently over the discovery of a wild man in the mountains above that place, who is supposed to be the long lost John Mackentire. About four years ago Mackentire, of Lebanon, while out hunting in the mountains east of Albany with another man, mysteriously disappeared and no definite trace of him has ever yet been found. A few days ago a Mr. Fitzgerald and others, while hunting in the vicinity of the butte known as Bald Peter, situated in the Cascades, several miles above any settlement, saw a man resembling the long-lost man, entirely destitute of clothing, who had grown as hairy as an animal, and was a complete wild man.

He was eating the raw flesh of a deer when first seen, and they approached within a few yards before he saw them and fled. Isaac Banty saw this man in the same locality about two years ago. It is believed by many that the unfortunate man who was lost became deranged and has managed to find means of subsistence while wandering about in the mountains, probably finding shelter in some cave. A party of men is being organized to go in search of the man.[6]

Then, of course, there was the type of wild man frequently featured in a "freak show." According to Ricky Jay: "In our own century, and until very recently, carnivals and sideshows featured the 'geek.' Presented as a wild man, a sort of missing link not truly human, the geek would eat snakes and mice and bite the heads off live chickens and drink their blood." In fact, Jay says, "the act was often faked, relying on trickery for its effects." He adds: "Occasionally a conjurer could entice a *real* or 'glomming' geek, as legitimate counterparts were called, to do the act—usually by providing drink or drugs to the performer."[7]

Still other wild man accounts are supposed to represent proof of the Abominable Snowman or its North American counterpart, Bigfoot. (The Bords indicate they believe "Jacko" may have been a "young Bigfoot," and that the creature identified as the "lost John Mackentire" was more likely another of the imagined species.[8]) Are there giant, manlike creatures inhabiting isolated regions of the earth? Those who hunt such creatures—who style themselves "cryptozoologists" point out that previously unknown animals (like the mountain gorilla of the Belgian Congo, discovered in 1901[9]) do occasionally come to light.

Yeti. For more then three centuries, the Sherpa tribespeople who live in the region of the Himalayan Mountains between India and Tibet have expressed belief in a legendary wild man or apelike creature they call the *Yeti.* Because of its reputed foul smell, it eventually became known to westerners—through explorers and mountaineers—as the Abominable Snowman. According to one source, "He is tangled in a web of fantasy, religion, legend, chicanery, and commercialism." Not surprisingly, "The Yeti is a highly commercial legend, perhaps even Nepal's principal foreign currency earner."[10]

The Yeti are described as ranging from the height of a normal man up to eight feet tall, are covered with hair, and have a conical head and large feet. The creatures are said to be shy and therefore are only rarely seen and are never captured. Yeti relics, such as a pelt and scalp, when scientifically examined have turned out to come from, respectively, a bear and a Nepalese serow (a chamois goat). Peter Byrne, described as a "colorful" explorer and Yeti seeker, tells how he enticed a monk at an isolated monastery to become intoxicated so Byrne could steal a finger from a mummified "Yeti paw." Tested many years later, it yielded "inconclusive" results but was thought most likely to have been human.[11]

One of the earliest sightings of a "wild man" in the region was made in 1925 by a Greek photographer named N. A. Tombazi, who only glimpsed the figure and made no pictures. He said he did not believe in the "delicious fairy tales" about the Yeti, and years later offered a theory that the "wild man" could have been simply a hermit or ascetic. As Daniel Cohen comments in *The Encyclopedia of Monsters*: "There are Buddhist and Hindu ascetics who seek out the desolation of high places. They can live at altitudes of fifteen thousand feet and can train themselves to endure cold and other hardships that would kill the average person." Cohen adds: "They can and do walk about naked or nearly so in the frigid mountain air. So Tombazi might really have seen a wandering ascetic, as he first thought."[12]

A 1986 photograph taken by British physicist Anthony Wooldridge near the India-Tibet border fared no better. Wooldridge and others believed they had captured the first Yeti on photographic film. Unfortunately, subsequent photo-surveying evidence proved—by the British physicist's own admission—"beyond a reasonable doubt that what I had believed to be a stationary, living creature was, in reality, a rock."[13]

Alleged encounters by Nepalese children are intriguing but ultimately no more convincing than Western children's reports of poltergeists or other entities. For example,

One Sherpa girl, Lakhpa Domani, described an incident to a Peace Corps volunteer, William Weber, who was working in the area of Machherma village in the Everest region. The girl said she was sitting near a stream tending her yaks when she heard a noise and turned round to confront a huge apelike creature with large eyes and prominent cheekbones. It was covered in black and red-brown hair. It seized her and carried her to the water, but her screams seem to have disconcerted the creature and it dropped her. Then it attacked two of her yaks, killing one with blows, the other by seizing its horns and breaking its neck. The incident was reported to the local police and footprints were found. Weber says: "What motive could there possibly have been for a hoax? My conclusion was that the girl was telling the truth."[14]

But Weber's view of motives for hoaxes—like those of other laypersons, as we have seen throughout this book—is naive: The girl might simply have been looking for attention.

As in the foregoing case, footprints are the most tangible and most common form of evidence for the Abominable Snowman's existence. Unfortunately the "footprints" photographed by Frank Smythe in 1937 reveal that the trail "was indisputedly a bear's,"[15] and the celebrated photos by mountaineer Eric Shipton, taken in 1951, depicted the trail of a mountain goat.[16] Confusion regarding the tracks can be caused by several factors, such as snow melting, causing the tracks to enlarge and become distorted before refreezing.[17]

The noted mountain climber Sir Edmund Hillary (who, together with his Sherpa guide, Tenzing Norkay, was the first to conquer the Himalaya's Mt. Everest) conducted an expedition to either document or debunk the fabled creature. Hillary was accompanied by Marlin Perkins (the late, beloved host of TV's "Wild Kingdom") and others. Hillary's team searched the area and reviewed the evidence for the Snowman's existence, including the various "relics" mentioned earlier. The outcome was that Hillary denounced the whole concept of the Yeti as nonsense. Monster enthusiasts were angry, but Hillary's prestige and background gave him credibility. As a consequence, after 1960, according to Cohen, "interest shifted to other monsters, particularly Bigfoot in the United States and Canada."[18]

Bigfoot. Like the Yeti, Bigfoot is described as a large, hairy, apelike creature, equated with the legendary American Indian Sasquatch (or "hairy man") which is said to live in caves in British Columbia and the Pacific Northwest.

Also like the Yeti, Bigfoot leaves behind large footprints, varying considerably in size and structure, even possessing anywhere from two toes to six—exactly the variety one would expect from independent hoaxers.[19] Indeed, just how easy it is to perpetrate a hoax involving a set of Bigfoot tracks is illustrated by a case that took place in 1930 near Mount St. Helens, Washington. Some people who had been picking berries returned to their cars to discover huge, manlike tracks circling the area. Excitedly, they reported the tracks to nearby forest rangers, but for more than half a century the tracks remained a mystery. Then in 1982 Rent Mullins, a retired logger who had been working for the Forest Service at the time the tracks appeared, confessed that he had been involved in faking the giant footprints. As a prank, he had carved from a piece of wood a pair of nine-by-seventeen-inch feet. A friend of Mullins, Bill Lambert, had then strapped them onto his own feet and tromped about the area where the berry pickers' cars were parked.[20]

In recent years, much more realistic footprints have appeared, curiously following extensive published descriptions of what genuine Bigfoot tracks should be like. Notably, in 1982, oversized footprints, complete with dermal ridges (the ridges that on the hands produce fingerprints), were discovered in the Mill Creek watershed of Oregon's Blue Mountains. The discovery was made by a new Forest Service patrolman, Paul Freeman, and were hailed by cryptozoologists as providing startling new proof of Bigfoot's existence. However, investigation at the time by the U.S. Forest Service, and later by noted Bigfoot authority Michael Dennett, turned up considerable evidence that the tracks were fakes, part of an elaborate hoax.

Forest Service wildlife biologist Rodney L. Johnson visited the Mill Creek site the day immediately following the discovery and noted that the pine needles and other fine forest litter had been brushed away before the imprints were made and that the tracks were insufficiently deep for a heavy Bigfoot-type creature. Johnson also reported that "in several cases, it appeared that the foot may have been rocked from side to side to make the track," and that the "toes on some tracks appeared wider" from one print to another. Furthermore Johnson observed that dermal ridges were suspiciously clear in areas of the foot that would be expected to be worn and even calloused. Finally, Johnson found that the stride (indicated by the distance between footprints) "did not change with slope," as would be expected, and that there was "no sign of heel or toe slippage on the steep gradient."[21]

Other evidence soon mounted against the tracks' authenticity. A professional tracker was brought in on the case but despite "excellent" conditions for observation and an exhaustive search of the vicinity failed to discover any continuity of the trail beyond the immediate impressions. The tracker, Joel Hardin, stated that "the tracks appeared and disappeared on the trail with no sign [traces] leading to or away from the area." He concluded the tracks were a hoax.[22] Moreover, Dennett conducted a background investigation on Freeman and discovered that not only did he have an astonishing propensity for discovering Bigfoot tracks and other traces but claimed to have had at least two face-to-face encounters with the creature. Astonishingly, Freeman, who reportedly once worked for an orthopedic shoe business, where he could have learned the techniques of making molds of feet, actually admits to having previously made false Sasquatch footprints.[23]

Dennett commissioned a cobbler to make him a set of "feet" complete with dermal ridges (the cobbler used one of his customers with size-16 feet to produce the model). Dennett then made Mill Creek-like impressions.[24]

Another hoax, skeptics say, is behind Roger Patterson's famed 16mm color film taken in October 1967, although it has been called "one of the most momentous events in the annals of Bigfoot hunting."[25] Patterson, a longtime Bigfoot enthusiast who had frequently "discovered" the creature's tracks, was riding horseback with another Bigfoot buff in northern California's Bluff Creek area. Suddenly they encountered a Sasquatch which frightened their horses, causing them to rear. Patterson jumped clear as his horse fell, and grabbed the movie camera from his saddlebag. He briefly managed to film the creature that strode away, a few frames recording its hairy, pendulous breasts that identify it as a female of the legendary species. Although one mystery-promoting book proclaims the film was never "proved to be a fake,"[26] it is important to note that, as proponents have the burden of proof in such cases, it was never proved genuine. In fact, the stride of the creature seems exaggerated, "almost,"

Cohen states, "as if a bad actor were trying to simulate a monster's walk." Dr. John Napier of the Smithsonian Institution, an expert in primate biology and anatomy, seemed to sum up the opinion of many when he quipped, "I couldn't see the zipper."[27]

Certainly there have been hoaxes involving persons dressing in realistic fur suits. Just such a hoax occurred near Mission, British Columbia, Canada, on May 1, 1977. Janet and Colin Bord's *Bigfoot Casebook* provides a photograph of the suit, modeled by Bigfoot investigator Dennis Gates. The hoax came only a few months after four Cashton, Wisconsin, youths admitted to a similar stunt. With the help of the others, one of them dressed up as a Bigfoot-type creature and affixed wooden Bigfoot "feet" to his shoes.[28] Yet another such hoax occurred in 1986 when a Pennsylvania man donned fake fur and a "wolfman" mask and alarmed nighttime drivers by appearing suddenly in their car headlights.[29]

A report of a Bigfoot could cause a wave of hysteria, as occurred after a nine-foot-tall monster with shining eyes was reported in the vicinity of Silver Lakes, Michigan, by a fruit picker named Gordon Brown. As the Bords relate it:

> The day following Gordon Brown's experience, more locals saw it and heard its typical "baby crying" noise, and on 11 June three 13-year-old girls out walking in daylight were confronted by the creature on a lonely road in Silver Creek township. Joyce Smith fainted, and Patsy and Gail Clayton were rooted to the spot with fear. Apparently satisfied with the impression it had made, the monster lumbered off into the bushes. Overnight Sister Lakes changed from a rural community of 500 inhabitants into a teeming tourist center. Hundreds of "hunters" and sensation-seekers flocked into the area, every shop ran a Monster Sale, cafes sold Monster Burgers, the local radio station played Monster Music interrupted by the latest monster reports, and a double-bill horror show played at the movie house. One shopkeeper advertised a special monster-hunting kit. For $7.95 the keen hunter could buy a light, a net, a baseball bat and, to clinch matters, a mallet and a stake. Teenagers were prone to dress in old fur coats and goof around in public places, but surprisingly no one was hurt, though Sheriff Robert Dool said:

"I had to order hunters away because it's getting mighty dangerous; three thousand strangers prowling about at night with guns. . . ." Such circumstances are not likely to produce high-quality reports, since people are keyed up and expect to see Bigfoot. In this state of mind they are very likely to see something which they interpret as Bigfoot but which someone unaffected by the atmosphere realizes is nothing of the sort.[30]

(Again recall from chapter 2 the case of the one hundred sightings of the non-existent panda.)

Among the most elaborate hoaxes must surely be counted that of the Minnesota Iceman, a Sasquatch-type creature encased in a block of ice and exhibited at fairs and carnivals. Viewing it through the ice's foggy surface in 1968, two famous crypto-zoologists, Ivan Sanderson and Bernard Heuvelmans, were impressed. Heuvelmans thought the creature was "most probably" a Neanderthal man who had been living fewer than five years before. Alas, the creature was only a rubber figure crafted by Howard Ball, a top Disneyland model-maker. (I once saw the creature as a separate side-show exhibit at a fair. The ice had partially melted away, exposing part of the figure. I felt it: it was obviously rubber.[31])

Hoaxes and questionable reports aside, the fact remains that no credible capture of the creature has ever been recorded, nor has anyone ever recovered a carcass or even partial skeleton. Insists Cohen, "Surely the creatures die."[32]

"*Loys's Ape.*" Not to neglect *South America*, there is the strange, controversial photograph of an apelike creature photographed in the 1920s by Francis de Loys. Here are his own words from the *Illustrated London News*:

> I was exploring at the time the untrodden forests in the neighborhood of the Tarra River, itself an affluent of the Rio Catatumbo in the Motilones districts of Venezuela and Colombia, and I came across two animals the nature of which was new not only to myself but to the native woodsmen of my party. At a bend of a western minor affluent of the Tarra River these two animals broke upon the exploring party then at rest and, owing to the violence of their attitude had to be met at the

point of a rifle. One of the two was shot dead at very close range; the other one, unfortunately wounded, managed to escape and disappeared in the jungle, the great thickness of which prevented its recovery. The animal shot dead was examined, sat into position on a packing case, measured, and immediately photographed from a distance of 10 ft. Its skin was afterwards removed and its skull and jaws were cleaned and preserved. The hardships met with by the party on their long journey across the forest, however, prevented the final preservation of either the skin or the bones.

At first examination it was found that the specimen was that of an ape of uncommon size, whose features were entirely different from those of the species already known as inhabiting the country.[33]

Loys said the creature was 1.5 meters (over five feet) tall and weighed 50 kg (over 112 lbs.). He added that it was "entirely devoid of any trace of a tail." When a French anthropologist received Loys's report and accompanying photographs (showing the animal seated on a crate and propped up with a stick), he promptly proclaimed it a new species of ape and christened it *Ameranthropoides loysi*.[34]

In response, Sir Arthur Keith, Fellow of the Royal Society, denounced Loys's specimen as a hoax. He found it suspicious that Loys had lost the evidence, failed to take suitable notes of the animal's characteristics, and neglected to photograph the animal with something of known size to indicate scale. "If it was genuine," Sir Arthur said, "there would have been a man in the picture for comparison." It was his view that the creature was simply a large spider monkey, with its tail either removed or hidden by the crate. That remains the prevailing view of primate biologists.[35]

Loys's "new species" of ape—like the legendary "wild man," Yeti, and Bigfoot—intrigues us especially because of its putative kinship with us. For the same reason, certain other notable hoaxes have captured the popular imagination for a time, like the Cardiff Giant (a supposedly fossilized man, unearthed in 1869) and the Piltdown Skull (allegedly that of the "missing link" between ape and man, "discovered" during 1911–15).[36] No doubt others will follow.

Night Creatures

They inhabit the night—at least they haunt the nightmares of those inclined to believe in such creatures. They are werewolves, vampires, and zombies, supernaturally monstrous manlike beings of frightening aspect who are included here not because they are widely perceived as real but rather in the interest of completeness. (Hence their treatment will be relatively brief.)

Werewolves. The term *werewolf* means literally "man-wolf" (from the Old English *wer*, "man," and *wulf*, "wolf") and describes either a human being who has been turned into a wolf by sorcery or one who makes the transformation (whether by will or otherwise) from time to time. In European folk belief the werewolf preyed on humankind each night but returned to human form at the light of dawn. It could only be killed by shooting it with a silver bullet.[37]

Werewolves were a part of the witch craze of the sixteenth and seventeenth centuries. For example, in France in the early 1500s, three men were put on trial for transforming themselves into werewolves and killing sheep. They were convicted and burned at the stake.[38] Near the end of the century, in 1598, a French beggar named Jacques Roulet was also tried as a werewolf. Discovered hiding in the bushes near the mutilated body of a teenage boy, half-naked and smeared with blood, Roulet admitted to the murder; however, invoking a popular belief of the time, he blamed a magic ointment that he said had caused him to become a wolf (whether physically or mentally is unclear). Although he was sentenced to death, on appeal the Parlement of Paris instead committed him to an insane asylum for two years.[39]

The concept that a human could turn into a wolf seems to have originated with the simple wearing of an animal robe for warmth, with people coming to believe that the man wearing the skin took on the animal's powers. Eventually the popular imagination conceived of bewitched men who, under the full moon's irresistible power, grew hairy coats, fangs, and claws and otherwise took on the aspect of a beast. The wolf was a popular form of such a metamorphosis in Europe.

In fact, there are two medical conditions that undoubtedly

helped foster belief in werewolves. One is a disease, a hormonal disorder known as Cushing's Syndrome, which can produce enlargement of the hands and face, together with rapid and copious growth of hair on the latter and an accompanying "acute emotional agitation." According to Rachleff, "Individuals afflicted with this disease, either because of ostracism or because of the psychotic ramifications of their illness, were, in the past, forced to live apart from society."[40] Then there is the psychiatric disorder known as lycanthropy—the delusion that one has been transformed into a wolf—which can cause one to become sadistic and even engage in cannibalistic or necrophilic behavior.[41] No doubt the murderer mentioned earlier, Roulet, suffered from lycanthropy.

The moon is not a factor (except perhaps a psychological one) in cases of "real" werewolves,[42] but something of the concept nevertheless survives in the popular notion of "moon madness." Also known as the lunar effect, it is the supposed influence the moon exerts on people's behavior. As psychologist Terence Hines explains:

> It is especially held that the full moon accentuates or increases the probability of all sorts of odd and troublesome behavior. Suicides, admissions to mental hospitals, arrests for public drunkenness, and crimes of various sorts are all said to increase when the moon is full. It is also widely believed, especially among maternity ward personnel, that more babies are born when the moon is full than during the other phases of the moon. The moon's gravitational influence is usually the mechanism used to explain the alleged effects of the full moon. After all, proponents say, the moon's gravity influences the oceans, which are largely water. Therefore, since the human body contains a great deal of water, the moon's gravity must also influence the human body. This in some unspecified way results in moon madness. But in fact the moon's gravitational influence on the human body is infinitesimal—equivalent to the weight of a single mosquito being added to the weight of a normal individual. Gravity is a weak force. As you hold this book, you are outpulling the entire planet Earth.[43]

According to Hines, however, when the proponents' studies are scrutinized "methodological or statistical flaws have appeared that invalidate the conclusion," and the overall data on the effect "shows overwhelmingly that the moon's phase has no effect on human behavior."[44]

I have never seen a werewolf *per se*, but during my stint in a carnival I did witness the sideshow exhibit billed as "Atasha the Gorilla Girl." Inside the tent the spectators saw "Atasha" standing at the rear of a large cage. As the carney "talker" chanted a magic spell, Atasha slowly took on the features of a gorilla— a very realistic one—which suddenly rushed forward out of the unlocked cage! This caused the spectators to fall back in fear, some of them running wildly from the tent—a fact which did not go unnoticed by the milling crowd outside, and which gave a boost to the next round of ticket sales.

Although the metamorphosis occurred before spectators' eyes, it was nevertheless a magic trick, a fact signalled cleverly at the beginning of each show. Atasha, the talker said glibly, was in "a legerdemain condition." This seemed to go right over the heads of most people, but *legerdemain* (French for "light of hand") is a term indicating a magician's trickery. How was the apparent transformation done? A magician would answer, "Very well, thank you." Seriously, the secret is given in various magicians' texts,[45] and perhaps that is where it should remain for all but the most persistently curious.

Vampires. Another creature of the night is the legendary vampire, "a living corpse or soulless body that comes from its burial place and drinks the blood of the living."[46] Although belief in vampires is found worldwide, it is typically a Slavic concept, hence the setting of Bram Stoker's *Dracula* in Romania. Indeed, Stoker's novel was inspired by the horrific deeds of a real-life Romanian nobleman, as we shall see.

Although tales of the "living dead" can be traced back to ancient Greece, and some evidence suggests that vampire legends derive from the concept of the earlier werewolf, the quintessential Count Dracula as portrayed in Stoker's novel derives from the Romanian Vlad Tepes. Colin and Damon Wilson provide a brief historical sketch that helps to clarify the derivation:

For more than four centuries the Turks had dominated eastern Europe, marching in and out of Transylvania, Walachia, and Hungary and even conquering Constantinople in 1453. Don John of Austria defeated them at the great sea battle of Lepanto (1571), but it was their failure to capture Vienna after a siege in 1683 that caused the breakup of the Ottoman Empire. During the earlier stages of this war between Europe and Turkey, the man whose name has become synonymous with vampirism—Dracula, or Vlad the Impaler—struck blow after blow against the Turks, until they killed and beheaded him in 1477.

Vlad Tepes (the Impaler), king of Walachia (1456–62, 1476–77), was, as his nickname implies, a man of sadistic temperament, whose greatest pleasure was to impale his enemies (which meant anyone against whom he had a grudge) on pointed stakes; the stake—driven into the ground—was inserted into the anus (or, in the case of women, the vagina), and the victim was allowed to impale himself slowly under his own weight. (Vlad often had the point blunted to make the agony last longer.) In his own time he was known as Dracula, which means "son of a dragon" or "son of the Devil." It is estimated that Dracula had about one hundred thousand people impaled during the course of his lifetime. When he conquered Brasov, in Transylvania, he had all its inhabitants impaled on poles, then gave a feast among the corpses. When one nobleman held his nose at the stench, Vlad sent for a particularly long pole and had him impaled. When he was a prisoner in Hungary, Vlad was kept supplied with birds, rats, and toads, which he impaled on small stakes. A brave and fearless warrior, he was finally killed in battle—or possibly assassinated by his own soldiers—and his head sent to Constantinople. Four hundred twenty years later, in 1897, he was immortalized by Bram Stoker as the sinister Count Dracula, no longer a sadistic maniac, but a drinker of blood.[47]

In addition to this real-life model and earlier tales of the "undead," the concept of vampirism is also indebted to at least two other factors. First is the disease known as *hemothymia*, characterized by a bizarre craving for blood. There are even instances of murder apparently carried out purely for the thrill of watching blood spill from a wound.[48] Second, there is the South

American *desmodus rotundus*, or vampire bat, a tiny furry mammal with sharp teeth that is actually able to "siphon blood from a sleeping victim" (that usually being an animal rather than a human). This is the source for the legendary vampire's ability to transform himself into a bat.[49]

Even so, occultists like to suggest that vampires might really exist. The Wilsons cite the story of an eighteenth-century Serbian man, Peter Plogojowitz, whose body was exhumed and, except for a somewhat sunken nose, "was completely fresh" and even had "some fresh blood in his mouth."[50] However, just such characteristics are frequently said to describe the "incorruptible" bodies of saints, for example, that of St. Sperandia (1216–1276), which was found intact well after her burial and exuded a "blood-fluid."[51] Roman Catholics would not appreciate the suggestion that their saints were actually vampires! In contrast to the corpse of St. Sperandia, which was exhumed two years after her death, that of Plogojowitz had been interred little more than ten weeks.[52] (Actually, bodies occasionally are found "incorruptible"—not only those of vampires and saints but also ordinary people—due to a variety of reasons.[53])

The claim that Plogojowitz was a vampire supposedly came from nine people who had died following a one-day illness and who "said publicly," according to an account of 1725, "while they were yet alive, but on their deathbed, that the above-mentioned Peter Plogojowitz, who had died ten weeks earlier, had come to them in their sleep, laid himself on them, and throttled them, so that they would have to give up the ghost."[54] In fact, the evidence suggests that the villagers died of a plague,[55] that Plogojowitz's imagined role came from a dream that his son had of his father visiting him (the son was one of the victims of the contagious disease),[56] and that rumor, hysteria, and the prevalence of fanatical belief in vampires in the area did the rest.

Zombies. Still another creature of the night is the zombie, a mindless, walking corpse. An element of the Haitian cult of *vodun*, or voodoo, the zombie (or zombi) is a human being whose soul is "stolen" by a practitioner of black magic:

The sorcerer digs up the body after its interment, using it as he wishes. It is believed that if the zombi is allowed to eat food flavored with salt, or, in some districts, if he is allowed to look on the sea, he will return to his grave. It is held that, if necessary, a zombi can be turned into an animal, slaughtered, and the meat sold in the market, whence derives the assertion often met with among Haitian peasants in documenting belief that they have not only seen zombis but have bought their flesh. This, it is thought, can be distinguished by the fact that such meat will spoil much more readily than ordinary meat.[57]

The zombie legend was popularized by Hollywood with the 1932 movie *White Zombie*, starring Bela Lugosi. Since then it has rivaled in popularity the vampire, the undead mummy (played by Boris Karloff), and the Frankenstein monster. According to the Wilsons, "No one who has seen a film like *King of the Zombies* can ever forget the shot of a zombie marching on like a robot while someone fires bullet after bullet into its chest."[58] But what about "real" zombies?

Stories about zombies are difficult to investigate. Many are anecdotal accounts similar to Elvis Presley sightings or tales of angelic visitations or extraterrestrial encounters. Some investigators insist that persons targeted as enemies may be "zombified" by the use of some "quick-acting poison,"[59] whereas Owen S. Rachleff, in *The Occult Conceit*, insists: "The cataleptic status achieved by some of the celebrants in voodoo sometimes becomes so severe as to be permanent."[60] Yet another theory, one advanced by the director of Port-au-Prince's Psychiatric Center, holds that so-called zombies have merely been drugged and so enslaved as agricultural workers.[61]

It may be that, as with reports of other strange creatures, not all accounts of zombies have a single, simple explanation. Least likely, of course, is the supernatural notion that zombies really are the "walking dead."

Denizens of the Deep

Among the remote areas of the earth, the seas and large lakes offer sanctuaries for fabled creatures like mermaids, sea serpents, and lake monsters of the Loch Ness variety. Each of these has certainly caught the popular imagination and is worthy of a concise discussion here.

Mermaids. In the Middle Ages there was widespread belief in the mermaid (after the Middle English words *mer*, "sea," and *maide*, short for *maiden*, meaning "an unmarried girl or woman"). The fabled sea-dwelling female was especially common to the folklore of maritime Europe and was invariably a supernatural creature. According to *Funk & Wagnalls Standard Dictionary of Folklore, Mythology, and Legend:*

> Mermaids are usually depicted as having the head and body of a woman to the waist, and a tapering fish body and tail instead of legs. A carving on Puce Church in Gironde, France, however, shows a young mermaid with lower body divided and two tapering tails instead of legs. They live in an undersea world of splendor and riches, but have been known to assume human form and come ashore to markets and fairs. They often lure mariners to their destruction, and are said to gather the souls of the drowned and cage them in their domain. Those who seek fact underlying every belief have offered the manatee or the dugong, warm-blooded sea mammals, as the original for the mermaid, relying on analogy more than on sailors' ability to differentiate between a seacow and a fish-woman.[62]

Although obviously a purely legendary being, the mermaid has nevertheless been placed on exhibit—albeit by showmen and hucksters. What is typically displayed as a mermaid (or occasionally some other bogus creature) is a type of fake known among hoax experts as a "Jenny Haniver," made by joining parts of different species by taxidermy. The most famous "mermaid" of this type—a composite made by grafting the upper part of a monkey onto the lower half of a fish—first surfaced in 1822, being alleged to have come from Calcutta, India, three years previously. P. T. Barnum obtained the fake in 1842 and christened it the "Fejee Mermaid," exhibiting it for many years. His advertisements pictured it as a living creature in its alleged native state. (Now in "rather decrepit condition," it reposes in the Barnum Museum in Bridgeport, Connecticut.[63])

Another such fake, known as the Dorchester Mermaid, was exhibited in that city by Melvin T. Freeman (formerly Boston's assistant water commissioner). This bogus creature also came from the Orient, "where manufacture of mermaids seems to have been a profitable business for a time."[64]

Sea Serpents. That there are great denizens of the deep no one can dispute. There is the giant manta ray (frequently twenty feet across), the whale shark (sixty or more feet long), and still other great creatures (without even mentioning the blue whale).[65]

While there are numerous early accounts of great "sea serpents," often described as having multiple humps, it is usually difficult to theorize about what was actually seen. In one instance it may have been a school of porpoises viewed at a distance, or in another simply the product of an overworked imagination or even a deliberate tall tale. The lack of photographs is one problem, the absence of a single authenticated remnant another.

Sometimes the identity of a sea monster can be inferred, as illustrated by the following story. During World War II, a handful of shipwrecked members of the Royal Navy and Indian Army found themselves adrift in a small raft in the remote South Atlantic. After a few days sharks appeared, then after three more days vanished. In their place appeared a great monster with huge tentacles. At length, it snatched one of the Indian men, "hugging him like a bear." The others tried to save him but to no avail, as the creature slowly sank away with its prey.

Is the story true? If so, according to one source, "Today it is possible to speculate that the voracious monster was a giant squid, perhaps the most fiendishly equipped of all the great marine creatures that lie hidden beneath the oceans." Thirty-foot specimens which have floundered on Newfoundland's shores are "probably relative midgets."[66]

I mentioned the lack of authenticated remnants. In fact, there are many reports and even photographs of *apparent* carcasses such as "the remains of an enormous monster that came ashore" at St. Augustine, Florida, in 1896. Noting that it could "scarcely afford the expense" of sending a scientist to Florida to view it, Smithsonian Institution experts decided that the badly mutilated, six-to-seven-ton creature was a whale. However, the photos, a detailed description, and preserved bits of the reportedly *invertebrate* creature were examined seventy-five years later and determined to have been a giant octopus, although that conclusion was largely ridiculed by the scientific community.[67]

Many of the sea monsters, including one that washed ashore in Scotland in 1808 and known as the Stronsa Beast, have turned out to be the rotting carcasses of basking sharks. According to *Arthur C. Clarke's Mysterious World*: "The dead basking shark decays in the most deceiving manner. First the jaws, which are attached by only a small piece of flesh, drop off leaving what looks like a small skull and thin serpentlike neck. Then, as only the upper half of the tail fin carries the spine, the lower half rots away leaving the lower fins which look like legs." As this source concludes, "Time after time this monsterlike relic has been the cause of a sea serpent 'flap.' "[68]

Quite a different creature was the source of giant, three-toed footprints first discovered along a Florida beach near Clearwater in 1948 but reappearing from time to time over the years. Zoologist/cryptozoologist Ivan T. Sanderson pronounced the tracks genuine, made, he opined, by a type of giant penguin, which he dubbed "Florida Three-Toes." Yet witnesses who claimed they had seen the strange creature said it had a "head shaped like a hog's." The mystery went unsolved until free-lance writer Jan Kirby interviewed a Clearwater businessman named Toni Signorini about the tracks.

Signorini admitted to Kirby that he and his late partner, Al Williams, had perpetrated the hoax. Williams was inspired by some photos of dinosaur tracks he saw in *National Geographic* magazine and, with Signorini's assistance, attempted to fashion a set of fake feet out of concrete. After several failed attempts they turned to a foundry worker who made them a pair of cast-iron monster feet, measuring eleven by fourteen inches and weighing about thirty pounds. These were affixed to a pair of black sneakers. Although they were heavy, Signorini discovered that by "swinging" his feet he could accomplish strides of up to six feet. His biggest problem with the heavy shoes, he explained, was: "I had to be very careful not to get out of the boat too soon when Al rowed me to the beach."

According to monster investigator Michael Dennett,

> Signorini's story is unquestionably authentic. Not only does his narrative fit the events, it turns out that both Williams and he had revealed the story to numerous people over the years. Moreover, his cast-iron feet are identical to the plaster casts of "Florida Three-Toes" held by Sanderson in 1948 newspaper photos.[69]

Lake monsters. Some of the world's large lakes are reputed to host sea-serpent-like creatures, the most famous of which is "Nessie," the Loch Ness Monster. A creature was reported in the great Scottish lake as far back as the sixth century when St. Columba supposedly saved a man's life by commanding the attacking monster to depart. (Such pious legends of saints—some of whom could fly, others being able to live without eating—are today given little credence.[70]) The extent of subsequent encounters is disputed before 1933, when the modern wave of sightings began.

On May 2 of that year the *Inverness Courier* carried an account by an anonymous correspondent (actually one Alexander Campbell), "Strange Spectacle in Loch Ness," telling how an unnamed couple had seen the waters of the loch disturbed by "no ordinary denizen of the depths" at least "judging by the state of the water in the affected area." It later turned out that Campbell's account was greatly exaggerated: that only one of the two persons had seen anything, and that the one who *had,* described it as seeming to be caused "by two ducks fighting."[71]

Nevertheless, more "sightings" soon followed—albeit some were of a floating log or school of fish. The monster was variously described: at lengths of 6 to 125 feet, with shapes ranging from that of a great eel to a creature with a hump or humps (up to nine), and in colors including silver, gray, blue-black, black, and brown. It was also endowed—or not—with such features as fins, flippers, mane, tusks, or horns.[72]

Hoaxers have been attracted to the monster along with tourists. One hoax involved the appearance of monster tracks, curiously resembling those of a hippopotamus. Indeed, they had been produced using a cast made from a hippo's hoof![73] Fake photos have abounded, including the classic Nessie photo: the so-called surgeon's photograph, taken in April 1934 by London gynecologist Robert Wilson; in 1994 two reseachers learned the photo had been made by photographing a model (constructed from a fourteen-inch toy submarine, some plastic wood for the head and neck, some gray paint, and a lead ballast strip).[74]

Other photos may not be hoaxes but instead depict some natural object such as driftwood or a swimming deer. A motion picture film taken in 1960 by monster hunter Tim Dinsdale was analyzed by the Royal Air Force's Joint Air Reconnaissance Intelligence Center (JARIC), which concluded that the moving object, seen from a mile away, could be a motorboat. Indeed, Dinsdale reported the object was a reddish-brown color, to which Ronald Binns says in The Loch Ness Mystery Solved: "An object which appears reddish brown at such a distance is clearly something which is relatively brightly coloured. Reddish brown is a reasonable colour for a motor boat, but an unusual one for a Loch Ness monster."[75]

An underwater photo taken in 1972 by Robert Rines and a crew from his Academy of Applied Science garnered considerable media attention for its supposed depiction of a "flipper" from an unknown creature. As it happens, the computer-enhanced pictures were found to have been "significantly altered to give the impression of the flipperlike objects that appear in the published version."[76] The unaltered pictures could depict virtually anything. In addition, expert review of the academy's sonar evidence, which Rines claimed as support for his interpretation of the "flipper" photograph, discredited the supposed proof of a lake monster's existence.[77]

Despite the extensive searches over the years, no authentic trace of the monster has ever been discovered. As Time magazine once reported, "There is hardly enough food in the loch to support such leviathans," and, "in any case, there would have to be at least twenty animals in a breeding herd" in order for the species to have continued to reproduce over the centuries.[78]

The same problems apply to other lake monsters. That includes the Lough Leane (Ireland) aquatic monster and the sea serpent Morgawr—both known from photographs depicting "strikingly similar" monsters and suspected of being "shot using the same technique, that of a sculpted plasticine monster stuck onto a pane of glass in front of the camera."[79] Other lake monsters include "Champ" (Lake Champlain, New York-Vermont), "Manipogo" (Lake Winnipegosis, Manitoba), "Ogopogo" (Lake Okanagan, British Columbia), and "Issie" (Lake Ikeda, Japan).[80]

Other Monsters

Many additional monsters remain besides those already discussed. For one example, consider the Jersey Devil, a phantom monster also known as the Leeds' Devil. Some indicate the latter name came from its origin at Leeds' Point in Southern New Jersey, others that it came from the woman who gave birth to it in 1735 (a Mother Leeds). In any event legend states that the woman had too many children (twelve by one count) and said if she had one more she wished it would be a devil. It was: born with the hooves and head of a horse (or dog or ram), batlike wings, and a long forked tail, it became a bogeyman of the southeastern New Jersey area known as "the Pine Barrens." Supposedly in 1740 an exorcism was performed that was allegedly good for a century; in 1840 it returned, feeding on sheep and chickens.[81] It left its footprints across roof tops and in other places of difficult access (reminiscent of "the devil's hoofprints" discussed early in chapter 4). As well, "its cries [were] often heard; if shades were left undrawn at night, it would come and look in people's windows; it was seen sporting in the surf with mermaids, or sitting gibbering on chimneys."[82]

In January 1909, the Jersey Devil was revived as a hoax by one Norman Jefferies, the publicity manager for a private Philadelphia museum, who was "much in disrepute in newspaper offices in that city because of previous stunts."[83] First, there appeared in a small-town paper in south Jersey a report of a new sighting of the legendary creature by a local farmer's wife. Then the Associated Press disseminated the story, whereupon

[r]eputable citizens described in detail his horrific form, the
great wings, the frenzied countenance, half human and half
animal, the long tail, the eleven feet, the deadly vapors which
were exhaled in a mixture of fire and smoke. The fiend was
ubiquitous. He was seen all over the southern part of the State.
He was seen in the rural parts of Pennsylvania, Delaware and
Maryland, all on the same night.[84]

Soon the devil had been trapped and, still alive, was put
on display by Jeffries at the Arch Street Museum. Crowds
gathered and (like the "Gorilla Girl" mentioned earlier), "When
the curtain of the devil's cage was drawn, the beast with a roar
leaped forward, and the crowd cleared the way for a new influx
of customers." To create his devil, Jeffries obtained an imported
kangaroo from a Boston animal dealer and affixed some fake
wings using a harness; to prompt the leap, a boy hidden at the
rear of the cage prodded the unfortunate animal with a stick.[85]

Subsequent hoaxes involving the Jersey Devil or its hysterical
offspring—for example, a "flying lion" of 1926—occurred in the
state. Noting the "return" of the creature in 1932, hoax authority
Curtis D. MacDougall states: "It was the occasion for much
burlesque journalism, but to John McCandless of Swarthmore,
Pennsylvania, the experience was a terrifying one. Five miles
north of Dowington he was attracted by mysterious moans and
observed in the brush a hideous form, half-man, half-beast, on
all fours and covered with hair." MacDougall adds: "McCandless
and a score of friends hunted with pistols and guns for a week,
as other persons of the vicinity, mostly small children and farmers'
wives, said that they, too, had seen the monster."[86]

Another exhibited monster was the remarkable "hodag" that
was captured alive at Rhinelander, Wisconsin. The term (a
combination of *horse* and *dog*) reflected its creation: a dog over
which three local pranksters had stretched a decorated horse's
hide. MacDougall says, "This interested eastern scientists and
circus owners, and the hodag created a sensation for weeks and
months." Later a stuffed successor was exhibited at fairs, and
its image survived on picture postcards in northern Wisconsin
for many years.[87]

Other monsters that could be mentioned are the Lamia (a demonic monster with a woman's face that lured seventeenth-century travelers to their death),[88] the Sucking-Monster (a giant of American Indian mythology who sucks in people), Fire-Moccasins (another Indian ogre who sets fire to whatever he walks about), the hippogriff (a cross between a griffin and a horse), a winged elephant (a mythological creature of the Hindus), and so on.[89]

Then there are what I call one-of-a-kind monsters—not necessarily seen by only one person but at least confined to a single "flap" in a relatively limited geographical area. Perhaps the best source of these (although the book treats "classic" monster cases and other allegedly paranormal phenomena as well) is Jerome Clark's *Unexplained! 347 Strange Sightings, Incredible Occurrences, and Puzzling Physical Phenomena.* Some of the one-of-a-kind creatures are the "Flatwoods Monster" (reported near Flatwoods, West Virginia, in 1952, by three boys who described a grotesque monster, its head in the shape of the "ace of spades"), the "Lake Worth Monster" (sighted at Lake Worth, Texas, in 1969, and resembling a "big white ape"), "Momo" (for Missouri Monster, a seven-foot, black, hairy, bipedal creature first encountered by three children in 1972 near Louisiana, Missouri), a "Thunderbird" (a gigantic flying creature with a serpentlike body and a face like an alligator, allegedly photographed in 1890 with its thirty-six-foot wings "nailed against the wall of the *Tombstone Epitaph*," although the newspaper cannot find such a picture), and others.[90] No doubt many, perhaps all of these, are figments, only as real as the imagination that would give life to them allows. Certainly until an authentic creature is captured or its body recovered, and is studied by qualified scientists, skepticism must prevail.

Recommended Works

Binns, Ronald. *The Loch Ness Mystery Solved.* Amherst, N.Y.: Prometheus Books, 1984. Comprehensive debunking of the "Nessie" myth.
Bord, Janet, and Colin Bord. *The Bigfoot Casebook.* Harrisburg, Pa.: Stackpole Books, 1982. Wide-ranging but overly credulous presentation of Bigfoot claims.

Cohen, Daniel. *The Encyclopedia of Monsters*. New York: Dodd, Mead & Co., 1982. An A to Z compendium of monsters of all types.

Dennett, Michael. "Evidence for Bigfoot? An Investigation of the Mill Creek 'Sasquatch Prints,' " *Skeptical Inquirer* 13, no. 3 (Spring 1989): 266–67. Excellent investigative report on a major Bigfoot case involving supposedly unfakeable footprints.

Heuvelmans, Bernard. *On the Track of Unknown Animals*. Cambridge, Mass., MIT Press, 1972. A cryptozoologist's examination of the evidence for many animals whose existence is unrecognized by science.

Leach, Maria. *Funk & Wagnalls Standard Dictionary of Folklore, Mythology, and Legend*. New York: Harper & Row, 1984. A standard reference work on folklore and mythology, including legendary creatures.

Robbins, Rossell Hope. *Encyclopedia of Witchcraft and Demonology*. New York: Crown, 1959. Reference book on the occult, including discussions of such creatures as vampires.

Thompson, C. J. S. *The Mystery and Lore of Monsters*. New York: Barnes & Noble, 1994. Discussion of all types of monsters, including so-called human "monsters" (i.e., the products of genetic defects).

Notes

1. C. J. S. Thompson, *The Mystery and Lore of Monsters* (New York: Barnes & Noble, 1994), pp. 27, 30, 32–34.

2. Joe Nickell, "Magic in the Carnival," *Performing Arts in Canada* 7, no. 2 (May 1970): 41–42.

3. Thompson (n.1) cites "Ulysses Aldrovandus. Opera omnia. Bononiae. 1599–1668." This post-Aldrovandus date is explained by the fact that "after his death a number of other volumes were compiled from his manuscript materials under the editorship of several of his pupils" (*Encyclopedia Britannica*, 1960, s.v. "Aldrovandi, Ulisse").

4. Janet Bord and Colin Bord, *The Bigfoot Casebook* (Harrisburg, Pa.: Stackpole Books, 1982), pp. 25–26, 153. The detail of the creature being lodged in jail is omitted from the Bords' account.

5. Gordon Stein, ed., *Encyclopedia of Hoaxes* (Detroit: Gale Research, 1993), pp. 246–47, citing John Green and Sabina W. Sanderson, "Alas, Poor Jacko," *Pursuit* 8, no. 1 (January 1975): 18–19.

6. Quoted in Bord and Bord, *The Bigfoot Casebook*, p. 26.

7. Ricky Jay, *Learned Pigs & Fireproof Women: A History of*

Unique, Eccentric and Amazing Entertainers (London: Robert Hale, 1986), p. 294.

8. Bord and Bord, *The Bigfoot Casebook*, pp. 25–26.

9. Bernard Heuvelmans, *On the Track of Unknown Animals* (Cambridge, Mass.: MIT Press, 1972), p. 21.

10. Simon Welfare and John Fairley, *Arthur C. Clarke's Mysterious World* (New York: A & W Visual Library, 1980), p. 14.

11. Peter Byrne, interviewed on TV program "Unsolved Mysteries," aired July 30, 1994 (not the original broadcast).

12. Daniel Cohen, *The Encyclopedia of Monsters* (New York: Dodd, Mead & Co., 1982), pp. 6–7.

13. Michael Dennett, "Abominable Snowman Photo Comes to Rocky End," *Skeptical Inquirer* 13, no. 2 (1989): 118–19.

14. Welfare and Fairley, *Arthur C. Clarke's Mysterious World*, p. 15.

15. Heuvelmans, *On the Track of Unknown Animals*, p. 81.

16. Cohen, *The Encyclopedia of Monsters*, p. 7.

17. Ibid.

18. Ibid., p. 9.

19. Joe Nickell in Robert A. Baker and Joe Nickell, *Missing Pieces* (Amherst, N.Y.: Prometheus Books, 1992), p. 256. The data comes from a variety of sources, notably Bord and Bord, *The Bigfoot Casebook*, passim.

20. Michael Dennett, "Bigfoot Jokester Reveals Punchline—Finally," *Skeptical Inquirer* 7, no. 1 (Fall 1982): 8–9.

21. Rodney L. Johnson, quoted in Michael Dennett, "Evidence for Bigfoot? An investigation of the Mill Creek 'Sasquatch Prints,'" *Skeptical Inquirer* 13, no. 3 (Spring 1989): 266–67.

22. Joel Hardin, quoted in Dennett, "Evidence for Bigfoot?" pp. 267–68.

23. Dennett, "Evidence for Bigfoot?" pp. 268–71.

24. Ibid., p. 271.

25. Bord and Bord, *The Bigfoot Casebook*, p. 80.

26. Joyce Robbins, *The World's Greatest Mysteries* (New York: Gallery Books, 1989), p. 109.

27. Cohen, *The Encyclopedia of Monsters*, p. 17.

28. Bord and Bord, *The Bigfoot Casebook*, pp. 127, 128.

29. Janet Bord and Colin Bord, *Unexplained Mysteries of the 20th Century* (Chicago: Contemporary Books, 1989), p. 32.

30. Ibid., p. 70.

31. Eugene Emery, "Sasquatchsickle: The Monster, the Model, and the Myth," *Skeptical Inquirer* 6, no. 2 (Winter 1981–82): 2–4; Cohen, *The Encyclopedia of Monsters*, p. 25.

32. Cohen, *The Encyclopedia of Monsters*, p. 9.

33. Francis de Loys, quoted in Welfare and Fairley, *Arthur C. Clarke's Mysterious World*, p. 143.

34. Welfare and Fairley, ibid., pp. 143–44.

35. Ibid., pp. 144–45.

36. Stein, *Encyclopedia of Hoaxes*, pp. 13–15, 16–18.

37. Maria Leach, ed., *Funk & Wagnalls Standard Dictionary of Folklore, Mythology, and Legend* (New York: Harper & Row, 1984), p. 11; Francis X. King, *Mind & Magic* (London: Crescent, 1991), p. 114.

38. Owen S. Rachleff, *The Occult Conceit* (Chicago: Cowles, 1971), p. 216.

39. Gordon Stein, "Werewolves," *Fate*, January 1988: 33.

40. Rachleff, *The Occult Conceit*, p. 215.

41. Stein, "Werewolves," p. 37.

42. Rachleff, *The Occult Conceit*, p. 215.

43. Terence Hines, *Pseudoscience and the Paranormal* (Amherst, N.Y.: Prometheus Books, 1988), pp. 156–57.

44. Ibid.

45. The secret is given in Albert A. Hopkins, ed., *Magic: Stage Illusions, Special Effects and Trick Photography* (New York: Dover, 1976), pp. 532–35. It is also given in my account of the Atasha show: "Magic in the Carnival" (see n.2).

46. Leach, *Funk & Wagnalls Standard Dictionary*, p. 1154.

47. Colin Wilson and Damon Wilson, *Unsolved Mysteries: Past and Present* (Chicago: Contemporary Books, 1992), pp. 372–73.

48. Rachleff, *The Occult Conceit*, pp. 214–15.

49. Ibid., p. 214.

50. Wilson and Wilson, *Unsolved Mysteries*, pp. 374–76.

51. Joan Carroll Cruz, *The Incorruptibles* (Rockford, Ill.: Tan Books, 1977), p. 48.

52. Ibid.; Wilson and Wilson, *Unsolved Mysteries*, p. 375.

53. Joe Nickell, *Looking for a Miracle* (Amherst, N.Y.: Prometheus Books, 1993), pp. 85–93.

54. Quoted in Wilson and Wilson, *Unsolved Mysteries*, p. 375. Another source gives 1728 for the date of Peter Plogojowitz's death: see Martin V. Riccardo, "Vampires an Unearthly Reality," *Fate*, February 1993: 63.

55. Rossell Hope Robbins, *Encyclopedia of Witchcraft and Demonology* (1959), cited in Wilson and Wilson, *Unsolved Mysteries*, p. 377.

56. Riccardo, "Vampires an Unearthly Reality," 63.

57. Leach, *Funk & Wagnalls Standard Dictionary*, pp. 1161–62, 1195.

58. Wilson and Wilson, *Unsolved Mysteries*, p. 413.

59. Ibid., pp. 413–17.

60. Rachleff, *The Occult Conceit*, p. 218.

61. *Reader's Digest Mysteries of the Unexplained* (Pleasantville, N.Y.: Reader's Digest Assn., 1982), p. 113.

62. Leach, *Funk & Wagnalls Standard Dictionary*, p. 710.

63. Stein, *Encyclopedia of Hoaxes*, pp. 259–62; Curtis D. MacDougall, *Hoaxes* (New York: Dover, 1958), p. 138.

64. MacDougall, *Hoaxes*, pp. 138–39.

65. Welfare and Fairley, *Arthur C. Clarke's Mysterious World*, p. 68.

66. Ibid., pp. 71–72.

67. Ibid., pp. 74–76, photo p. 75. See also Jerome Clark, *Unexplained!* (Detroit: Visible Ink Press, 1993), pp. 156–61.

68. Ibid., p. 81.

69. Michael Dennett, "Monsters on the Beach: A Hoax Revealed," *Skeptical Inquirer* 14, no. 2 (Winter 1990): 120–21.

70. Joe Nickell, *Looking for a Miracle* (Amherst, N.Y.: Prometheus Books, 1993), pp. 231–63.

71. Ronald Binns, *The Loch Ness Mystery Solved* (Amherst, N.Y.: Prometheus Books, 1984), p. 12.

72. Ibid., passim; Rupert T. Gould, *The Loch Ness Monster* (London: Geoffrey Bles, 1934), passim.

73. Joe Nickell, *The Magic Detectives* (Amherst, N.Y.: Prometheus Books, 1989), pp. 91–92.

74. Tom Genoni, Jr., "After 60 Years the Most Famous of All the 'Nessie' Photos Is Revealed as a Hoax," *Skeptical Inquirer* 18, no. 4 (Summer 1994): 338–40.

75. Binns, *Loch Ness Mystery Solved*, pp. 107–25.

76. R. Razdan and A. Kielar, "Sonar and Photographic Searches for the Loch Ness Monster," *Skeptical Inquirer* 9, no. 2 (1984–85): 147–58.

77. Ibid.

78. "Myth or Monster," *Time* 20 (1972): 66.

79. Mark Chorvinsky, "Our Strange World: The Lough Leane Monster Photograph Investigation," in two parts, *Fate*, March 1993: 31–35 and April 1993: 31–34.

80. Welfare and Fairley, *Arthur C. Clarke's Mysterious World*, pp. 100–15.

81. Leach, *Funk & Wagnalls Standard Dictionary*, pp. 547–48; Stein, *Encyclopedia of Hoaxes*, p. 253; *Reader's Digest Mysteries of the Unexplained*, p. 165.

82. Leach, *Funk & Wagnalls Standard Dictionary*, p. 548.

83. MacDougall, *Hoaxes*, p. 32.
84. Quoted in ibid., p. 33.
85. Ibid., p. 33.
86. Ibid., p. 34.
87. Ibid., pp. 17–18.
88. Ibid., caption to illus. facing 126.
89. Leach, *Funk & Wagnalls Standard Dictionary*, pp. 742–43.
90. Clark, *Unexplained!* (n. 67), passim.

8

Fairyland Encounters

Various types of wee creatures supposedly inhabit the earth with mankind, including different types of fairies as well as elves, gnomes, and others. In this chapter we look primarily at fairies, who are not infrequently encountered in studying the paranormal, giving particular attention to alleged abductions by fairies and photos of the little creatures.

Fairies on the Loose. The term "fairy" derives from the Latin word *fata*, "fate," and denotes a group of supernatural beings who live in close contact with men and women and interact with them—for good or ill.[1] Known by various names, fairies are found all over the world, although they are especially common in West European and Asian culture and are less so in Africa and America. According to a standard reference source:

> The fairy has the same general characteristics wherever he is found. He is usually diminutive, often very small but sometimes pygmylike. He can become invisible at will, often by putting on a magical cap. He usually lives underground in a burrow or under a hill, or in a heap of stones. Usually he is clothed in green; sometimes his skin and hair are green. White is also associated with fairies, and frequently solitary fairies are clothed in brown or gray. Fairies are rarely harmful; even when they abduct children they do not harm them. If fairies are mistreated, they retaliate by burning houses, despoiling crops. They delight in playing pranks: milking cows in the fields, soiling

251

clothes on the line, appropriating food, curdling milk. But they are helpful, too, for they often take food and money to the poor, give toys to children, work countermagic to break spells laid by witches.[2]

There are two major groups of fairies: those who actually live in fairyland (which is ruled by a king and queen although the latter is usually dominant) and a more varied group, associated with a particular place (such as the salamander fairy who lives in fire and the bucca who lives in mines); among the latter group is the "household familiar" (such as the dwarf and the brownie) who is attached to a particular household.[3]

Fairies interact with humans in five main ways: (1) the mortal falls in love with a fairy; (2) the fairy exchanges a fairy infant for a newborn baby; (3) fairies help people; (4) fairies harm people; and (5) fairies abduct human beings.[4] As we shall see, in the cultures that believe in them, fairies provide explanations for certain events that in other cultures would be explained quite differently.

Skipping over the first of the five ways fairies interact with people, and taking up the second, we come to the subject of the *changeling*: the fairy infant exchanged for a human one. Fairies supposedly want their children suckled by human mothers (although an alternate explanation is that fairies wish to sacrifice mortal children to the Devil). Folklorists suggest that "such stories are probably nothing other than explanatory stories to account for the abnormal appearance or abnormal behavior of the human child by saying that it was a changeling." To prevent children from being exchanged, certain charms, such as a pair of scissors, the Bible, or some garlic, were placed near the infant.[5] No doubt such charms were usually effective!

Stories of fairies assisting people evoke some of the guardian angel tales of today. For example, "A Jutland peasant, trying in vain to free his horse stuck in the mud, suddenly is surrounded by fairy folk who easily free the animal."[6] Again, "In France a fairy rescues a lady whose jealous husband had imprisoned her."[7] Sometimes fairies merely reward people for their kindnesses (such as leaving out food offerings) by giving money or other gifts.[8]

When fairies harm people it is usually for some perceived harm done to them, such as failing to keep a clean house or neglecting to leave out food and drink. The nature of the fairy punishment is usually some form of mischief. For example, in mines they may pelt the laborers with stones, and in the home they often knock pans from their shelves, extinguish candles, or roll up rugs and mats.[9] In short, they may do just those sorts of things that today would be classified as a "poltergeist outbreak" (as we discussed in chapter 3).

Perhaps the most interesting fairy activity as far as today's paranormal investigator is concerned is the kidnapping of mortals. Either they are taken bodily to the fairies' subterranean abode, or they are lured there by bewitching them.[10] The parallels with modern UFO "close encounters" and abductions by ETs are obvious.

Consider, for example, this encounter, related firsthand by a Rev. Arnold J. Holmes to Sir Arthur Conan Doyle (an avid spiritualist and believer in fairyland) in Doyle's *The Coming of the Fairies*. One night, the Rev. Holmes was on his way home when, he states:

After passing Sir Hall Caine's beautiful residence, Greeba Castle, my horse—a spirited one—suddenly stopped dead, and looking ahead I saw amid the obscure light and misty moonbeans what appeared to be a small army of indistinct figures—very small, clad in gossamer garments. They appeared to be perfectly happy, scampering and tripping along the road, having come from the direction of the beautiful sylvan glen of Greeba and St. Trinian's Roofless Church. The legend is that it has ever been the fairies' haunt, and when an attempt has been made on two occasions to put a roof on, the fairies have removed all the work during the night, and for a century no further attempts have been made. It has therefore been left to the "little people" who claimed it as their own.[11]

Rev. Holmes continued:

I watched spellbound, my horse half mad with fear. The little happy army then turned in the direction of Witch's Hill, and mounted a mossy bank; one "little man" of larger stature than the rest, about 14 inches high, stood at attention until all had passed him dancing, singing, with happy abandon, across the Valley fields towards St. John's Mount.[12]

Another fairy-sighter who wrote to Doyle (in response to his publicized interest in the subject) was a Mrs. Ethyl Enid Wilson, who announced:

> I quite believe in fairies. Of course, they are really nature spirits. I have often seen them on fine sunny days playing in the sea, and riding on the waves, but no one I have ever been with at the time has been able to see them, excepting once my little nephews and nieces saw them too. They were like little dolls, quite small, with beautiful bright hair, and they were constantly moving and dancing about.[13]

Let us look at one more encounter before moving on to fairy abductions. This account is abridged from Miss Eva Longbottom's narrative:

> I have seen many fairies. . . . They are of various kinds, the ones I see. The music fairies are very beautiful. "Argent" describes them, for they make you think of silver, and they have dulcet silvery voices. . . . Then there are dancing fairies. Their dancing is dainty and full of grace, a sweet old style of dance, without any tangles in it. I am generally alone when I see them, not necessarily in a woodland, but wherever the atmosphere is poetical. They are quite real.[14]

What are we to make of such accounts? As a beginning we can look at the unabridged first sentence of Miss Longbottom who said, "I have seen many fairies *with my mind's eyes*" (emphasis added). Blind from birth, she supposedly "saw" the fairies clairvoyantly, whenever the "atmosphere" was "poetical." This is a clear indication of fantasy proneness, despite her protestations that the fairies "are quite real." Mrs. Wilson's account, too, contains indications that she was "different": "I quite believe in fairies," she stated, as if to assert her independence and invite attention. That she had "often seen" the little entities when others with her had not is corroborative evidence that hers was a fantasy-prone personality.

And as to the Reverend Holmes, we note that he arrived at a spot where fairies were *expected* according to a longstanding legend. Also, the conditions of "obscure light and misty moonbeams" provided an ideal setting for his imagination to conjure up visions, much as a crystal ball does for the diviner.[15] Moreover, he would seem to have possessed "a very religious background" which is often a characteristic of the fantasy-prone personality, as well as a flair for pictorial imagery and dramatic narrative ability.[16] All of the percipients, it should be noted, came from a culture that promoted belief in fairies and encouraged such anecdotal accounts. In another place and time, these same people might have seen ghosts or been abducted by UFOs.

And speaking of abductions, Doyle does not include accounts of fairies kidnapping his respondents, but it is a simple step from close encounters to closer contact, even abductions. (Recall that the "Great Airship Wave" of the late 1890s featured a report of an attempted kidnapping by alien creatures.) Folklorist Thomas Bullard noted striking parallels between abductions by fairies and those by extraterrestrials; looking at the latter first, we have this summary of Bullard's findings:

I. At night in a remote area or at home, a witness sees a UFO and tries to flee. II. He enters a zone of strangeness as surroundings lose normal appearance, machines misbehave, his volition is impaired and his memory blanks out. Strange humanoid beings appear and float or carry him inside the UFO. III. He enters a uniformly lighted operating room where one or more alien beings subject him to a medical examination, sometimes of a painful character. IV. Afterwards he may see long tunnels and other parts of the ship, or travel a great distance in a short time to a dark and desolate other planet, then to a light and airy realm, both of which have buildings. Among the aliens he may also see a human being, and receive messages. On returning to earth, he finds a memory gap and injuries, and may receive later visits and extranormal manifestations.[17]

Now note the similarities with abductions by fairies:

> I. At night in a remote area or in the vicinity of a fairy mound the witness II. Finds his surroundings unfamiliar as he encounters mist or is "led astray," or loses his volition as he hears enchanting music. He encounters one or more unusual beings who invite or lure him away with them, and afoot or by some unusual conveyance, he passes through a dark tunnel, takes a ride in darkness or sails on a stormy voyage to an other-world inside the mound or across the sea. III. He enters a dimly or indirectly lighted hall, room or otherworldly country, and joins a society of beings in feasts, dances, games or pleasures, or assists a woman in childbirth, which is often painful. While there he may see a captive human, and acquire extranormal powers of knowledge. V. He becomes a captive or returns after supernatural lapse of time, which causes him to turn to dust, or he receives later punishment for powers gained while in fairyland.[18]

Proponents argue that such parallels as may exist are either "weak" (Bullard admitted they were at best "oblique and speculative") or that fairy encounters may actually have been UFO encounters. For example, Jerome Clark says of one 1938 sighting by Irish schoolboys, "If this incident had occurred a decade later and been reported somewhere other than Ireland, it probably would have been treated as an encounter with UFO occupants." Again, of a case that transpired in 1959, in which a man clearing land saw a little red man, three feet tall, dart from beneath his bulldozer and scamper across the field, Clark states: "Only the Irish locale kept this from being treated as a UFO incident, though no UFO was seen."[19]

Skeptics, on the other hand, believe the parallels show that UFO encounters and abductions are no more credible than those involving fairies, which, in their opinion, are too silly for words. Robert Sheaffer, a noted UFO skeptic, wrote a delightful, tongue-in-cheek essay, "Do Fairies Exist?" published in the Skeptical Inquirer,[20] in which he uses UFO reports to, supposedly, establish the existence of the little people. Pretending to rail at the skeptics for their neglect, Sheaffer says he intends to form an organization called the Anomalous Phantasmagorical Research and Observation Network (APRON), which he describes as "a loose association of skilled field investigators and Tarot card readers" whose principal activity will be "public relations."[21]

In addition to ufology, fairies also seem to figure in some cases of "mysterious disappearances" (a genre of accounts in which there is a suggestion that the disappearance was paranormal[22]). Take the case of David Lang; as Robert Schadewald summarizes the story:

> On the afternoon of September 23, 1880, a Tennessee farmer named David Lang stepped off the face of the earth. He walked into his pasture to look at his horses and with his wife and children and friend Judge August Peck looking on, he vanished! The stunned onlookers rushed to the spot where he was last seen but could not find a trace of him. There was no hole in the ground, no subterranean cave, nothing to explain his disappearance. He was just gone. It was reported that as time passed a circle of stunted yellow grass grew at the spot where David Lang disappeared and sometimes members of the family could hear his voice calling weakly for help from inside the circle.[23]

In some versions of the story the circle of grass was not stunted but "had grown high and thick in a circle 20 feet in diameter"[24]—a description which evokes a "fairy ring," a dark green circle occasionally found in the turf of a field or lawn (caused by the fungus *Marasmius oreades*), popularly believed to be the fairies' dancing place or an entrance to fairyland.[25] (Some also suggested fairy rings as an explanation for southern England's famed crop circles—swirled patterns in wheat and other grain fields. Others thought them "UFO nests" or landing spots, but each year the designs became progressively more elaborate and eventually a pair of hoaxers admitted to having started the craze.[26])

Was David Lang kidnapped by fairies? The folklore motifs (narrative elements) in the story suggest so; these include "fairy rings on grass," "entrance to fairyland through fairy ring," "mortal abandons world to live in fairyland," and "extraordinary glen: mysterious shouting heard."[27] On the other hand, occult writer Colin Wilson is willing once again to go out on a limb in search of his own route to never-never land: Observing that "some ufologists have suggested that UFOs may originate in another dimension—a space-time world running parallel to our own that may contain living creatures, just as our world does," Wilson opines: "David Lang, the Tennessee farmer who disappeared without trace, may have fallen into this parallel dimension."[28]

Unfortunately, neither fairies nor extraterrestrials made away with David Lang. He never vanished at all, because he never existed. In his book *Among the Missing*, Jay Robert Nash debunks the old Lang tale but asserts it was based on the true story of one Orion Williamson. As Nash claims:

> Over the years, a thorough investigation on the part of the author and his staff revealed, Williamson's name and place of residence have been changed for various reasons by several writers. This began when a wandering salesman named McHatten from Cincinnati was trapped by a snowstorm in 1889 in Gallatin, Tennessee. With nothing to do except drink, McHatten sat in the Sindle House Hotel and rewrote the Williamson story in an attempt to make a bit of extra change by selling it as an original report. He changed Orion Williamson's name to David Lang, the site of his disappearance from Selma, Alabama, to Gallatin, Tennessee, and the date of the occurrence from July 1854 to September 1880.[29]

Nash adds, however, that "Orion Williamson was no figment of the imagination but a real, live resident of Selma, Alabama— until, of course, he slipped into eternal mystery." While maintaining that "Orion Williamson" actually existed and that the "basic facts" of the story were true, Nash admits that "Ambrose Bierce thought the whole thing farcical and wrote a satire about the odd happening. . . ."[30]

Now it is Nash who is in error. I conducted an investigation of the matter, assisted by an Alabama state archivist, the Dallas County court clerk, and a Selma librarian. Exhaustive searches of the 1850 and 1860 censuses, various compendiums of Alabama records, local deeds, and other records failed to document the existence of either "Orion Williamson" or his alleged neighbor (according to Bierce) Armour Wren. Mr. Nash refused to reply to my challenge that he either prove his claims or at least clarify how he obtained his information. (His account provides the name Orion, for example, for the man described by Bierce only as a "planter named Williamson.")[31]

In fact, just like the tale (related in chapter 6), about the boy who vanished while fetching water and left his abruptly ending tracks in the snow, the Lang/Williamson yarn is another Bierce short story. Titled "The Difficulty of Crossing a Field," it was one of a trilogy (including "Charles Ashmore's Trail," the basis for the proliferating tracks-in-the-snow stories) grouped under the heading "Mysterious Disappearances" in Bierce's *Can Such Things Be?*[32] There is no evidence that Bierce based such stories on earlier tales, much less that he believed such tales to be true.[33] Interestingly, Bierce—who himself disappeared in 1913[34]—may have been aware that his own name was virtually a synonym for disappearance. According to the *Oxford English Dictionary*, one meaning of *ambrose* is that it is equivalent to *ambrosia*; and according to a reference book on the occult, "In many countries if a person disappears and cannot be found, he is supposed to have eaten ambrosia and been turned by it into a fairy."[35]

In the next section, we continue our search for the elusive fairies with a look at some photographs of the little people made by two young girls. Citing photographic experts, Conan Doyle pronounced them genuine, but would his literary creation, the great skeptical detective who lived at 221-B Baker Street in victorian London, have thought so, or would he have found the mystery of the photographs quite elementary?

At Cottingley Glen

Sir Arthur Conan Doyle began his book *The Coming of the Fairies* with the statement, "The series of incidents set forth in this little volume represent either the most elaborate and ingenious hoax ever played upon the public, or else they constitute an event in human history which may in the future appear to have been epoch making in its character." The events Doyle was speaking of were the taking of two photographs depicting fairies, which he learned about in early May 1920, but which had been made three years previously.[36]

The earliest written record in the case may be a letter to a young lady friend of Doyle's, a Miss Scatcherd, from a Miss Gardner. Referring to her brother, she said, "You know that Edward is a Theosophist" (that is, one who believed knowledge of God came not from historical revelation nor from scientific inquiry but from mystical insight). Miss Gardner mentioned her brother's recent "bereavement" (apparently the death of his wife) and continued:

> I wish you could see a photo he has. He believes in fairies, pixies, goblins, etc.—children, in many cases, really see them and play with them. He has got into touch with a family in Bradford where the little girl, Elsie, and her cousin, Frances, constantly go into woods and play with the fairies. The father and mother are skeptical and have no sympathy with their nonsense, as they call it, but an aunt, whom Edward has interviewed, is quite sympathetic with the girls. Some little time ago, Elsie said she wanted to photograph them, and begged her father to lend his camera. For long he refused, but at last she managed to get the loan of it and one plate. Off she and Frances went into the woods near a water-fall. Frances " 'ticed" them, as they call it, and Elsie stood ready with the camera. Soon the three fairies appeared, and one pixie dancing in Frances' aura. Elsie snapped and hoped for the best. It was a long time before the father would develop the photo, but at last he did, and to his utter amazement the four sweet little figures came out beautifully![37]

Miss Gardner continued:

> Edward got the negative and took it to a specialist in photography who would know a fake at once. Skeptical as he was

before he tested it, afterwards he offered 100 pounds down for it. He pronounced it absolutely genuine and a perfectly remarkable photograph. Edward has it enlarged and hanging in his hall. He is very interested in it and as soon as possible he is going to Bradford to see the children. What do you think of this? Edward says the fairies are on the same line of evolution as the *winged* insects, etc., etc. I fear I cannot follow all his reasonings, but I knew you would be keenly interested. I wish you could see that photo and another one of the girls playing with the quaintest goblin imaginable![38]

Soon Doyle, who said the letter "filled me with hopes" as to the possibility of seeing the photos, received copies from Edward Gardner's cousin, a Mr. Broomfield, with the proviso that "the pictures are being copyrighted." In a subsequent letter, Broomfield said, "I do not see any opening for fraud or hoax," although he admitted that at first sight he thought the pictures "appeared too good to be true!" Doyle was fast convincing himself that the photos were genuine. He showed the pictures to the great physicist (and spiritualist) Sir Oliver Lodge, who suggested that the figures were superimposed. But Doyle argued "that we had certainly traced the pictures to two children of the artisan class, and that such photographic tricks would be entirely beyond them, but I failed to convince him."[39]

The "two children of the artisan class" that Doyle described (or "Elsie, and her cousin, Frances," as Miss Gardner referred to them in her letter) were two schoolgirls from the village of Cottingley (near Bradford, in Yorkshire) who often played in nearby Cottingley Glen. In 1917, when the photographs were made, Elsie, daughter of Arthur Wright (an electrician) and his wife May, was sixteen, and Frances Griffiths was ten. Now it happened that Elsie had actually been employed in a photographic studio near her home. Doyle and Gardner dismissed the implications of this fact by claiming she only worked at the counter and ran errands. It was later discovered that she also retouched photographs, but the fairy photos were clearly unretouched, experts attested; neither were they double exposures or apparently faked in any other way. Even so, Elsie's mother told investigators that her daughter was "a most imaginative child, who has been in the habit of drawing fairies for years." At the time Edward Gardner met her, she was working in a greeting card factory.[40]

Doyle published an article, "Fairies Photographed—An Epoch-making Event," in the London *Strand* for Christmas 1920, and followed it a year later with *The Coming of the Fairies* (from which book we earlier looked at some testimonials about fairy encounters). The book included three more photographs made at the request of Doyle and the prompting of Gardner. Gardner had been apprehensive, since three years had passed and "I was well aware that the processes of puberty are often fatal to psychic power." But they were rewarded with "three more wonderful prints" which could not have been faked, Gardner claimed, because the photographic plates had been secretly marked as a safeguard against being switched.[41]

Nevertheless, a reporter for the *Westminster Gazette* was suspicious. In an article in the January 12, 1921, issue, he described Elsie as evasive:

> Like her parents, she just said she had nothing to say about the photographs, and, singularly enough, used the same expression as her father and mother—"I am 'fed up' with the thing."
>
> She gradually became communicative, and told me how she came to take the first photograph.
>
> Asked where the fairies came from, she replied that she did not know.
>
> "Did you see them come?" I asked; and on receiving an affirmative reply, suggested that she must have noticed where they came from.
>
> Miss Wright hesitated, and laughingly answered, "I can't say." She was equally at a loss to explain where they went after dancing near her, and was embarrassed when I pressed for a fuller explanation. Two or three questions went unanswered, and my suggestion that they must have "simply vanished into the air" drew the monosyllabic reply, "Yes." They did not speak to her, she said, nor did she speak to them.[42]

The *Gazette* article continued:

When she had been with her cousin she had often seen them before. They were only kiddies when they first saw them, she remarked, and did not tell anybody.

"But," I went on, "it is natural to expect that a child, seeing fairies for the first time, would tell its mother." Her answer was to repeat that she did not tell anybody. The first occasion on which fairies were seen, it transpired, was in 1915.

In reply to further questions, Miss Wright said she had seen them since, and had photographed them, and the plates were in the possession of Mr. Gardner. Even after several prints of the first lot of fairies had been given to friends, she did not inform anybody that she had seen them again. The fact that nobody else in the village had seen them gave her no surprise. She firmly believed that she and her cousin were the only persons who had been so fortunate, and was equally convinced that nobody else would be. "If anybody else were there," she said, "the fairies would not come out."

Further questions put with the object of eliciting a reason for that statement were only answered with smiles and a final significant remark "You don't understand."

Miss Wright still believes in the existence of the fairies, and is looking forward to seeing them again in the coming summer.[43]

The girls continued to maintain the authenticity of the photographs, but skeptics were chipping away at the girls'—and later the elderly women's—story. In early 1921 "a lady photographer connected with the Bradford Institute" produced a fake photograph to show how Elsie and Frances might have done theirs; indeed Ina Inman's production, Doyle said, "was so good that it caused us for some weeks to regard it with an open mind."[44]

Little that was new about the photos transpired for fifty years, until Elsie, being interviewed on a 1971 BBC television program, admitted coyly that she "would not swear on the Bible that the fairies were really there." Later, in a letter to Brian Coe, a noted photographic expert, she said: "I admit that I may not believe in fairies. As for the photos, let's say they are figments of our imaginations, Frances's and mine." But she stopped short of an outright admission that the photos were faked.[45]

And in a 1976 Yorkshire Television program, when asked if the photos were fake, Frances responded: "Of course not. You tell us how she [Elsie] could do it—remember she was sixteen and I was ten. Now then, as a child of ten, can you go through life and keep a secret?" Of course Frances was no longer ten, but apparently she could still keep a secret. In the more than half a century since the photos were made, Frances had become Mrs. Frank Way, and spent considerable time abroad with her soldier husband. Elsie had married a Scottish engineer named Frank Hill, and lived with him in India.[46]

A new development came in 1977. Fred Gettings was looking through a 1915 children's book titled *Princess Mary's Gift Book* when he saw a drawing of dancing figures that illustrated a poem titled "A Spell for a Fairy." Although wingless, the photos appeared to have served as the models for Elsie's fairies.[47]

In 1978 Robert Sheaffer published the results of a computer analysis which showed that the fairy figures were not three-dimensional but rather had the characteristics of paper cutouts. The only exception was the gnome figure in the second photograph, which could have been an in-the-round model such as a toy figure. The photo-analyst William Spaulding concluded that the photos "represent a crude hoax."[48]

Another blow to the photos' credibility came with an examination of the original glass-plate negatives by Kodak of London's Brian Coe. Coe demolished several of the claims made by Conan Doyle's "experts" including the alleged 1/50 second shutter speed used for the first photograph. In fact an exposure of 1½ to 2 seconds would have been required, during which time the motion of the fairy's wings should have produced blurring (like that of the waterfall in the background). Yet the fairy figure is "frozen" the way a paper cutout would be. Doyle's "experts" claimed the figures *were* in motion in the various pictures, but they were simply fooling themselves (possibly confusing the lack of perfect focus for blurring caused by motion).[49]

Finally, in a 1982 article in *The Unexplained*, Joe Cooper reported that Elsie and Frances had confessed to faking the Cottingley photographs. Cooper had been assisting Frances with her autobiography. However, the two women responded, not by denying the truth of Cooper's statements, but by claiming that the confessions Cooper cited were "unauthorized." The authorized versions—actual signed statements—were given to Geoffrey Crawley for a major review of the case published in the *British Journal of Photography.*[50]

Even so, the two would still not tell all. They did reveal that the pictures had begun as a "practical joke" which they said "fell flat on its face." They had agreed to withhold the truth until all the major authenticity advocates (Doyle, Gardner, and the latter's son Leslie) had died. They refused to disclose the actual techniques they used in making the pictures, saving that for books they were in the procress of writing; however, both died before their books were completed.[51]

Nevertheless, little remained to be told. They admitted that Elsie, the artist of the two, had adapted the figures from *Princess Mary's Gift Book.* In September of 1981, as Frances sat with Cooper in a coffee shop, she told him about the first photograph (in which she is seen, suspiciously, looking into the camera while tiny fairies dance before her): "From where I was, I could see the hatpins holding up the figures. I've always marveled that anyone ever took it seriously."[52]

In other words, it was not really the *photographs* but the scene that had been faked. Doyle and Gardner had done what so many paranormalists have done: exaggerate the difficulty of faking a phenomenon as a means of promoting it as authentic. (Conspiracy theorists, incidentally, do much the same: overstating the difficulty of a single person accomplishing something in order to involve more people.)

Ironically, Doyle had actually considered the very method Elsie and Frances used! In *The Coming of the Fairies* he wrote: "Elsie could only have done it by cut-out images, which must have been of exquisite beauty, of many different models, fashioned and kept without the knowledge of her parents, and capable of giving the impression of motion when carefully examined by an expert." Doyle added, "Surely this is a large order!"[53] Actually, what *really* happened was not very difficult at all.

Other Wee Folk

In addition to the fairies that appeared in the Cottingley photographs, photo number two depicted Elsie amusedly watching a gnome. Like fairies, gnomes are underground beings, but have a "deformed and dwarfish" appearance.[54] Elves are also diminutive supernatural entities but are usually distinguished from fairies by being somewhat more troublesome or mischievous; for example, in England a knot of tangled hair was termed an "elflock."[55] The term sprite is sometimes applied to an elf or fairy.[56] So is nymph, which in classical mythology was a nature spirit, supposedly a beautiful young woman who danced and made music; nymphs are thought to have evolved in popular belief into the diminutive fairies of European folklore.[57]

Amusingly, in light of the proven bogus nature of the Cottingley photos, a "clairvoyant" friend of Edward Gardner spent a week with Elsie and Frances and supposedly corroborated their ability to see the little people.[58] In fact, Gardner said of the gentleman: "Seated with the girls, he saw all that they saw, and more, for his powers proved to be considerably greater." It must have been quite a sight seeing each trying to outfake the other! Not surprisingly, they did not see precisely the same. For example, in a field, the girls and the clairvoyant both saw gnomes who "were making weird faces and grotesque contortions" at the group. Stated the (unidentified) clairvoyant, "the forms appeared to Elsie singly—one dissolving and another appearing in its place. I, however, saw them in a group with one figure more prominently visible than the rest."[59]

The clairvoyant also claimed he saw various fairies, "a water sprite" (an "entirely nude female figure" inhabiting the glen's waterfall), as well as a water fairy, wood elves, a brownie, and "a group of goblins." The latter, we are told, "differ somewhat from the wood elves, having more the look of gnomes, though they are smaller, being about the size of small brownies."[60]

Dwarfs represent yet another community of diminutive supernatural entities who inhabit the underground. Although they resemble men, their skin is wrinkled and leathery, and they have wide mouths and long beards (fully developed at three years of age and gray at seven).[61] The folklorist Rev. S. Baring-Gould described an encounter he said he had with dwarfs as a child:

> In the year 1838, when I was a small boy of four years old, we were driving to Montpelier on a hot summer day over the long straight road that traverses a pebble-and-rubble-strewn plain, on which grows nothing save a few aromatic herbs. I was sitting on the box with my father when, to my great surprise, I saw legions of dwarfs of about two feet high running along beside the horses; some sat laughing on the pole, some were scrambling up the harness to get on the backs of the horses. I remarked to my father what I saw, when he abruptly stopped the carriage and put me inside beside my mother, where, the conveyance being closed, I was out of the sun. The effect was that, little by little, the host of imps diminished in number till they disappeared altogether.[62]

Even Conan Doyle, in *The Coming of the Fairies*, responded wryly: "Here, certainly, the advocates of sunstroke have a strong, though by no means a final, case."[63]

We should not neglect leprechauns, especially since I once met a young woman who told me—with a perfectly straight face—that she and her little daughter had together seen a leprechaun. (This was after we appeared together on a television talk show during which the woman claimed to have had sexual encounters with a ghost. Obviously the woman had a proclivity for seeing fantasy-type creatures.[64])

This report notwithstanding, the leprechaun is a member of the fairy-tribe that inhabits Ireland. He is envisaged as an old man and "is by profession a maker of brogues; he resorts in general only to secret and retired places, where he is discovered by the sounds which he makes hammering his brogues." Moreover, "He is rich, like curmudgeons of his sort, and it is only by the most violent threats of doing him some bodily harm, that he can be made to show the place where his treasure lies; but if the person who has caught him can be induced (a thing that always happens, by the way) to take his eyes off him, he vanishes, and with him the prospect of wealth."[65]

In *The Coming of the Fairies*, Doyle presents an account of a leprechaun encounter by a "Miss Winter, of Blarney, in Cork":

> We received communications from a fairy named Bebel several times, one of them lasting nearly an hour. The communication was as decided and swift as from the most powerful spirit. He told us that he was a Leprechaun (male), but that in a ruined fort near us dwelt the Pixies. Our demesne had been the habitation of Leprechauns always, and they with their Queen Picel, mounted on her gorgeous dragon-fly, found all they required in our grounds.
>
> He asked most lovingly about my little grandchildren, who visit us frequently, and since then he has been in the habit of communicating with them, when we have yielded the table to them entirely, and just listened to the pure fun he and they were having together. He told them that the fairies find it quite easy to talk to the rabbits, and that they disliked the dogs because they chased them. They have great fun with the hens, on whose backs they ride, but they do not like them because they "jeer" at them.[66]

I suspect that this lady was indeed "of Blarney," i.e., that she had the proverbial gift of "blarney" (or "smooth talk"). I can only say that when I was traveling with a girlfriend in Ireland in January 1971, in the very area of the Blarney Castle that the lady described, I saw not a single leprechaun lurking about. However, I note from my travel journal of the time, "We're told that many people, 'particularly around [the county of] Mayo,' actually believe in leprechauns."[67]

How do people see the wee creatures? Many, like the clairvoyant mentioned earlier, or the blind woman cited still earlier (who saw fairies in her "mind's eyes"), are clearly people with vivid imaginations—some, no doubt being fantasy-prone personalities. Children's ability to fantasize is well known. Doyle misunderstood this when he stated: "If the confidence of children can be gained and they are led to speak freely, it is surprising how many claim to have seen fairies."[68]

Other psychological factors include those discussed much earlier, including waking dreams, *folie à deux*, and contagion (see chapter 2). The power of suggestion is inherent in all of these.

There is even the possibility of psychedelic influence. Certain hallucinogenic drugs, like the tryptamines, have a distinctive characteristic: A "tendency to produce visions of or encounters with non-human entities." One person who has experimented with such drugs reportedly saw "elves" on multiple occasions, sometimes as "more creaturely" than others.[69] Another person reported encounters with elf-like beings while using the hallucinogenic drug LSD and psilocybin mushrooms: "There are generally three to five of them, and they are always at the periphery of my vision. Their initial appearance reminds me somewhat of the cartoon character 'Gumby' but as they speak the colors and shapes of their bodies change. . . . They radiate a feeling of great happiness and love."[70]

Drugs do not *place* concepts of elfin beings in the mind; rather, hallucinatory experiences can be triggered by hallucinogens or by "the vast pharmacopoeia of similar mind-bending stimulants available since prehistoric times."[71] Hallucinations may also result from such environmental conditions as sleep deprivation, starvation, fatigue (including heat exhaustion), extreme stress, and grief.[72] Whether we see elves and fairies—or monsters, ghosts, demons, ETs, or other entities—depends on the culture around us and the nature of our own minds.

Recommended Works

Doyle, Arthur Conan. *The Coming of the Fairies*. 1921; reprint New York: Samuel Weiser, 1979. Account of the Cottingley fairy photographs and allegedly supportive accounts of fairy encounters by a gullible proponent.

Keightley, Thomas. *The World Guide to Gnomes, Fairies, Elves and Other Little People*. New York: Avenel Books, 1978. Illustrated survey of wee creatures from around the world.

Nickell, Joe. "Ambrose Bierce and Those 'Mysterious Disappearance' Legends," *Indiana Folklore* 13, no. 1-2 (1980): 112-22. Includes debunking of Andrew Lang/Orion Williamson "disappearance"— a case with fairyland implications.

Randi, James. "Fairies at the Foot of the Garden," chapter 2 in *Flim-Flam! Psychics, ESP, Unicorns and Other Delusions*. Amherst, N.Y.: Prometheus Books, 1982. Thorough skeptical analysis of the Cottingley fairy photographs and how they deceived Sir Arthur Conan Doyle.

Sheaffer, Robert. "Do Fairies Exist?" *Skeptical Inquirer* 2, no. 1 (Fall/Winter 1977): 45–52. Satirical look at UFOs, pretending to use UFO reports to establish the reality of fairies.

Notes

1. Rosemary Ellen Guiley, *Harper's Encyclopedia of Mystical & Paranormal Experience* (New York: HarperCollins, 1991), p. 198; Maria Leach, *Funk & Wagnalls Standard Dictionary of Folklore, Mythology, and Legend* (New York: Harper & Row, 1984), p. 363.

2. Leach, *Funk & Wagnalls Standard Dictionary*, p. 363.

3. Ibid.

4. Ibid., p. 364.

5. Ibid., p. 365.

6. Ibid., p. 364.

7. Ibid.

8. Guiley, *Harper's Encyclopedia*, p. 198.

9. Ibid.; Leach, *Funk & Wagnalls Standard Dictionary*, p. 364.

10. Leach, *Funk & Wagnalls Standard Dictionary*, p. 364.

11. Arthur Conan Doyle, *The Coming of the Fairies* (1921; reprinted New York: Samuel Weiser, 1979), pp. 155–57.

12. Ibid., p. 157.

13. Ibid., p. 167.

14. Ibid., pp. 168–69.

15. Richard Cavendish, ed., *Encyclopedia of the Unexplained* (London: Routledge & Kegan Paul, 1974), pp. 222–23.

16. Robert A. Baker and Joe Nickell, *Missing Pieces: How to Investigate Ghosts, UFOs, Psychics, and Other Mysteries* (Amherst, N.Y.: Prometheus Books, 1992), p. 223.

17. Thomas Bullard, doctoral dissertation, in Keith Thompson, *Angels and Aliens* (New York: Fawcett Columbine, 1991), pp. 124–25.

18. Ibid., pp. 124–25.

19. Jerome Clark, *Unexplained!* (Detroit: Visible Ink Press, 1993), pp. 121–22.

20. Robert Sheaffer, "Do Fairies Exist?" *Skeptical Inquirer* 2 no. 1 (Fall/Winter 1977): 45–52.

21. Ibid., p. 51.

22. For a discussion, see Joe Nickell, "Ambrose Bierce and those 'Mysterious Disappearance' Legends," *Indiana Folklore* 13, no. 1–2 (1980): 112–22.

23. Robert Schadewald, "David Lang Vanishes . . . FOREVER," *Fate*, December 1977, p. 54.

24. David Wallechinsky and Irving Wallace, *The People's Almanac* (Garden City, N.Y.: Doubleday, 1975), p. 1371.

25. Leach, *Funk & Wagnalls Standard Dictionary*, p. 365; Stith Thompson, *Motif-Index of Folk Literature*, rev. ed., 6 vols. (Bloomington: Indiana University Press, 1955).

26. See Joe Nickell and John F. Fischer, "The Crop-Circle Phenomenon: An Investigative Report," *Skeptical Inquirer* 16, no. 2 (Winter 1992): 136–49.

27. Nickell, "Ambrose Bierce," p. 121, n. 15.

28. Colin Wilson, *Enigmas and Mysteries* (Garden City, N.Y.: Doubleday, 1976), p. 130.

29. Jay Robert Nash, *Among the Missing* (New York: Simon & Schuster, 1978), p. 330.

30. Ibid.

31. Nickell, "Ambrose Bierce," pp. 114–20.

32. Ambrose Bierce, *Can Such Things Be?* (1893; reprint New York: Albert & Charles Boni, 1924).

33. For a discussion, see Nickell, "Ambrose Bierce," pp. 70–72.

34. See Joe Nickell, *Ambrose Bierce Is Missing and Other Historical Mysteries* (Lexington: University Press of Kentucky, 1992), pp. 19–34.

35. Cora L. Daniels and Prof. C. M. Stevens, eds., *Encyclopedia of Superstitions, Folklore and the Occult Sciences* (1903; reprint Detroit: Gale Research, 1971), p. 1255.

36. Doyle, *The Coming of the Fairies*, pp. 13–15.

37. Miss Gardner, quoted in ibid., pp. 15–18.

38. Ibid., p. 18.

39. Ibid., pp. 18–26.

40. Ibid., pp. 59–92; see also James Randi, *Flim-Flam! Psychics, ESP, Unicorns and other Delusions* (Amherst, N.Y.: Prometheus Books, 1987), pp. 15–16, 36.

41. Randi, *Flim-Flam!* pp. 16–19; Doyle, *The Coming of the Fairies*, p. 94.

42. "Do Fairies Exist? Investigation in a Yorkshire Valley," *West-*

minster *Gazette*, January 12, 1921, reprinted in Doyle, *The Coming of the Fairies*, pp. 60–70.

43. Ibid.

44. Doyle, *The Coming of the Fairies*, p. 73.

45. Randi, *Flim-Flam!*, p. 31.

46. Colin Wilson and Damon Wilson, *Unsolved Mysteries Past and Present* (Chicago: Contemporary Books, 1992), pp. 86–87.

47. Ibid., pp. 87–88.

48. Randi, *Flim-Flam!*, pp. 31–32. See also Robert Sheaffer, "The Cottingley Fairies: A Hoax?" *Fate*, June 1978: 76–83; Gordon Stein, ed., *Encyclopedia of Hoaxes* (Detroit: Gale Research, 1993), pp. 181–83.

49. Randi, *Flim-Flam!*, pp. 22–23.

50. Clark, *Unexplained!*, p. 77.

51. Ibid.

52. Wilson and Wilson, *Unsolved Mysteries*, p. 88.

53. Doyle, *The Coming of the Fairies*, p. 71.

54. Leach, *Funk & Wagnalls Standard Dictionary*, p. 456.

55. *Encyclopedia Britannica*, 1960, s.v. "Elf."

56. *Webster's New International Dictionary*, 1955, s.v. "sprite."

57. Leach, *Funk & Wagnalls Standard Dictionary*, p. 806.

58. The alleged clairvoyant's report is given in Doyle, *The Coming of the Fairies*, pp. 108–22.

59. Ibid., p. 108.

60. Ibid., pp. 108–22.

61. Leach, *Funk & Wagnalls Standard Dictionary*, p. 331.

62. S. Baring-Gould, quoted in Doyle, *The Coming of the Fairies*, p. 129.

63. Doyle, ibid.

64. "The Christina Show" was taped in Miami on July 29, 1992; our discussion was over dinner afterward (with parapsychologist Kerry Gaynor and others).

65. Thomas Keightley, *The World Guide to Gnomes, Fairies, Elves and Other Little People* (New York: Avenel Books, 1978), pp. 371–72.

66. Quoted in Doyle, *The Coming of the Fairies*, pp. 163–64.

67. Joe Nickell (in company with Carole Beale), travel journal, entries of January 7–8, 1971.

68. Doyle, *The Coming of the Fairies*, p. 127.

69. "Gracie's Visible Language" (by "Gracie & Zarkov"), *Gnosis Magazine* (Winter 1993): 60–63.

70. Diane McCloud, "Close Encounters of the Elf Kind," ibid., p. 63.

71. Owen S. Rachleff, *The Occult Conceit* (Chicago: Cowles Book, 1971), p. 180.

72. Ibid., pp. 179–81; Baker and Nickell, *Missing Pieces,* pp. 18–19.

Afterword

Robert A. Baker

Where do entities come from? After reading this far it should be obvious: from within the human head, where they are produced by the ever-active, image-creating human mind. Spirits, ghosts, poltergeists, devils, demons, angels, aliens, monsters, and fairies— all are human mental products and, deviant and bizarre though they may be, all are permutations and variations of the human form, i.e., they are basically "humanoid." Entities are essentially projections of ourselves and, if Stuart E. Guthrie in his recent book *Faces In the Clouds* (Oxford University Press, 1993) is correct, not only are all religions anthropomorphic but man also creates all of his entities in his own image.

The answer to the question "Why do they appear?" is, however, a trifle more complex. It requires that we consider a number of basic facts about human nature. First, we are social creatures from the day we come into the world until the day we depart. Our very existence is humanly interactive and we are, by design and necessity, totally dependent upon our fellow creatures. If at any time we find ourselves isolated from our fellow human beings we quickly form kinships with the other life forms around us. We endow every living—and nonliving—thing with human characteristics, i.e., the time "flows," the ocean "roars," days are "hot" and "cold," birds "sing," water is "wet," and the stars "look down"—just as if stars had eyes to see with. Anything and everything we experience is personified or anthropomorphized. We see it from the only perspective possible for us: a human one. We thus create sea gods; wind gods; the god of fire, lightning, storms, earth; and eventually a god of all the lesser gods—the "one God." We form close bonds with animals and bestow upon them our own motives, needs, and desires. When we fall asleep and dream, we then create dream-creatures and dream-people as well as our own alter-ego: the dream-self. If we find ourselves too long alone we create, quite naturally, invisible companions: imaginary playmates like Calvin and his toy tiger Hobbes. Adults, on the other hand, may take comfort in Harvey, their large and invisible white rabbit. Our need for company is so pervasive and profound that if companions do not exist, we invent them. A neglected literary and psychological masterpiece, Raoul Faure's *The Spear In the Sand* (Harpers, 1946), tells the story of a modern Robinson Crusoe minus a Friday. Finding himself alone on a tiny uninhabited island paradise, Sansal, the young scientist hero, as time passes, gradually creates for himself an imaginary mate who soon becomes as real as himself. In real-life situations wherein people have found themselves suffering from social (as well as sensory) deprivation, similar things occur. Admiral Byrd, alone in the Antarctic, also hallucinated companions, as did Wildred Theisger crossing the Empty Quarter alone (*Arabian Sands*, Dutton, 1959). Isolated miners, trapped below the surface for several days, without water, food, light, or human contact, quickly hallucinate powerful visual scenes not only of companions and rescuers but of other nonhuman entites as well.

Because the world we live in is such a fearful, dangerous, and unpredictable place, quite frequently we are driven to invent protectors for ourselves in the form of powerful and benign gods and goddesses. We also plead with them for mercy and favors. We further enjoy imagining ourselves as all-powerful, all-conquering, and dominant. We overcome our fear and trembling with dreams of being Superman or Wonder Woman. When we discover death and disintegration, our minds rebel and invent a soul and an afterlife with a heaven. Haunted by our fears we create a host of guardian angels to protect us from worldly harm. Drifting into dreams we quickly encounter another reality. Or altering our awareness with alcohol and other more powerful drugs, alternate realities with other strange inhabitants emerge.

Except for small variations within very narrow limits, when we ingest a drug it affects us alike both physiologically and psychologically. Ingesting LSD or DMT or MIMA can quickly bring about the appearance of entites of various degrees of strangeness. When John Lilly ingested ketamine (Vitamin K) he not only saw extraterrestrials but Buddha as well. When anthropologists ingest some of the phenethylamines they tend to see elves. Exactly which entities we will experience seems to depend upon those that our particular culture supplies. Mental habits, expectations, and psychological conditioning also play vital roles in exactly "who" or "what" is seen.

Stressors, either physical or mental, can spawn a nation of entities. Shock, trauma, pain, fatigue, fear, excessive cold or heat, hunger, and thirst are all reliable means for producing wraiths and phantoms, demons and angels, and spirits bearing messages from beyond. Only those individuals already deranged are impervious to such stressors. As Sargant observed in *The Mind Possessed* (Heinemann, 1973), abnormal behavior brought on by stress "is particularly true, not of the insane but of the sane, not of the severely mentally ill but of normal, ordinary, average people who make the best possible material since a normal person is responsive to other people and is reasonably open to their influence" (p. 195). Those who are mentally ill are usually preoccupied with their own internal scenarios and are, therefore, closed to the external world.

Sleep and dreaming, as well as so-called hypnosis or suggestibility, clearly show that certain mental states include a need to fabricate a cast of imaginary characters just as we do in our dreams. Visions of the Virgin Mary, ghostly friends and enemies, angels and demons, and other dream entities we know issue directly from our waking needs and common concerns. Depersonalization, role-playing, and personification, all of which are involved in the production of alternate personalities in the so-called multiple personality disorder (MPD), are also psychological operations essential to the creation of entities. MPD, most certainly, is a handy thing to have if one wishes to escape personal responsibility for one's actions. One can always create an alternate personality of a malevolent bent to blame for our heinous or unforgiveable acts. One can carry this ploy to such extremes that one can also be possessed by demons, the dead, or even another living spirit. Reveries, waking dreams, trances, hypna-gogic and hypnopompic states—all are psychological conditions intrinsic to inspiring and creating our interactions with ghosts, spirits, visions, fairies, angels, and extraterrestrials.

Physical illnesses, high fevers, and severe pain can also trigger the appearance of beings from within who often show up in the form of helpers, guides, guardians, or angels. They may also inspire a host of internal voices bringing us messages of comfort and joy from heaven, the past, the future, or from outer space. We heed them at our peril. Meditation, prayer, or mediumistic trances are also conducive to the summoning forth of various religious or spiritual entities. This is the common technique used by those marvellous New Age comedians who call themselves channelers. In anomalistic circles it is also well known that body chemistry can play a role in entity creation. If certain nutrients essential to the proper functioning of the central nervous system are insufficient or missing entirely from our diet, all sorts of visions may occur. In many primitive tribes prolonged frenetic dancing accompanied by hyperventilation can quickly bring about physical and nervous exhaustion, as well as a high degree of blood and brain alkalosis. Brain alkalosis, in turn, is well known to produce suggestible behavior, trance states, and visions (Sargant, 1973). In 1937 Schmeing, a German biochemist, argued that clairvoyance is inhibited by adding calcium to one's diet, i.e., second sight is caused or abetted by a calcium deficiency in the blood. Although unproved, it is a fascinating supposition. Cedric Wilson, an American pharmacologist, in 1958 reported that ergotropic drugs, e.g., dexamphetamines and caffeine, depress ESP ability, whereas trophotropic drugs such as valium, et al., appear to enhance it (Hilary Evans, *Alternate States of Consciousness*, 1989). It is also likely that such drugs may have similar effects on the brain's ability to produce entities. Certainly the psychedelics are very much involved. Concentrated rhythmic breathing, i.e., hyperventilization, leads to a build-up of carbon dioxide which causes hallucinations, feelings of expansiveness, and, if prolonged, unconsciousness. It is noteworthy that the psychiatrist John Mack in his treatise on alien abductions (*Abductions*, Scribners, 1994) himself engages in this breathing practice and encourages his student abductees to do likewise so that they will encounter more of the aliens. Mack refers to the practice as "LSD without the drug."

Perhaps the most fascinating of all the progenitors of entities is the condition noted earlier: sensory deprivation. Whenever we are deprived of normal sensory inputs, e.g., sights, sounds, smells, muscular tension, and the like, for a reasonably lengthy period, we will invariably experience hallucinations, i.e., false perceptions, emotional disturbances, and intellectual impairment. The most common hallucinatory experience, it appears, is that of establishing contact with other beings. When the scientist John C. Lilly placed himself in his isolation tank filled with water at body temperature and isolated both body and brain in a minimum-stimulus environment, he immediately encountered extraterrestrial deities who showed him his future. Further experiments with ketamine reinforced his contact with these beings as well as leading him to conversations with God, Buddha, and other supernatural creatures (*The Scientist*, Lippincott, 1978). As noted earlier, explorers of arctic wastes caught in "white-outs" (blinding snowstorms) also experience other realities and encounter strange and nonexistent entities.

Fatigue and exhaustion resulting from intense or sustained physical effort such as are experienced in combat, mountain climbing, forced marches, et al., can also induce hallucinatory states filled with apparitions. Forced wakefuless leads to the release, after two or three days without sleep, of natural brain chemicals similar to psychedelic drugs that will produce a hallucinatory state. Sleeplessness, when combined with emotional stress and sensory deprivation, will also enhance the appearance of imaginary beings.

Pain, injury, fatigue, and strong emotion combined with physical stress can also create heavenly saviors or guardian angels in the world of the religiously devout. For the religiously inclined, entities sustain, support, and reinforce one's faith. Such divine creatures seem to be fairly common and are frequently reported by contemporary Christians. According to a recent *Time* magazine survey (27 December 1993, p. 56) 69 percent of the American population believe in angels and 32 percent reported personal contact. Even though the time, place, and circumstance of many such encounters seem far removed from religious settings, stories like the following are common:

> Two women, seeking to climb Mt. Everest, after a hard day's trek in the foothills, were following a narrow and dangerous trail in a driving rainstorm. In the words of one of the women, "It was raining so hard we could barely see a hundred feet in any direction. I had gone on ahead of Francesca, and I came to a stream. It was moving really fast and there was no bridge, just a series of stones. You had to jump from one to the next. I got out in the middle, and then I just froze. The next stone was just too far to jump and I was slipping. Once in this ice-cold water I would have been swept away, drowned—
>
> "Suddenly, a bearded man, a saddhu, appeared beside me; he was wading in the water, bracing himself on a long wooden staff. He spoke to me in perfect English, that funny kind of accented English educated Indians speak. 'Here let me help you,' he said. He took my arm and helped me the rest of the way across the stream.
>
> "I sat down on a rock, real shaky from almost falling in the water. A minute later Francesca came across the stream to where I was.
>
> " 'It's a good thing that saddhu helped me,' I said. 'What saddhu?' Francesca asked. I looked around and there was no one there.
>
> " 'I watched you cross the stream,' Francesca said. 'There was no one else there. You started to lose your balance in the middle, and then after a few moments, you pulled it all together. I tried to call you, but the sound of the water was too loud. But there was no one out there with you.' " (Paraphrased from Robert Schukthesis, *Bone Games* [International Publishers, New York, 1986, p. 99])

Francesca was right. There was no saddhu. The narrator created her savior to intervene precisely when and where he was needed. Nor did it matter that the guardian angel showed up in the guise of an Indian saddhu. Guardian angels come, it seems, in many shapes and forms, and the more devout the believer, the more frequently they may be expected on the scene. Such entities not only validate and reinforce one's devotion and belief, but their seemingly "physical" appearance also eases the anxieties of doubt. More typical of the guardian angel stories, however, but also showing up in disguise is this story taken from the pages of *FATE* magazine, where such accounts are common:

> One night in June 1986, a mother driving her five-year-old daughter along a steep gravel road in Oregon, slipped over the edge into a deep ravine. Halfway down the cliff slope the daughter was thrown free, but the mother was pinned in the van and was knocked unconscious.
>
> The five-year-old, barefoot, bruised and bleeding, managed to climb in the darkness up the steep side of the cliff. Half way to the top she found a hole in the cliff face, crawled in and fell asleep. The next morning she was found at the top by a passing motorist who summoned help. The rescue team who brought up the badly injured mother had to use rock-climbing gear to get up the cliff face. The five-year-old told her father that a young boy holding a black puppy helped her climb the cliff, find the hole, and he then disappeared. (Paraphrased from *FATE*, November 1986, p. 19)

In anecdotes like these we will never know what really happened. Unless one investigates personally it is impossible to separate fiction from fact. In this "very good story," however, you can be sure there is much more of the former than of the latter.

In this same category is the tale told by one of my clients who asked me if such things as "guardian angels" were either possible or real. According to him, when he was either three or four years old a space heater overturned in his bedroom and set fire to the rug and curtains. Despite his terrified screams, his mother downstairs listening to the radio failed to hear him. Suddenly an elderly, gray-haired woman plucked him from his bed, smothered the flames with his blankets, put him outside in the hall, and then suddenly disappeared. Running downstairs, he alerted his mother, who told him later that the elderly lady who had saved him and disappeared was his maternal grandmother who had died several years before. He remembered this incident years later when on extended combat patrol in Vietnam after starting down a jungle path while "in country." Suddenly a gray-haired woman appeared in front of him blocking his path, hands extended to shove him backwards, while shaking her head. Just as suddenly she disappeared. Completely unnerved, he stopped and, peering carefully at the ground, spotted an almost invisible trip-wire on the path ahead. Had he failed to stop he would not have survived the booby trap. Being somewhat skeptical and hard-headed, he was looking for a rational explanation for the two strange events.

After a few questions the client admitted that he didn't actually remember the childhood event himself; it was told to him years later by his mother. As for the combat experience, he also admitted that he had been without sleep for nearly thirty hours, was exhausted and bone weary, and subconsciously well aware of the need to probe all paths for mines and booby traps. The fact that it was also twilight, and that his platoon had been ambushed earlier in the day also enhanced his susceptibility to having his senses and perceptions betrayed. My explanations, he agreed, were much more plausible than the notion that his heavenly granny was standing guard. My client, however, is a rare exception among the many. The belief that angels are all around us, watching over us, protecting us from all the arrows and horrors that flesh is heir to, is considerably more comforting and reassuring than the sad scientific fact that our senses are not always reliable, our minds play tricks on us, and wishful thinking cannot and will not change the world.

Among angel believers one often encounters very rational and sober citizens who scoff at other paranormal and superstitious claims. But as far as angels, life after death, and heaven are concerned, they believe. There is an element in their thinking that argues against science, reason, and psychology. Science just can't explain everything, they insist. Some visions, some entities just can't be accounted for: They are simply too profoundly mysterious. But what they're really saying is that they are frightened of the truth. If the truth shows that their faith is misplaced and there are no guardian angels to protect them, what will they do? These individuals remind one of Shel Silverstein's poem "Batty":

> The Baby Bat
> Screamed out in fright,
> "Turn on the dark,
> I'm afraid of the light."

(From *A Light in the Attic* [Harper & Row, 1981])

Science and reason, they hold, will take us only so far. Unlike most skeptics, they prefer not to know.

Persuading such dedicated believers that the human mind is brimful of gods, ghosts, demons, ogres, witches, fairies, monsters, aliens, angels, elves, as well as other unnameable weird and bizarre humanoids—all of which are unreal but easily available if one merely asks them to put in an appearance—is not an easy task. Drugs, meditation, prayer, suggestion, relaxation, hypnosis, regression—any and all such imagination-arousing, hypnagogic exercises will take us quickly to alternate realities, foreign dimensions, and the farthest limits of the human imagination. Seductive and entrancing as they are, however, we must remember that they are not (nor have they ever been) anything more than false and insubstantial creation of the restless human imagination. As we have seen in this book, Nickell is acutely aware of this and has performed an invaluable service with this latest collection of case studies.

In fact, with regard to these delusionary beings, few writers have given them much attention. Other than the present work, I know of only one other attempt to catalog and account for these imaginary creatures. Hilary Evans, a few years ago, devoted two books to the subject: *Visions, Apparitions, Alien Visitors: A Comparative Study of the Entity Enigma* (Aquarian Press, 1984); and *Gods, Spirits, Cosmic Guardians: A Comparative Study of the Encounter Experience* (Aquarian Press, 1987). Using his considerable skills as collector, curator, and classifier, Evans also provided an extensive and fascinating catalog of imaginary beings. At the time the two books were written, Evans was undecided whether the entities were or were not due to psychological processes. Evans also frankly admitted that most of his case reports were anecdotal, that many of them were spurious, and that many of his reporters and witnesses were either lying or were deluded. Furthermore, many of the reported experiences relied entirely upon the unsupported testimony of a single observer.

As a typical example, Evans provides the case of Glenda, a twelve-year-old who came home from school one day, went up to her room, and encountered a "spacewoman" who seemed concerned about Glenda's well-being. While most people would dismiss Glenda's entity as a figment of her imagination, Evans refuses and insists that we take these reports seriously. We should not, he says, relegate them to the domain of the psychologist too quickly. They may be, according to Evans, exactly what they claim to be, i.e., spirits of the dead, extraterrestrial visitors, or ministering angels. Until we can prove they are *not* real, Evans insists, we do not have the right to discount this firsthand testimony. One could, of course, argue extensively that we *do* have such a right. Evans himself, curiously enough, as his work progressed, reached this conclusion on his own. Though he had earlier denied that the experience was psychological, after many long and convoluted arguments with himself and assays of the damnable facts, Evans concludes at the end of his second book that the entity experience is basically psychological after all. In his words, "My own view is that there is no need to hypothesize either an external supermind nor an externally occurring encounter experience: I suggest that we contain the necessary resources within us" (p. 267). After a third book, also devoted to extraordinary experiences, *Altered States of Consciousness: Unself, Otherself, and Superself* (Aquarian Press, 1989), Evans concludes we are better off not fooling ourselves. In fact, he chides believers with the statement: "It is even arguable that, whatever the obscure purposes of the universe, the fact that we have been given this earthly life implies an implicit instruction to live it as best we may, and that to seek to escape or transcend it is to miss the point of existence" (p. 239). As for our ability to manufacture entities and experience altered states of conscious-

ness (ASCs), Evans avers, "ASCs are short-term means to immediate ends; once that end is achieved we should come back
to reality where we belong—just as nature, in her wisdom, sees
to it that we do. . . . Most of us, once the trance or the dance
or the ecstasy or the dream is over, come back to our usual state
of consciousness; our subconscious self sees to that. And though
it may have been exciting out there in Wonderland, it's just as
well to be back home where we belong, in our usual state of
consciousness" (p. 243).

Evans's book and this present survey are in no way super-
numerary, nor are they repetitious; they are, instead, comple-
mentary. The problem with Evans's earlier cases is that so many
of them, while admittedly anecdotal, are also heavily biased literary accounts. Many of these are second- and thirdhand reports
filled with falsifications and missing details. In many of the cases,
were these "missing pieces" of evidence available, there would
be no mystery. A striking example of this is the story of the
three Kentucky women purportedly abducted by a UFO. In
Evans's book the case remains an unsolved and unfathomable
mystery. Upon being properly investigated in person, at first by
Billig and later by Baker and Nickell, it becomes a nonevent,
i.e., there was no UFO, no aliens appeared, and no abduction
occurred. The value of Nickell's *Entities* rests upon the fact that
his representative cases are based upon personal, on-the-scene
investigations by the author himself. Nickell, though he loves
mysteries, loves them most and best when and after he has solved
them. All of his many readers and admirers—myself included—
are delighted that this is so.

Robert A. Baker
Professor Emeritus
Lexington, Kentucky
September 1994

Index